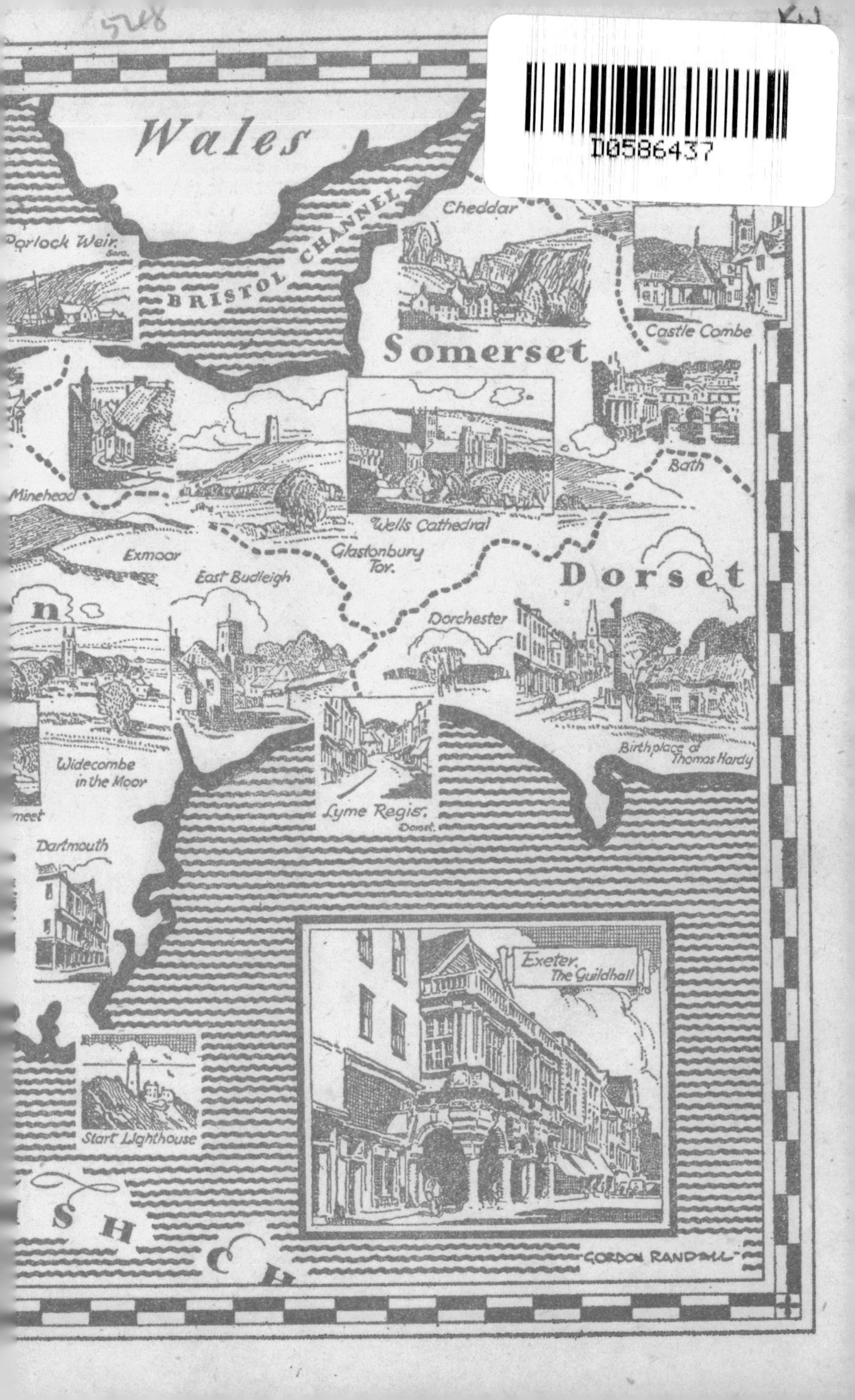
Wales
BRISTOL CHANNEL
Porlock Weir.
Cheddar
Castle Combe
Somerset
Minehead
Bath
Wells Cathedral
Exmoor
Glastonbury Tor.
East Budleigh
Dorset
Dorchester
Widecombe in the Moor
Birthplace of Thomas Hardy
Lyme Regis.
Dorset.
Dartmouth
Exeter. The Guildhall
Start Lighthouse
GORDON RANDALL

Xmas 1950

A SON OF ENGLAND

NORMAN WYMER

A BREATH OF ENGLAND

THE SOUTHERN SHIRES

LUTTERWORTH PRESS
LONDON and REDHILL

First Published 1948

PRINTED IN GREAT BRITAIN BY THE WHITEFRIARS PRESS LTD.
LONDON AND TONBRIDGE

To My Wife

MARY JEAN

in memory of many happy
trips together through the
glorious English countryside

Author's Note

IN presenting this book, I would like to take the opportunity of thanking all those, in each of the ten counties I have visited, from Cornwall to Kent, who have welcomed me into their midst, and thereby given me an insight into their life and work, their traditions and country lore; those people, in fact, about whom I now write.

Particularly grateful am I to those who have so kindly read the various chapters in MS. form; their many suggestions have proved invaluable. In this respect I would especially mention Miss Maxwell Fraser, whose own books on the countryside are as full and informative as one may hope to find, and a delight to read.

Finally, I would like to acknowledge the kindly help and consideration afforded to me at all times by my publishers, whose idea it was that I should write this book.

One more remark. With the nation's larder in its present state, it is quite possible that certain of the customs and doles connected with food may have been suspended for a time, as, indeed, has actually happened in some places. I have, however, included such customs, on the grounds that in normal times they still take their place in the life of the people, and will do so again, I hope, when happier days return.

NORMAN WYMER.

SUSSEX,
1947.

Contents

Illustrations

All the photographs not acknowledged separately below were taken by the Author, and are his copyright.

Illustrations

Illustrations

Introductory

PRECIOUS HERITAGE

WHEN the craftsmen of the Middle Ages first started building homes for the people out of stone or rock, hewn from the very ground on which they were to stand, or from oak beams and wattle hurdles, reinforced with chopped straw and cow-dung, the story of England's countryside began in earnest.

Villages sprang up ; independent villages whose inhabitants had no clear picture of the scenery outside their immediate neighbourhood, and who knew little of what was going on but a few miles away, except, perhaps, what they had gleaned from the hearsay talk of the pilgrims passing through. For no one in those days would have thought of travelling for pleasure ; the risks and discomforts were altogether too great.

In such circumstances, then, the villagers preferred to work together, and so make themselves self-supporting and independent of the outside world. They had, indeed, no alternative, cut off as they were from the rest of England. Thus, each village would form its own band of craftsmen, who would be entirely dependent on local resources ; its own farming programme ; its own administration and system of justice, although here a number of districts would often be brought together under the same sphere of influence by the Lord of the Manor.

Thus they grew up as individual units, so that the pilgrims and merchants, passing on their long and weary treks, must have noticed many differences with every few miles of trackway. They would have found a people varying in their work and customs, in their speech and outlook ; they would have found them varying in their everyday life almost as much as their localised architecture varied with the change of soils and with the mood and temper of the natives.

Yet, though these were the people who gave England her unified character and her greatness, even to-day, when we may travel two hundred miles or more by fast car in a single day, we can still detect that traditional variation. Like the pilgrims before us, we may yet find a world of difference between one village and another ; between one town and another ; between one county and another.

As we pass from county to county through the length and breadth of the British Isles we shall, if we travel intelligently, find many shades of the past. We shall find people still talking the local dialect that their ancestors gradually devised through the process of centuries ; still clinging to customs whose origins are lost in antiquity, or which date back to the time when the villagers worshipped strange gods ; still fulfilling the same work for which their districts first became famous generations back. We shall notice a wide diversity of both scenery and architecture, and we shall come upon, from time to time, some small town or village that once played a notable part in British history, but which now lies forgotten by all but the comparatively few men and women who yet delight to make it their home.

It is, of course, in the counties as a whole that we shall notice the greatest variation to-day, and, as we move from one to another, let us linger awhile in each

Such a system was intended in the first place, I imagine, merely as an emergency measure, for in Georgian days this westernmost corner of Britain was a barren land, uncultivated and sparsely housed. While the " tinners ", with their earnings of but a few shillings a week, experienced increasing difficulty in finding a home for their families, the landed gentry, on the other hand, had vast acres lying idle which they were anxious to see developed. So it was that landowner and tinner got together.

While the former saw in this a profitable way of raising the value of his estates, the latter counted his blessings, and proceeded to become miner by day and builder by night. Devoting every moment of his precious leisure hours to the task, he would erect, with his own hands and with a devotion so typical of the craftsman, a home for his family as worthy as his personal skill and endurance would allow. This done, he might then turn his attention to outbuildings, and to cultivating the soil itself, until in time whole colonies had sprung up on land that had once been useless ; and the face of Cornwall changed accordingly.

Needless to say, a man wishing to benefit by this system was careful to name three of the youngest and healthiest lives he could think of. For in that way he could, at least, be reasonably certain of enjoying the fruits of his labours for the rest of his life, while always he cherished the hope that his children after him might also benefit by his long years of sweat and toil. More often than not his ambition was rewarded, and sometimes such homesteads would pass down as far as the third generation. Still, it by no means always worked out like that ; instances have been recorded of all three lives dying almost before the last slate had been laid on the roof. In such an event the peasant was at the mercy of the landowner. While some might insist upon the payment of an extortionate fine before the lease could be renewed, others, more generous-minded, would allow the unfortunate man to name two, or maybe even three, further individuals.

It is some years since the last lease of this kind was granted, and many of the existing holders are becoming not a little anxious as to the health of their remaining " lives ".

" You're looking some wisht, me 'andsome ! " the cottager may say as he peers anxiously into the face of the last of his chosen three. " You look like a winnard on a perch," and he will shake his head, sad in the knowledge that at her passing all that he—and his father before him—has loved and worked for may be taken from him.

All over Cornwall we may find clusters of cottages, hamlets and farms—and I have even come upon one or two thriving inns and hotels—that owe their origin to this strange system. For, until quite recent years, the leasing of land on lives was fairly general throughout the county. It is in the mining area, however—that rather bleak belt, stretching along the north coast from Land's End, through St. Just, barren Zennor (so barren that it is said that a cow at Morvah, nearby, was once forced to eat the bell rope in order to keep alive), Hayle, and on to Camborne and Redruth, the tinners' " capital "—that we find the most examples.

It was in this belt that the Phœnicians first started their tinning activities in the days before the Roman occupation, thereby laying the foundations of our first export industry. From the time of their arrival until wellnigh the end of the Victorian era, tin-mining formed one of the county's main industries. Not only was Cornwall the only source of supply for the whole of Europe, but it was here that the entire system of mining in general, with its " captains " and complicated underground workings, was gradually evolved, to spread, in time, to the farthest corners of the earth as more and more Cornishmen left their native land to pass on their secrets. The coal mines of the industrial North and Midlands and of Somerset ; the gold fields of South Africa ; and the silver workings of Cobalt in Canada, all can trace their origin to this Celtic corner of England.

Although but two mines are working to-day—the South Croft, between Camborne and Redruth, and the Geevor at St. Just—there is still an important mining school at Camborne. With the advent of machinery, much of the old tradition has passed away. Even so, we may still find men adopting a lore and language that have been handed down to them through the process of centuries, just as such towns as Helston, Liskeard, Truro, Penzance, and Lostwithiel stand to remind us of the days when the tinners had their own " parliament ", and when offenders were tried by their special courts, the guilty being condemned to the stannary prisons. Although " cages " are now in more general use, we may yet see the tinners descending the " bal " in their " kibbles ", precarious-looking iron containers—not unlike high buckets—perhaps three feet high and four feet in diameter ; and, if we follow them deep down into the bowels of the earth, we may perhaps hear one or two of the old stock reverently singing some Methodist hymn as they set about their work, just as their ancestors had done ever since John Wesley paid his thirty-one visits to Cornwall, and so brought a new breath of life to her inhabitants. It was not far from the tinners' capital, at Gwennap, that Wesley made some of his most stirring calls, and every Whit-Monday for more than a hundred and fifty years men, women and children have assembled here in their thousands to hold a service in his memory.

One old tinner told me that his job takes him something like two thousand feet below ground, and that water has to be constantly pumped from his mine at the rate of about one thousand gallons a minute. Work is carried out here in shifts. After holes have been drilled some five or six feet into the rock, and charged with explosives, the mine is cleared. Then, when the danger period is over, a second shift descends to clear up the ore and put in further charges. And so it goes on. Meanwhile the ore has to be crushed, sampled, washed in convex " buddles ", and separated from the waste on a washing-table.

" What do you do with the waste ? " I asked.

" The tailings ? " The old man smiled. " We get pitchblende from them, I tell 'ee, and that gives us uranium."

One of the most remarkable things about Cornwall is her wide diversity of climate, which, in turn, affects not only her scenery, but also the life of her people. While along parts of the north coast the Atlantic gales may rip the slates from the very roofs, cause whole buildings to collapse unless they are really soundly built, and make most forms of vegetation virtually impossible, except in the more sheltered hollows ; in the south the sun will shine upon an azure blue sea with a warmth and loveliness reminiscent of the French Riviera. I shall always remember being welcomed by roses and wallflowers, freshly cut from the garden, when I went to stay with an aunt at Mevagissey one New Year's day : it made such a pleasing contrast to the howling wind and driving rain (persisting, though it was August, with undiminished vigour for no less than three days) that greeted my arrival at Tintagel, with its widely-exploited King Arthur links welcomely relieved by the magnificent coastal scenery of Barras Head, now safe in the hands of the National Trust.

As I say, the climate has left its mark on the people. Somewhere about seventy years ago a little group from the Scilly Isles—which, though cut off from the mainland, are, nevertheless, Cornish—packed up a quantity of their locally-grown narcissi, and sent them in a hat-box to Covent Garden to see how they would be received. In doing so they laid the foundations of what has since grown into a flourishing industry, spreading to many parts of the mainland, so that to-day, in early spring, we may see whole fields of daffodils, narcissi, violets, and anemones at such places as Penzance, Gulval, Ludgvan, Paul, Boskenna, Lamorna, and in various other places around Mount's Bay—where, incidentally, a fossilized forest lies submerged under the sea—while as far east as the valley of the Tamar, on Devon's border, we shall find bulb farms where a single bulb may be worth as much as £5. Some of these fields slope gracefully towards the cliff tops to make a picturesque contrast with the sea below and St. Michael's Mount in the distance ; others lie comparatively flat to add a blaze of colour to the inland beauty. South Cornwall in springtime is a sight to behold.

With thousands of acres given up to the growing of spring flowers and early vegetables, the average annual consignment for market now runs into more than a million wooden packages, where the one lone hat-box had once sufficed.

North Cornwall, too, derives certain benefits from the weather. While the peculiar sea-sand washed up by the storms around Harlyn Bay, Polzeath, and Constantine is used to provide mineral salts for fertilizing the fields, along Daymer Beach whole villages will turn out in their bathing-suits every spring tide to gather seaweed for the production of penicillin. In no other part of England, I believe, is such seaweed to be found, although other varieties are gathered along many stretches of both the Cornish and Devon coasts for medicinal purposes.

" 'As 'ee never *eaten* seaweed, then ? " an elderly harvester asked me in surprise, as I watched him piling the stuff into his basket.

I confessed that I had not.

" Naw ? Why, 'tis as dear as saffron in these parts. What 'ee wants is to get me old woman to cook 'ee up a dish. Boil it for hours 'er will. Topped up with a spot of lemon juice or butter, and served, steaming hot, with mutton, why there's nothing like it, I tell 'ee."

It was from the sea, as from the tin mines, that Cornwall gained the greater part of her prosperity in the past, and all round her two hundred miles of rugged coastline—often most threatening, but always most superbly wonderful—we come upon harbours of all sizes and descriptions, and little sandy coves, that serve to remind us of the days when son would follow father to sea as surely as the night followed the day.

At the top of the cliffs near Newquay, too, we may still see an old stone hut where, in days gone by, a huer might spend hours at a time gazing out to sea, watching for the distant approach of a shoal of pilchards. Early that morning a number of boats had set sail with their nets—some of them as much as five hundred yards long and weighing, with their corks, ropes, and lead " sinkers ", close on three tons—from a nearby harbour, their crews laughing and joking, and happily singing their seasonal songs in cheerful expectation of a good catch. Patiently they would remain at anchor within sight of the cliffs until, at last, the huer blew his bugle, and shouted " Hevva, hevva ! " through his special trumpet. Immediately the cry was heard, the little stretch of beach below, quiet and deserted but a few moments before, would become the scene of feverish excitement as men, women, and children of all ages came hustling and bustling from the nearby cottages. From the cliff-tops the huer would wave a club in each hand, first this way and then that, to guide the boats on to the right course, while the " lurker "—the man in charge of the fleet—waited expectantly for the order to " shoot the seine ". Then the fishermen would begin to pay out their nets, while the oarsmen proceeded to row the boats, as hard as they could, in a semicircular direction. As soon as the pilchards had been safely encased, the work of " tucking " would begin. A small net would be fastened to one of the craft, lowered into the seine net, and then drawn taut again by means of ropes on its farther edge. As thousands of pilchards were thereby brought to the surface, bands of men, each armed with a " whisket ", would busily scoop up the fish into their boats as fast as they could go. No sooner was a boat filled than it was on its way back to the shore for the " blowsers " to unload it and cart the pilchards to the fish cellar for salting.

The development of deep-sea trawling in the English Channel in recent years has, alas, all but ended the inshore pilchard fisheries by breaking up the shoals, so that most fishermen now find it more profitable to go farther out to sea and work with drifters. Even so, we may still occasionally find them working from some southern cove in the traditional way, just as we shall yet find huers keeping watch over the autumn mackerel shoals, studying the every movement of the gannets, which, if anything, are even more fish-conscious than they.

As a fisherman once remarked, in the case of mackerel it is often a question of Nature chasing Nature. The

" They laid the foundations of what has since grown into a flourishing industry "
—Daffodil time in West Cornwall.

CORNISH INDUSTRIES :

Left : " Holes are drilled some five or six feet into the rock " —a tinner at work.

Above : " More interesting still are the china-clay pits"—looking down upon a pit near St. Austell.

Right : " It was the Caradon Moors that furnished the granite for old Waterloo Bridge."

“We come upon harbours of all sizes and descriptions”—looking down upon St. Ives.

mackerel are following the streams of whitebait, while the gannets, in turn, swoop down on to the water after the mackerel. Thus, by watching the behaviour of these birds, the huer can often judge the depth at which the shoal is moving under the sea. Here speed is more important than ever. The mackerel tides are often short and, unless the cliff watcher is prompt with his instructions, the fishermen may be unable to take to their boats in time, in which case they must wade, waist-deep, into the sea to pay out their nets.

Sons no longer follow their fathers to sea with such regularity. Tackle and boats are becoming increasingly costly to maintain, while the prices paid for the fish make the industry unprofitable. Thus many of the younger generation are turning to work on the land instead, while others are finding their salvation in hiring out yachts and dinghies to the hundreds of holiday-makers that now invade the county each summer. In the little ports and harbours all around the coast the village boat-builders are as busy as ever, though the number of fishing-smacks grows less. Once-flourishing centres of fishing activity have declined into comparative obscurity ; even at such places as Newlyn, Looe, Penzance, Mousehole, St. Ives, and Mevagissey —which may be considered to comprise the main centres to-day—the number of boats lessens almost year by year.

Yet, despite all these outward signs of decline, the fisherman, and all that he stands for, still forms an essential part of Cornwall's make-up, just as the many and various harbours and coves are ever unique ; each so different from the next ; each delightful, if only on account of that very difference. Small wonder that in the Penwith Peninsula—that spine of granite with its richly wooded valleys, coves, and megalithic remains, stretching westwards to Land's End from St.

Ives in the north and Penzance in the south—colonies of painters, with Mousehole, Lamorna, Newlyn, and St. Ives as their headquarters, should have been inspired to introduce a new school of artistic expression in recent years. Only in Brittany are such places to be seen, and there the similarity is most marked.

Though the ways and methods may be changing, the pilchard fishery is still the one on which the fisherman pins his faith that it may help to redeem an otherwise poor season. Here modern ways have helped him a little, for, in recent times, a canning-factory has sprung into being close by the quay at Mevagissey, where men and women are busily engaged canning more than twenty " lasts ", each containing perhaps ten thousand fish, every week.

But, if their methods are changing, their old superstitions and customs die hard. Start eating a pilchard from its head towards its tail, and the fisherman will grab you by the arm and declare in horror that such a practice is simply courting disaster : you must *always* begin at the tail.

" My dear life, if 'ee do that, anything might happen ! " he will tell you ; and he firmly believes it, as he also believes that it is unlucky for him to see a hare or rabbit—either dead or alive—a clergyman, or a woman, when he is about to put to sea. At such times his womenfolk are always careful to keep well away from the boats, they, too, believing implicity that their appearance will mean " no fish to-day ".

Strong in their religious beliefs, the fishermen regard the presence of a clergyman as a warning from the Almighty. They are not even quite happy if they sight a church when out to sea, and few there are who will be persuaded to go fishing on Sundays. Nor do they consider that others should do so. At St. Ives, I am told, a free fight once took place between the local fishermen and a party of holiday-makers who offended against these unwritten laws, and at Mevagissey they will tell you quite proudly of the time when they flatly refused to go to the aid of a man who got into difficulties on the Sabbath.

Before ever they drop their nets, the Cornish fishermen will reverently offer their prayer to God : " Lord, spare our labour and send them in with a blessing ", while many of them, like the tinners on land, will help to while away their long hours of patient waiting with the singing of Methodist hymns and, perhaps, even with reading passages from the Bible. Every autumn, too, they will hold their thanksgiving services, when their little village churches may be decorated with various tackle, from lobster-pots to tarred nets, from oilskins to anchors, to form a fitting background for their offerings of fish.

For all that, the fisherman is no prude. He will knock back a pint at the " local " as well as anyone, smoke incessantly, and tell his quota of " stories ". He has his other side, as the many relics of the old smuggling days will tell. There is hardly a cove along the whole lengthy coastline where illicit goods have not, at some time or other, been brought in from France and elsewhere at dead of night, to be hidden away at some secret spot inland. At Falmouth we may find the quaint brick furnace, known as " the King's Pipe ", where the contraband tobacco was burnt, while at Mevagissey are a number of houses with their front doors in the roof: an idea especially conceived for the convenience of the smugglers.

The owner of one of these houses told me that hers had been built for her grandfather, who, it seems, had been an offender on no small scale. Set on to the side of a cliff, this house has two ways of approach—by the sea at the back and by a steep path at the front. By thus compelling the " Preventive Man " to make his way to the top of the house, the smuggler was able to gain a few more minutes in which to make his escape below. By the time the knock had been answered, and the intruder led through the house and convinced that all was well, the smuggler would be well away.

It is not only along the southern coast that such activities took place. Up in the north, between Polzeath and Port Isaac, set in a hollow between two hills, lies Port Quin, ghostly, eerie, and almost unknown. For something like a century its cluster of stone cottages lay deserted. Not a man or woman would live there. It became as a place bewitched, with its roofs falling in, windows gone, and weeds growing everywhere ; a scene of utter desolation and ruin.

Many a Cornishman—if he has ever heard of Port Quin—will tell you, by way of a reason, that, somewhere about a hundred years ago, a terrible storm broke out off the coast just after the entire male population had put to sea. One after the other, the ships of their small but proud fleet were bashed and battered by the waves ; not a man was saved. When news of the tragedy reached the little hamlet, the womenfolk at once took to their heels, believing there to be a curse on the place.

Ask a native of one of Port Quin's neighbouring villages for his version, however, and he will shake his head and say " Nay, that weren't so." He will tell you that on the contrary, far from being heroes, the entire population were smugglers on a prolific scale, who, growing afraid, suddenly decided to scatter themselves to other parts of the county.

Now, after all these years, Port Quin is coming to life again. Its ruined cottages have recently been bought and are now being restored.

I asked one Cornish fisherman to tell me frankly whether any smuggling still takes place. He smiled and looked about him as if to make certain that nobody was listening.

" Well, I shouldn't perhaps be telling 'ee the truth if I said naw," he drawled. " I wouldn't say as though there weren't some out to get hold of an odd bottle of something on the quiet now and again if they got the chance."

" Do *you* do any ? " I asked him.

The old salt looked taken aback, but then laughed :

" Well, sir, it be like this. I be more awkwardly placed than some of t'others. It be my job to stop that sort of thing." And he added, confidingly, " You see, I be a coastguard ! "

As I say, the old order changes but slowly in Cornwall. Few things ever seem to die out completely in this delightful land. Even if smuggling is now virtually dead, the old days of sail, when Fowey was an important port from which the Crusaders set off for their Holy Wars, and when, in considerably later times, Falmouth became a flourishing packet station, are by no means entirely forgotten. To this day Falmouth remains even yet a port of call for the square-rigged sailing barques returning to Finland with their cargoes of Australian grain. At no other harbour in England, I believe, can such a sight be seen ; a picturesque reminder that, even in these days of " progress ", there is much that was good in the old ways of life. With these old-timers sharing the waters with heavily-gunned battleships, and with centuries-old buildings contrasting vividly with the many modern erections of less pleasing character, Falmouth, perhaps more than anywhere, presents a true meeting of the ways : a kind of cross-roads between the ancient and the modern.

If the town of Falmouth has been robbed of much of

its old world atmosphere by its rise to greater " popularity ", the beautiful wooded Helford River, not far off, winding its way to Gweek, and affording a passage to Port Navas, with its small cluster of thatched cottages at the bottom of the hill, and its oyster fisheries and river vista round the bend, more than atones.

By contrast with Falmouth, Fowey has hardly changed through the ages. Now a centre for yachting, boating, and salmon fishing, it is still the same quaint little port that once helped to swell the ranks of Queen Elizabeth's much-tested Navy.

But the Cornishman no longer thinks only in terms of tin and fish, though the sea may sometimes prove his inspiration in other fields, as at Kynance Cove, on the Lizard Peninsula, where small colonies of craftsmen may be seen fashioning all sorts of articles, from candlesticks and inkstands to tobacco jars and ash-trays, out of the peculiar serpentine rock of which the very cove is formed ; or as around the Land's End area, where they search the beaches for " Cornish Diamonds " to make into articles of jewellery.

Upon the inland slopes the farmer drives his plough with a greater sense of earnestness than ever, while here and there in the hollows below the village craftsmen continue to ply those trades that remain—in spite of machinery—ancillary to agriculture.

At Delabole we shall find slaters working the same slate pits as their ancestors knew four hundred years or more ago, while at Penryn we may visit quarries that have provided granite for monuments as far away as Turin in Italy. There are many quarries in Cornwall, and while it was from Luxulyan that the materials were taken for the Duke of Wellington memorials, it was the Caradon Moors that furnished the granite for old Waterloo Bridge.

More interesting still, though, are the china-clay pits, whose enormous white pyramids of sand stand out as landmarks for miles around St. Austell. From these eighty or so pits—quite the most important in Britain, and said to be the finest in the world—more than one million tons of Kaolin are produced each year for the making of pottery and china-ware, notepaper, cosmetics, medicines, rubber, linoleum, and numerous other articles.

It was a Plymouth chemist, William Cookworthy, who, in the eighteenth century, first discovered the presence of china-clay at Tregoning Hill. Since then it has been sent all over the world, and work has been going on almost without pause, by night as well as by day. While one group of men is busily superintending the finishing stages at the top of the pit, others will be hard at work at the bottom seeing to the early stages of a further batch. Then again, others too will be journeying backwards and forwards from top to bottom upon the little inclined railway ; and so it goes on from day to day ; from year to year.

Here in these pits we may see grandsons rubbing shoulders with their grandfathers at an industry that, to them, has no equal. For, as one old clay-worker—eighty-two, I think he said he was—told me proudly, a man born to the pits starts young and knows no retirement. So it seems !

Kaolin, he explained, is produced in six stages, of which the first comprises blasting holes into the sides of the rock with sticks of dynamite in a rather special way—a highly-skilled job in itself, since everything depends upon the amount of dynamite used. It would be so easy to blast the rock to smithereens, but such methods are of no avail here. Rather it must be merely loosened in a way that will enable the streams of water from the high-pressure hoses to seep into the cracks and so force the sandy clay to trickle down the side of the pit into a sump below.

But that is only the first stage. Now starts a series of cleansing processes as the clay is moved from tank to tank before eventually being dried slowly and carefully in narrow kilns for perhaps two days and nights.

Hidden away in a small copse, just off the road back from the pits to St. Austell, is an ancient baptistery, while at Fool's Corner is a quaint stone, known as the Mengu Stone, which, it is believed, was placed there in the old days of feudalism to mark the boundary of three adjacent manors.

All over Cornwall we may come upon unusual features of one kind or another. Dotted about the highways, for instance, are something like five hundred ancient crosses, which, it is thought, were set up in prehistoric times and were later sanctified to the Deity. Upright pillars ending in a circle containing four holes at the top—a fascinating feature of the Cornish countryside—nowhere else in the world are they to be found in like number.

Tucked away in a hollow of Perranporth golf course—secluded and hard to find—is a little building with a curved roof, not unlike that of a Dutch barn. Inside, under lock and key, are the remains of what is said to be the oldest church in England. Only fragments of its four walls are left, but, on its altar, always adorned with vases of fresh flowers, candles are once more kept ever burning.

The man who looks after the place with such devotion to-day told me something of its strange history. Somewhere about one thousand four hundred years ago, it seems, an Irish saint named Piran—from whom Perranporth gets its name—called his followers together on the nearby sands, told them that he felt he was dying, and gave them his last blessing. Whereupon he collapsed. He was buried at the spot where he died, and the church was erected over his grave. For hundreds of years it stood secure. The huge sand-banks nearby did not threaten it, for the good reason that there was a freshwater stream between the church and the sands, and sand will never cross running water.

A few hundred years ago, however, the stream was diverted for domestic purposes, with the result that the sand soon engulfed the church, and for three or four hundred years it lay completely buried, before eventually being uncovered last century. At once thousands of people flocked to the site to make off with pieces of the ruins as mementos. So this building was erected over the remains, literally to prevent the church from being stolen.

Not far off is an old Cornish amphitheatre. A massive turfed affair with high ramparts, and capable of holding perhaps two thousand people at a time. It is said—though without any apparent authenticity—that it was here that some of the best of the Celtic dialect plays were staged in the Middle Ages.

Such plays, once a great feature of Cornish life, are seldom performed these days, but much of the old Celtic language is still in use, for all that. Get a Cornishman really talking, and it is often quite impossible to understand a word he is saying. For who but a Celt could guess that a " croust " means a snack lunch ; a " dag " a hatchet ; a " cundard " a water-pipe ; a " gunnies " a large excavation ; a " slab " a kitchen range ; or a " shiner " a sweetheart ? Yet these and many other words and phrases form part of his everyday parlance.

Many of the strange place-names—Come to Good, Cost is Lost, Hard to Come By, Pennywise, Penny Come Quick, and so on—are nothing more than derivations of Celtic words, as the prefixes, " tre ", " pol ", and

" pen " on so many Cornish names are of Celtic origin, " tre " meaning a dwelling-place or town, " pol " a pool, and " pen " a head or headland. Similarly, the various " Roselands " have no connection whatever with roses, but are merely corruptions of " rhos ", meaning a moorland.

At Gunwalloe, not far from Poldhu, where Marconi sat on a rock trying to get a signal from Newfoundland and later set up his first long-distance wireless station, is another church in the sands. Built on the foreshore, this might well have suffered an equal fate had not a special protecting wall been built in later years to preserve it from the waves.

While at Manaccan the villagers will point with pride to a fig tree growing out of the very walls of their church, at Newlyn East we may see a similar tree, that has given rise to a superstition so deep as virtually to prevent anyone from benefiting from its fruits except at the gravest risk. The story goes that on her arrival in Cornwall a certain female saint, by name Newlyna, looked around for a suitable spot whereon to build her church. When at last she had made her choice, she struck her staff into the soil to mark the position, taking, at the same time, the wise precaution of setting a curse upon anyone who dared touch it. Whereupon the staff took root and turned into a fig tree.

Ask a villager about his tree, and he will at once turn grave, and warn you that, assuredly enough, death will come to you within the year if you dare pick so much as one leaf.

" Do it if 'ee like," he will say, " but I warn 'ee, others have died for their folly ! "

To support his argument, he will tell you of the former vicar who died within a few months of pruning it ; of the disbelieving Australian who had a fatal collapse on his homeward voyage ; and of many other equally blood-curdling coincidences. But to him they are not coincidences !

It takes a lot to shake a Cornishman in his beliefs. At Veryan-in-Roseland the natives still avow that their little round, white-washed, thatched cottages, each proudly displaying a wooden cross, were deliberately made circular in shape in order to deprive the Devil of corners in which to lurk, and that the crosses were erected to give them Divine protection. Round Liskeard way, too, they will still point a warning finger to a group of enormous prehistoric stones, and tell you that those are the bodies of men who once played the old Cornish game of hurling on a Sunday, and who, after the style of Lot and his wife, were turned into rocks for their sins. Indeed, the stones have long become famous as the " Hurlers ".

Nor were they the only offenders to suffer such a fate, it seems. Near St. Buryan is a group known as the " Nine Maidens ", which, tradition has it, represent a like number of young women who let gaiety get the better of them, and went out dancing on the Sabbath.

That strange arrangement of stones near the Hurlers that goes by the name of the " Cheesewring " is also credited to the Devil. Who else, it is asked, would have piled up stones of so many tons weight in such a way that the largest of them, some thirty-four feet in circumference, was left on top with the smallest at the bottom ? The old stones of Cornwall, especially round Zennor—with its many cromlechs, logan stones, bee-hive huts, and the like, to remind us of the part played by primitive man in shaping the face of the county—certainly provide plenty of food for the fertile imagination. So do some of the natural rock formations, if it comes to that. The fishermen around Land's End will tell you that Gog and Magog are the petrified forms of giants, just as those at Kynance Cove, not to be outdone, will proudly point out the Devil's Pillar Box, the Witches' Kitchen, and many others with equally strange stories.

No matter where we go, there is always plenty to see. While at the Bedruthan Steps, near Newquay, almost terrifying in their magnificence, we may find the Queen Elizabeth Rock. Near Bolventor we shall stand beside the thirty-acre Dosmary Pool, imagining the Cornishman, Tregeagle, to be still beside us, laboriously endeavouring to bale out the water with a limpet shell in fulfilment of a punishment for his crimes. Tradition has it that the pool is bottomless, and cottagers of nearby hamlets still say that it is Tregeagle howling in his anguish whenever they hear the wind sweeping across the lonely moors.

At Truro we shall come upon the exquisite Mansion House, whose Bath Stone, of which it is built, was presented by Ralph Allen, " the Man of Bath ". An American visitor once considered it so beautiful that he went straight home and arranged for it to be copied in detail in his own land.

On Bodmin Moor, that long and lonely stretch, with its barrows and earthworks, and its hills, Brown Willey and Rough Tor, providing two of the highest points in Cornwall, we shall find the little grey stone Jamaica Inn that Miss Daphne du Maurier made famous in her novel. Bleak and forbidding—very different from the galleried Tudor affair portrayed in the film—anything might have happened there ; as, indeed, it is possible to imagine that anything might still happen anywhere on Bodmin Moor, lovely though it is in its bleakness.

While St. Neot can boast some of the oldest and finest stained glass in the country, Wadebridge can claim to have the only bridge whose foundations consist simply of bale upon bale of wool, this material proving the only one to hold firm in the shifting sands of the Camel estuary. Though to-day the bridge, with its some fifteen arches, forms part of a quite busy main road, it still stands as secure as ever.

Perhaps most interesting of all, though—if only on account of the important part they have played in the life and outlook of her people—are the many old wells with which Cornwall so richly abounds. In the days before Christianity was brought to England, all and sundry would come from far and wide to these wells, firm in the belief that their waters contained spirits that would absolve them of their sins, rid them of their maladies, and generally protect them from future harm. Indeed, such an integral part of their lives did they become that when, at last, Christianity did arrive, many of them were re-dedicated to the various saints. Thus, from meeting-places for the adoration of strange gods, they gradually became transformed into centres of Christian worship. Not that all the wells are pagan in origin—far from it. Some of them were started by the saints themselves, as, for instance, St. Keyne's Well at Liskeard, which is said to have issued forth when St. Cadoc struck his staff into the ground there. Staffs certainly seem to have had a way with them when driven into the Cornish soil !

With the building of the churches, the wells lost much of their importance. They were by no means to be deserted, however. On the contrary, with the march of time belief in their curative properties only strengthened, until soon each grew to be associated with one particular complaint. While the wells at Madron, Lewannick, St. Breward, and elsewhere, acquired reputations for curing sore eyes, those at Perranzabuloe and Buryan became no less notable for their successes with cases of rickets. Weaklings might turn to St. Austell, but those with whooping cough would make for St. Minver with as much confidence as those with wounds put their trust in the well at Sancreed.

St. Keyne's itself, besides possessing certain healing propensities, became the object of an unusual superstition among the young men and maidens for miles around. Believing that once they had become man and wife the one who drank first of its waters would hold the whip-hand and generally get the better of the deal, as it were, the newly-weds would invariably run, helter-skelter, for the well the moment the marriage ceremony was over. Nor did the menfolk always get it their own way in the chase, as might be imagined. Southey tells of a woman who took a bottle of the precious water to church with her, and stood placidly drinking it in the porch while her bridegroom puffed and blew his way to the well.

Equally effective, it seems, was the well at Altarnun, Cornwall's largest parish. Here lunatics were brought to their senses by a combination of magical waters, chill, shock, and general man-handling. Placed with his back to the well, the troubled man was knocked bodily in by a forceful blow on the chest, the ceremony being repeated, time and again, until at last his rage had subsided. More often, one would have thought, he would have been either dead or unconscious after a few rounds of this. Still, perhaps an unconscious man was sometimes mistaken for a cured one in the heat of the moment.

The wells were, in effect, the forerunners of the spas of Georgian days, and so deep was the Cornishman's faith that inns were often built nearby to provide accommodation for the many pilgrims so constantly making their way to them ; some of them coming as incurables, others just to make sure of things. Even to this day that faith is not entirely lost. Though many of Cornwall's wells have long since fallen into disuse, and serve only to remind us of an age that is past, we may yet find Cornishmen—and women, for that matter—who still prefer to put their trust in their local wells rather than in modern medicines; who still believe their waters to be enchanted. Maybe they are: try to find Holy Well, cleft in the rocks of Holywell Bay, and it is possible to believe anything! One moment it stands out clear before you; continue your course towards it, however, and it has disappeared again. I once made as many as three attempts in one day, yet, though I must have been almost beside it, I never found it.

But if the belief in the wells is not as strong as it was, Cornish men and women may still be found carrying on some of the old customs that have grown with them through the centuries, sometimes from ages so remote that their origin is a matter of but small importance.

Some of these customs, like the Padstow Hobby Horse, are as pagan as the wells, even though far more recent interpretations, such as the commemoration of shipwrecks and the like, have since been attributed to them.

If, on April 30, we stand by the harbour's edge at Padstow, and listen to the clock striking out the hour of midnight, we shall soon find ourselves in the company of a group of men and women with blackened faces who, but a short while before, had been eating, drinking, laughing, and generally making merry in the *Golden Lion* close by. In the stillness of the night we shall hear some shadowy figure call out a few names, to be answered at once by other shadows. These men and women are no other than a chosen team of singers who have come to herald the arrival of May and, with it, the hope of a good summer; the "gang", or members, of the Hobby Horse team.

Within a few minutes we shall find ourselves alone

again as the shadows make their way up one of the streets leading from the harbour, singing :

Unite, unite and let us all unite
For Summer is a-coming unto day,
And whither we are going we will all unite,
In the merry morning of May.

Outside each house they will stop and sing verses to each of the various members of the family inside, some of the verses hinting strongly, to say the least of it, for some small money contribution, as, for instance :

You've a shilling in your purse, and I wish it was in mine,
In the merry morning of May.

And so it will be most likely ; for, after completing their round, the singers snatch a few short hours of sleep from what is left of the night, before passing round the hat, so to speak, next morning.

At eight o'clock, or thereabouts, they will repair to the *Golden Lion* once more, to emerge again, two hours later, with their vicious-looking horse, whereupon the entire town of Padstow will become quite light-headed in their excitement. It is the day of days. Led by some hefty man, inappropriately dressed as a dainty-looking woman, and accompanied by the " gang " in their top hats and ridiculous assortment of clothes and floral adornments, the " hoss " dances its way through the streets of the town for hours on end, varying its antics with occasional wild dashes against some of the women onlookers to increase (according to superstition) their chances of fertility, and with periodic death falls. At each fall the crowds will break forth into a traditional funeral dirge calculated to bring about its resurrection. And so the ceremony will continue for as long as you like, or at any rate until their energy gives out, and the " gang " consider that a further visit to the " local " is indicated.

The importance attached to May Day dates back to

" At Veryan the little round, white-washed thatched cottages were deliberately made circular to deprive the Devil of corners in which to lurk."

" The ' hoss ' dances its way through the streets of the town "—the Padstow hobby horse.

"The shops barricaded as of old"--a hurling match at St. Columb.

"At Lanreath, they still bring in the Maypole."

earliest times. In the Middle Ages—and long before then—the peasant heralded it not only as the approach of summer, but also as the end of his winter privations. The cereals which he had threshed by hand in the autumn were giving out by now and, besides, he had grown uncommonly tired of the dried fish that, for long months, had provided the most substantial part of his meagre winter diet, while even the more wealthy were beginning to feel that they had seen enough of Cornish mutton. May Day, then, was a day of hope and expectation ; something calling for celebration, sober or otherwise. It was a day on which the children rejoiced as much as their parents, and to this day the boys and girls in the Penzance district will herald its dawn with the blowing of horns and bugles as their fathers and grandfathers did before them.

At Lanreath, too, they still bring in the Maypole, and after christening it with good old English ceremonies, dance around it as of old, cutting it up into skittles at the end of the month for their traditional game of ninepins.

Though held a week later, the Furry Dance at Helston, like the Padstow Hobby Horse, has undoubtedly sprung from this sense of relief. Here, on May 8, we shall find the streets gaily decorated with multi-coloured flags and bunting—a sorry exchange for the more appropriate boughs and tender-leafed branches used of old—as practically the entire town, from the oldest inhabitant, almost, down to the youngest child that is capable of moving unaided, dance their giddy way. In and out of the houses, round the corners, up the side tracks, into the back yards, they go, bowing and curtseying to all and sundry to bring them the luck of the season. No one in Helston would think of working on that day—it would be almost immoral. Besides, there is too much going on. Apart from the dancing, there is a fair and a ball, while the dances themselves are as many in number as they are detailed in execution. At one time we may see a group of children dancing with willow boughs in their hands ; at another, we shall turn our eyes upon the maid-servants and others of their kind ; then at midday, by contrast, will come the frock-coated gentry with their womenfolk dressed in brightly-coloured summer frocks, adorned with sprays of lily-of-the-valley. Not that it matters which party is dancing : it is the same spirit prompting the same gaiety—the inherent love of summer and all that it stands for in the farmer's calendar.

At Helston, too, they still beat the bounds in Rogation week ; a survival of the days when maps were unknown, and when the occasion of blessing the crops was made an opportunity for impressing upon all the boundary lines of their territory. In this respect the younger members of the community often had a thin time of it. Where a stream or river formed a terminal point, a boy might be thrown in bodily, and left to struggle out as best he could ; where a particularly prickly hedge was met with, he would probably be rolled in it ; he might even be expected to climb the roof of a house ; or, at points where there was no specific obstacle to surmount, he might be made the target for a round of stone-throwing. Yet, if the beating of the bounds was sometimes tantamount to downright cruelty, there was method in their madness. It was reckoned that treatment of this kind in early childhood would leave such a lasting impression upon the young memories as to prove a safeguard against disputes in the years to come. Certainly the young had every reason to remember the boundaries !

Needless to say, such methods no longer find favour. Indeed, at Helston the boot is on the other foot, as it were. Here the boys mark their boundaries with clods of earth and pieces of hawthorn, and give each pile a sound beating with a wand before passing on to the next. At Bodmin, on the other hand, where the ceremony is held less frequently, we may still see something of the old river-ducking when, at Saltings Pool, towards the end of a trek of several miles, a ball is thrown into the water, and all dash in after it in hopeful expectation of an award of ten shillings for the rescuer, or of fifteen shillings for he who succeeds in running back with it to the Mayor. This stage is actually part of the old hurling game that has long formed part of Bodmin's ceremony.

A kind of primitive football, bearing a distinct similarity to the old Roman game of *harpastum*, this hurling was, until comparatively recent times, a pastime which shared the Cornishman's affections only with wrestling. There were two varieties—hurling to goal and hurling to country—and it was in the latter that he really let himself go. Here the goals, often several miles apart, would take the form of some definite landmark such as the squire's house, an inn, or even, maybe, a church tower. Though details often varied with the districts, the object always was to get the ball to the opponent's goal by whatever means seemed the most appropriate at the time. Fierce and often extremely dangerous were the matches played between village and village. Neither houses nor rocks, neither bogs nor hedges, were allowed to prove impediments as the players battled their way mercilessly towards their objective, each side confident that the victorious village would meet with good fortune throughout the ensuing year ; all hopefully expectant of a well-earned reward at the end of the game, provided, more often than not, by the squire at whose house the ball was eventually delivered up. Not always friendly was the rivalry in the old days ; sometimes it was downright antagonistic. Still, in the main, everybody was happy ; broken limbs, with perhaps an odd death or two here and there, were of small account, and could hardly be expected to mar the proceedings. But that was in olden times ; things are different now.

At St. Columb Major every Shrove Tuesday we may yet see the houses and shops barricaded as of old in readiness for a hurling match that is to take place later that day between " Town and Country " ; between, that is, those who live in St. Columb itself and those whose homes are in the more outlying parts of the parish. Somewhere about tea time one of the more youthful members of the community will climb the lamp-post in the square to call for three cheers for the silver-coated wooden ball ; a moment later the little town will vibrate with a mighty roar from the voices of perhaps a thousand players, and a possibly even larger number of spectators. Not long afterwards the ball will be " hove up " into the air from a point in the centre of the town, whereupon the players will set-to with a will, and with a speed and cunning, and with an endurance, unknown to any but a traditional hurler. Here the goals, consisting of stone troughs on the Newquay and Wadebridge roads, are two miles apart, and the game will continue until at last some fast and youthful runner manages to dodge the rather more cunning old-timers who lie in wait for him in the most unsuspected places, and outwits them with his speed, to bring the ball safely to his opponent's goal. That is, of course, assuming that all have not previously submitted to physical exhaustion. But this does not often happen. The clothes of the players may be tattered and torn ; their bodies mud-spattered and cut, long before the end. But they have stout hearts these Cornishmen, and in any case, there is always the thought of the evening celebration to keep them going. For the " evening " is part of the show. Then the toast of the ball will be drunk after it has been immersed in beer.

At St. Ives, too—where rough storms sometimes pile up the sand on the beach so high as to maroon people in the nearby houses—we may see another form of hurling, played between goals. But, if this is a tame affair by comparison with the St. Columb Major ceremony, St. Ives has a number of other interesting old customs to make up. Here the guise dancers still carry out their New Year pagan processional through the streets, just as, at midsummer, like the people of Land's End and Penzance, they continue to hold their bonfire ceremonies. Once a regular feature of English country life, when children and animals would be dashed through the flames for luck or in the hope of curing them of some ailment, these bonfire meetings are, in effect, but Christianized survivals of the old Summer Solstice when men and animals were offered up in homage to the sun.

At St. Ives also, every five years, on the feast of St. James the Apostle, we shall find ten small girls dancing to the music of a fiddler before a mausoleum, built in the eighteenth century by an eccentric lawyer named Knill. For many years Collector of Customs at this little port, Knill became the prime mover in a treasure hunt around the Lizard. When, alas, the hunt failed, he consoled himself by building a mausoleum—some fifty feet high and now known as Knill's Steeple—and preparing a deed of trust whereby the children taking part in this strange ceremony were to receive £5 between them, and the fiddler £1.

The traditional fairs of " Summercourt ", " Corpus Christi " (maintained only at Penzance, because, it is said, news of the Reformation, with its subsequent changes, never reached this " outpost "), " Mazzard ", and " Long " still hold a place in the countryman's calendar, while parishes, both large and small, even yet cling to their time-honoured feast-days. And these are no ordinary feasts ; what with her pasties, saffron cake, " hoggans ", " fuggans ", " figgy hobbins ", marinated pilchards, and, of course, her delicious cream, the Cornish woman has many unusual dishes with which to whet the appetite.

A Cornish woman once told me that the pasty was originally made its unusual shape so that the tinner could carry it in his pocket while working underground. For a similar reason it is customary to cut the initials of the prospective owner in one corner of the pastry before baking. By eating from the opposite end, the tinner—and others, for that matter—can always be certain of picking up the right one again should he put it down on a ledge or elsewhere for a few minutes.

Expert as they are, though, at making up their dishes, in one or two parts the women prefer to let someone else do the actual baking. At Mevagissey, for instance, they still run a communal cookhouse, where their midday meal can be cooked for a penny a time on weekdays and for twopence on Sundays. Here the housewives will converge on the bakery from all corners in the early morning ; at noon, or thereabouts, they will be back again, and it is amusing to hear their happy, excited chatter and laughter as they hurry home with their steaming pies and puddings. I am told that when, some years ago, electric cookers first came to Mevagissey, few of the cottagers would have anything to do with such new-fangled contraptions.

It is easy to believe, for Cornwall and her people are unique. Indeed, as we reach the Tamar to cross into Devon, and realize that, but for some three miles of land in the north, Cornwall would be an island, and as we stop to ponder his strange ways of life, we begin to see why the Cornishman persists in regarding the rest of us as " furriners ".

Before we cross, let us linger a while by the banks of the Tamar, and imagine ourselves listening to the first verse of Cornwall's national song, *One and All*, which, like *Joseph Was a Tinner* and *As I Sat On a Sunny Bank*, is still widely sung. Let us imagine the words to be echoing from some far distant valley where, perhaps, a thousand or more are gathered together :

O rugged and bold are Cornwall's cliffs,
And rugged and bold are her men,
Stalwart and true when there's work to do,
And heeding not where or when ;
Braving the storm on ocean wave,
Or toiling beneath the ground,
Wherever the spot, whatever his lot,
The Cornishman staunch is found.

Therein does the Cornishman tell of himself and his countryside.

Two — *Red Earth and Cob*

A FEW miles across the border, we find the scene changing to an extent that is truly remarkable. Except in the bleak and lonely stretches of Dartmoor and Exmoor, the inland country becomes at once more wooded and more kindly, while the villages themselves, with their quaint little white-washed cob cottages, built of mud without any timber framework and thatched with locally-grown straw, provide a pleasing contrast with the more grim granite homes of parts of Cornwall. Houses of all sorts there are these days, but cob is Devon's vernacular.

The coastline, too, becomes more kindly as the steep, rugged rocks of Cornwall give way to red cliffs and many-coloured strata ; never so magnificent, but beautiful for all that.

On the Southern coast, especially along the stretch between Torquay and Beer, it is a curious fact that the villages two or three miles inland are infinitely older and more picturesque than those immediately by the sea. Indeed, so strange is the contrast that I recently asked a fisherman the reason.

" Cob is Devon's vernacular "—cob cottages in the shadow of the village church at Woodbury.

“That quaint little old-world town set in a hollow between beautiful wooded hills”—Dartmouth. The Naval College is on the right.

“Farming is the mainstay of Devon life”—haymaking in Devon.

"Pirates!" he half whispered, and almost appeared to stiffen himself as if to avoid a shudder.

"Pirates? What kind of pirates?"

"Algerians. Come over at dead of night, they did. Looking for slaves, they were. No one dared live by the sea in those days, I tell 'ee."

The old salt puffed at his pipe of evil-smelling tobacco and gazed seawards as he talked, until I quite expected him to shout a warning of an approaching vessel and see him and the rest of his companions drop their work and beat a hasty retreat inland.

"Of course that was a long time ago. We don't have to worry about them now," he went on as if to comfort me.

Still, it was not so very long ago, it seems. It is only in the last three hundred years or so that anyone has deemed it quite safe to live by the sea; only in the last three hundred years that the majority of the coastal towns and villages have sprung up. Before that, those who earned their living by the sea were careful to keep their wives and children at a safe distance inland lest they should be carried off as slaves; nor did they lose any time in getting back themselves as soon as dusk approached. Thus such villages as East Budleigh and Otterton which, to-day, appear to have no connection with the sea and are now of no importance in themselves, were once the homes of fishermen and saltworkers, and ports of no mean consequence. Indeed, it was from these two ports—before the harbour became silted up about the year 1450, and the course of the River Otter diverted as a result—that much of our wool was exported to the Continent in the days when the wool taxes provided a principal source of revenue and did much to finance the wars with the French.

The making of salt was then a thriving Devon

industry, and such towns as Salcombe Regis—where the work was carried on as far back as the time of Athelstan—Budleigh Salterton, and Saltash can all trace their origin to the old saltpans. Special platforms would be erected on the beach in such a way as to allow the high tides to beat over them. Then, after allowing a suitable time for evaporation, the workers would hurriedly return to sweep up the salt before the next tide. At Otterton, soon after the Norman Conquest, thirty-three men were engaged wholetime at this industry, and salt was sold at the Sunday market.

It seems hard to imagine that anyone in Devon should ever have been frightened of anything, when one thinks of the names of some of her most famous sons—Sir Francis Drake, Sir Walter Raleigh, General Monk, the Duke of Marlborough, Captain Scott, and a whole host of others.

In the little hamlet of Hayes, just out of East Budleigh, where his father was churchwarden in 1561, we may still visit the thatched farmhouse where Sir Walter Raleigh was born. Here we may see the four-poster bed in which he is said to have first seen the light of day, and the settle—a most rickety affair—in the kitchen from which he used to watch the farm produce being cooked on the spit (still there) over the large open fire. We may still see his smoke-room and one of his tobacco-jars, while on the front door we shall find the old flint which he used for lighting his famous pipe.

Raleigh had a special affection for his old birthplace, and cherished the thought of spending his retirement there, till the scaffold put an end to such hopes. At the farm they will show you a letter which he wrote to the Lord of the Manor, Richard Duke, with this idea in mind :

Mr Duke I wrote to Mr Prideux to move you for the purchase of Hayes, a farme sometime in my father's possession. I will most willingly give you whatsoever in your conscience you shall deeme it worthe and if you shall at any time have occasion to use mee you shall find me a thanckful friend to you and yours. . . . I am resolved, if I cannot interest you, to build att Colliton, but for the natural disposition I have to that place, being borne in that house, I had rather seat myself there than any wher els. . . .

Court the XXVI of July 1584

Your very willing frinde in all I shall be able

W. Ralegh

Incidentally, Raleigh was not the only one to cast longing eyes upon the farm ; an American once offered the owner a blank cheque to be allowed to dismantle the old home and transport it to his own country. The offer, happily, was rejected.

Not far from the farm, down the winding lane into East Budleigh, is the old vicarage—a cob building with walls some three-and-a-half feet thick—where the great Elizabethan learnt his lessons. A place of somewhat doubtful reputation in the past : the owner told me that it was once an important receiving-centre in the old smuggling days, a secret passage—unearthed at the beginning of last century—having proved a suitable hide-out.

A former vicar, it seems, was one of the central figures in a great intrigue, and a good story is told, showing the pains he took to hoodwink his parishioners while posing as the kindly shepherd of his flock and so gaining their esteem and affection. To help him in his exploits a ghost—that of one of his late lamented female relatives—was conveniently brought on to the scene. Night after night the wretched "woman" would be seen wandering through the village, draped in white from head to foot. So terrifying was the apparition that the villagers soon gave both church and vicarage a wide berth ; indeed, it was not long before they deemed it wiser to stay indoors altogether after dark. So far so good ; the vicar and his accomplices were left undisturbed to carry on their nocturnal activities. The fat was in the fire, however, when one night a " Preventive Man ", seeing a light in a downstair window of the vicarage, chanced to peer through, only to find vicar and ghost comfortably ensconced by the fire smoking their pipes !

Almost a stone's throw from the old vicarage is the church where, it is said, a carving of a sailing ship gave Raleigh his first dreams of adventure. In the house opposite was born Roger Conant, who, in 1623, founded Salem in America.

Though Drake's birthplace at Crowndale, near Tavistock, has long since vanished, we may still see his country seat, Nutwell Court, at Lympstone, as also may we yet gaze seawards from Plymouth Hoe, and ponder the admiral's famous game of bowls. Sail has given place to steam, but it is even now possible to capture something of the Elizabethan touch. To the Devonians Drake is ever the figure-head of the Royal Navy, but by the people of Plymouth he is remembered for something more—for bringing them water.

Like most great men of his time, Drake once rubbed Queen Elizabeth up the wrong way, and during his brief period of unpopularity at Court became Mayor of Plymouth, a post at which he appears to have excelled. Horrified at the idea of the inhabitants having to fetch their water from a spot something like a mile away, and having already been angered at the difficulty experienced in getting it for his ships when setting off on his voyages, he at once laid plans for building a reservoir and bringing water to the city from a point on Dartmoor some seven miles off. In recognition of his services the Devonians still hold periodic "Fyshyne Feasts", when the Mayor of Plymouth leads a pilgrimage to Burrator to drink Drake's health—first in spring water and then in wine —offering the toast: "May the descendants of him who gave us water never lack wine."

Just off the main Axminster road by Musbury stands the beautiful old stone Manor House, known as Asshe House, together with its tiny private chapel. Where the great Duke of Marlborough was born in 1650. It was an accident of fate that brought the Churchills to this spot from Minthorne in Dorset. The Duke's father, Sir William Churchill, had backed the wrong side in the Civil War, and had fallen upon hard times as a result of his Royalist sympathies. Thus he and his wife, Elizabeth, had packed up home and moved to Asshe House to live for a time with her parents and so save expenses.

A land of adventurers, Devon has certainly seen much movement in her time. Ask a native of Dartmouth—that quaint little old-world town set in a hollow between beautiful wooded hills at the mouth of the Dart—about the Naval College, and he will at once dismiss that as modern, and proceed to recall the days when young cadets were trained in the old *Britannia*, a wooden sailing ship of three decks. But he will not only talk of times that he himself can remember: he will tell you proudly—as if to convince you that Dartmouth has *always* been important—how it was from here that William the Conqueror set off on his last voyage, and Richard Cœur de Lion, after him, embarked on his great crusade. He will talk excitedly too of the time, in 1404, when Dartmouth turned out, almost to a man, to drive away the French invaders. To him Dartmouth is the only place.

Get chatting to a Brixham man, on the other hand, and he will point to a stone on the quay, declaring in his good-humoured way that, but for Brixham, the whole history of England would have been altered. For it was on this stone that William of Orange first set foot on English soil in his bid for the Crown after the miserable James II had made such a hash of things. To drive home his point, he will ask you to imagine, for the sake of argument, what would have happened if the inhabitants had decided to " turn nasty " by resisting the landing. Brixham folk are proud of their part in history, but then, so are those of Newton Abbot. They will not let you forget that it was here that Dutch William made his first proclamation to the people, and will lead you to the spot where he stood during this somewhat tense moment when the future of the Crown hung in the balance, the outcome depending, to a large extent, upon the reception accorded by the Devonians.

Then, again, Exeter will argue that she played her part in guarding England's destiny nearly a hundred years before that, when Drake, Frobisher, Hawkins, Raleigh, and many others held their councils of war in the oak-panelled room on the first floor of Mol's Coffee House—now occupied by an art dealer—in the shadow of the Cathedral. Indeed, it was here that many of the finer points of battle were thrashed out in the dark days before the Armada ; points that brought victory to British arms and glory to Devon's name.

By no means all Devon's famous men were adventurers, however. At Holne, on the edge of Dartmoor, where, incidentally, is an ancient dole stone, we may visit the old vicarage where that delightful character, Charles Kingsley, was born. When only four years old, he had delighted to dress up in a pinafore for a surplice and address stirring sermons to imaginary congregations from a home-made "pulpit" in his nursery.

His name will ever be linked with that of Devon. Bideford, and Clovelly, that fascinating little cove with its cottage windows and doors decorated with brightly-coloured fruit and flowers, all hand-carved by the famous Passion Players of Oberammergau, and where a donkey postman carries the mail up the narrow cobbled main street; Westward Ho! where Kipling was educated, and which later figured in *Stalky & Co.*; and South Zeal, where Dickens wrote part of the *Pickwick Papers* at the local inn—these must always be Kingsley's.

His father was Rector of Clovelly for a time from 1830. There, beloved of the fishermen, whenever the boats were going out he would go down to the quayside to conduct a special service for their benefit, when the words of the 121st Psalm would echo through the countryside with a fervour and sincerity unsurpassed.

Such scenes as these, like the Atlantic gales that so often spelt disaster for these North Devon fishing fleets, left their mark on young Charles, inspiring some of his finest work both in the pulpit and by the pen. Fierce seas still rage at times along this stretch of coast, and as we stand gazing out on Bideford Bay, let us recall Kingsley's epic description of

> the tiny herring-boats fleeing from their nets right for the breakers, hoping more mercy even from those iron walls of rock than from the pitiless howling waste of spray behind them; and that merry beach beside the town covered with shrieking women and old men, casting themselves on the pebbles in fruitless agonies of prayer, as corpse after corpse swept up at the feet of wife and child, till in one case alone, a single dawn saw upwards of sixty widows and orphans weeping over those who had gone out the night before in the fulness

of strength and courage. Hardly an old playmate of mine but is drowned and gone.

At Plympton we may picture the first President of the Royal Academy, Sir Joshua Reynolds, " wasting his time " at the local Grammar School by drawing the likenesses of his school fellows, while his father, who was master there, vainly endeavoured to train him for a medical career. While at Budleigh Salterton we shall be shown the house, Octagon by name, where Millais painted his famous picture, " The Boyhood of Raleigh ". His two sons and a local fisherman posed as the models, and the wall where they sat while the old salt recounted his tales of adventure still stands.

At Ottery St. Mary, too, we shall find links with both Coleridge and Thackeray. It was while his father was vicar here that Samuel was born in a house known as The Chantry, and it is said that Thackeray, who used to come here for many of his holidays while at Charterhouse, took the church as the subject for his Clavering St. Mary in *Pendennis*. More or less a replica in miniature of the cathedral at Exeter, it was in this church that the Parliamentary troops sought refuge for some five weeks in 1645, before eventually being driven out by the pestilence.

Devon is justly proud both of her past and of her many illustrious sons, and that is the secret of much of her charm to-day ; she even yet regards the old ways of life as the best, and shows it alike in her country and her people.

The days of the squirearchy are by no means past in this enchanting corner of the English countryside. Farming is the mainstay of Devon life, and most districts have their Lord of the Manor or Squire, who is respected according to the efficiency with which he runs his estate. To the countryman he is neither a

" Fishing is still second only to farming in importance "—a Devon fisherman-coastguard " bricking " his lobster-pot in readiness for the tide.

" What more beautiful than that quaint little cluster of stone-built thatched cottages? "—Buckland-in-the-Moor.

" It was in the forge here that Tom Pearse's grey mare is said to have been shod "—the forge at Widecombe-in-the-Moor.

figurehead nor a snob, but an employer for whom he will work tooth-and-nail, confident in the thought that while he is giving of his best his master will have his well-being at heart. It is a happy union ensuring the prosperity of all ; a union which once formed the basis of country life at its best in the days before industrialism cast its mass-production gloom over our island life and ways.

In Devon it is not necessary to have a letter of introduction before you say " good-morning " to your neighbour for the first time. The humble peasant, with corduroys tied up with string under the knees, likes you to pass the time of day with him as he clatters down the lane in his hob-nailed boots, homeward bound at the end of a long day in the fields. The old-fashioned courtesy still persists, and it is shown as much to the complete stranger as to the native.

As I say, this clinging to the old ways shows itself as much in the countryside as in the people. All over Devon we shall meet with instances of whole villages which are owned by one man, whose only wish is to preserve the beauty of the countryside while, at the same time, making his land an economic asset. In such cases land and buildings alike are sold by leasehold only, and in that way the lords are able to form a bulwark against the jerry-builders and other would-be despoilers. Thus, by their life and outlook, the Devonians are proving the traditions of the past to be the most effective means of combating the menaces of the present. The results are delightful.

A happy, cheerful people, they reveal their carefree spirits in their musical voices. No Devon church is ever hard-up for a good choir, although one vicar confessed to me that he always takes care to steer clear of Hymn 197 (Ancient and Modern) since he finds the natural tendency to modify an " oo " into an " ü " just a little disconcerting when a crowded congregation really gets into its stride and starts singing of "güd" and "güdness"; "füd" and "fülish".

Fascinating, this Devon brogue!—as fascinating as many of the words and phrases that mean so much to the native, but which are often quite unintelligible to the rest of us. Many a time have I been tied up by their quaint expressions. Particularly disturbing is the Devonian's refusal to recognize the masculine gender; everyone is "her"—or, rather, "'er"—whether man, woman or child. Likewise parents seem to have a rooted objection to referring to their female offspring as daughters; always are they "maids".

A man never grows old in Devon; he simply "gets up along", just as the lights are never put out at night, but are "douted". And even then it is not considered to be dark but "dimpsey". Ask a cottager the way anywhere, and she will point her thumb in the direction and, with a kindly smile, will say "'ee wants to go thicky way, 'ee do. Of course 'ee could go round there, but thicky way's best, I tell 'ee."

Call in on the same cottager one cold winter evening, and she will draw a chair up to her welcoming hearth, and bid you "catch yet". As the evening draws on, she may bring out a bag of sweets—"taffies", she will call them—and ask you to try one, assuring you that they make very "purty eating".

The Devon housewife has many delicacies which make "purty eating", and, just as in Cornwall the county dishes have largely sprung up around the life of the tinner, so here they are centred around the farm. Apple dumplings, the farmer's wife will tell you, are of Devon origin, as also are junket-and-cream and those elongated scones which glory in the name of "stiffs". Every day on every farm we may find enormous quantities of dumplings steaming away in large iron crocks upon the open hearths ; for the dumpling is the farm-hand's national dish, just as cider is his national drink.

When talking of food, it is well to be wary, though. Cream, for instance, is a touchy point. There is nothing that pleases the Devon woman more than that you should ask for Devonshire cream in Cornwall ; but she dislikes it intensely the other way round. So, too, is there a certain feeling on the matter of " stiffs ". Both Cornwall and Dorset make a " split ", but to her way of thinking they are entirely inferior, and afford no excuse for confusion. As for cider—well, here we are in danger of getting-up the back of the farmer himself. To suggest that the orchards of Hereford and Kent could possibly be in the same street as those of Devon is just insulting. Only grudgingly will he admit the claims of Somerset and then, doubtless, only on account of the other's close proximity.

Although the work is no longer done so universally throughout the county, the making of cider is still an autumn ritual on farms both large and small. For the native still prefers his " firkin " of " jungle juice " to a tankard of any beer. Nor has he any use for the bottled stuff of the multiple firms, which he classes as " woman's " ; what he wants is his good old " rough ". More often than not he will have his own cider tankard which, no matter what its size, he will always insist on calling a " firkin ", quite undeterred by the fact that, strictly, this is the equivalent of nine gallons.

Pretty potent is this Devon cider at times ; not to be recommended to an inexperienced drinker who is contemplating going out into the midday summer sun immediately afterwards. Indeed, its potency has been the cause of much amusement in the village pubs, where the hardened yokels find plenty to entertain them in watching the growing effects of their " juice " on strangers.

I shall always remember the scene in one bar. A somewhat fashionable youth with immaculately brushed hair—so fashionable that I glanced through the window expecting to see a lavish-looking car outside—had entered, and ordered himself a glass of cider—" some of your local stuff. Better try it while I'm here." He drank it down, but obviously did not think much of it, and so proceeded to call for a tankard of " mild and bitter ".

This was too much for one old yokel. He was up in a flash.

" Don't 'ee do that, I tell 'ee ! "

" And why, pray ? " The man with the hair was indignant.

" Only one man ever attempted that afore. 'Er cut 'er throat afterwards ! I *tell* 'ee."

The youth reluctantly took the tip, bought a packet of cigarettes instead, and went sheepishly out, much to the amusement of all.

As I say, the making of the cider is something of a ritual, and it is a job in which the farmer takes the greatest pride. Many and varied are the methods adopted ; antiquated to a degree some of the machinery used. In the old days the apples would be crushed to pomace by means of a horse-turned millstone ; now electrically driven grinding-machines are used instead. In Devon and Somerset, unlike other parts, the farmer likes to use straw—oat straw, for preference—to make his cider, since this helps to give it the required " kick ". After making a high, dome-shaped " cheese ", comprising alternate layers of straw and apples, the latter are left to rot. Then the press is clamped down, or the grinding machine set in motion, to crush the apples to pieces and so force the liquid to run through the straw into a wooden tub below, where it will be left to ferment before being strained off into the casks.

"So really the making of cider amounts to nothing more than turning everything bad!" I chaffed one farmer.

"Well, that be one way of looking at it, I suppose," he laughed. "Still, even if it is bad it's good too, I tell 'ee. Try some."

I did, and it was.

One of the secrets of good cider, he told me, lay in cleaning the casks with cold water, draining them well, and letting the air blow through.

"Mind 'ee, it takes a Devon man to make a cider that is neither sweet nor ropey."

"Ropey?"

"Aye, sharlegogs—sour."

Not all the cider is for human consumption. Among the first to taste of the precious juice are the trees that bore the season's fruit, for in most orchards the old custom of pouring cider round the roots to ensure fertility the following year is still kept up—the Devon farmer can never quite shake off his old beliefs.

By rubbing his hands with a piece of raw meat and then burying it in his garden, he still avows himself capable of banishing the most obstinate of warts. And if, perchance, that should fail—which would astonish him greatly—well, he has only to wait for the new moon, which will invariably do the trick. All that is necessary is to hold his hands to the sky, repeating three times the words "Moon, moon, I give thee my warts". Surely, they will be gone next morning. Strangely enough, such is, in fact, often the case.

Incidentally, they seem to be rather fond of the moon in Devon. In one or two parts, I am told, it is still customary for young damsels, anxious about their future, to stand with their backs to the moon and see how many images they can see in a hand mirror, each image representing one more year before they will finally find a husband. Nor is it only the moon that enjoys veneration: many a farmer will even yet declare that a bright noon sun on Christmas Day means a bumper apple crop next year.

Similarly, he whose child develops whooping-cough will at once take him to some spot where a sheep has lain all night, confident in the belief that the combination of wool and soil provides some magic healing property.

As I say, farming is Devon's lifeblood, and in villages everywhere children are introduced to the farm almost as soon as they can toddle. Indeed, by the age of eight they have already inherited, both traditionally and practically, a considerable understanding of livestock and crops, so that, as one farmer put it to me, they are virtually farmers from birth, with no thought of following any other occupation when their time comes to leave school.

The same is true to a great extent where the fisherfolk are concerned. It is nothing to see a boy of nine, or perhaps even less, get into a boat and put to sea on his own for hours on end. The mastery which these youngsters display in handling their craft even when the weather is quite wild—or, as the fisherman prefers to call it, "foosty"—is truly remarkable. But perhaps that is not surprising, for we must remember that we are in the land of Drake, and fishing is still second only to farming in importance.

All types of fishing are carried on along both the north and south Devon coasts—crabs, lobsters, herrings, mackerel, whiting, and so on—and it is interesting to watch these sons of the sea busily making their crab and lobster pots on the beaches, or their nets in the gardens of their cottage homes, in either late winter or early spring.

From May to September is the lobster season, and this is followed by herring-netting until Christmas, after which the " long lines ", with anything from a hundred to two hundred hooks to the line, are brought out. " Snifting " (spinning with a spinner) or " bobbing " for mackerel is an important branch, but it is upon the whiting that most fishermen pin their greatest faith, just as, in Cornwall, they turn to the pilchard.

But alas, as in Cornwall, fishing is declining. Beaches that could once boast twenty boats or more, each with crews of three or four to man them, now have no more than half-a-dozen fishermen all told, with two, or at best three, boats between them. The profits to be made are no longer enough to attract the younger generation to the same extent as in the past. As an instance, one fisherman told me that from a record season's catch of 360,000 herrings on his beach, no man earned as much as £20, while a good day seldom yields more than a few shillings per head.

Even so, the industry is by no means dead. At Brixham, possibly the county's greatest centre, I found that long years of war are leaving their mark in an unusual way—a beneficial way. When the Nazi hordes swept across the Low Countries, the fishermen of Belgium manned their craft and set sail for England. Some forty of them arrived at Brixham. Whereupon things began to happen. Sleepy Brixham, no longer able to rely on the pleasure-boating, which, in peace-time, had helped to keep the wolf from the door, awoke to a new realization. For the Belgians were soon to show that, given the right tackle, there was still plenty of money to be made from fish. Their boats were bigger and their engines more highly-powered. Thus did they prove themselves capable of bringing in greater and more profitable hauls.

The Belgians can fish from their own shores now, but the Brixham folk have not forgotten their lesson. Local boat-builders are looking to their designs, hopeful that bigger and better craft will bring renewed prosperity, not only to themselves but to other ports as well.

Among the most interesting of these ports is Beer. Once a great quarrying centre, it was from Beer that much of the stone was taken for building Devon's parish churches when, at last, Christianity became really established in England. Hitherto—that is between the era of the wells and the churches—it had been customary to erect a cross as a place of worship, a splendid example of which is to be seen at Copplestone—selecting some convenient spot such as the junction of four cross roads. When the church-building epoch arrived in all its glory in the Middle Ages, the Devon master masons, who were also their own architects, had their stone laboriously taken by packhorse from Beer to points within close proximity of these crosses : a long and weary procedure, demanding many burdensome journeys of great distance. By now imbued with a deep sense of religion, the masons were careful to build their churches as near to their cross as possible, often going so far as to enclose the latter within the graveyard. Thus have many of Devon's most prosperous towns and villages gradually sprung up, in the process of centuries, around what were once lonely meeting-places for scattered bands of worshippers. In many a churchyard we may yet see the old cross standing out, erect and dignified, mellowed by the ages, among the smaller gravestones, and I have more than once come upon one in a private garden ; a living reminder of a forgotten past. It is said that much of the material used in the construction of Exeter Cathedral was brought from Beer by packhorse, when the See of Devon and Cornwall moved from Crediton in the eleventh century, and the old Abbey church of St. Mary and St. Peter began to be remodelled and enlarged for the purpose.

It is said, too, that the people of Beer, like those of Bucks Mill, near Clovelly, are mostly of foreign extraction—the descendants of Spaniards whose ships were battered to pieces with the Armada, or of Flemish or Huguenot refugees who sought shelter here in the sixteenth century after being driven from their own countries by religious tyrannies.

Be that as it may, it was these and other refugees who first brought the art of lace-making to England. Those who sailed into Beer Cove lost no time in setting up their industry and in teaching the art to the villagers. In course of time the craft spread throughout the county, with Honiton assuming the position of lace-maker's " capital " by virtue of its convenient position as a collecting and distributing centre at a time when transport was all but non-existent.

Lace-schools were soon set up throughout the length and breadth of Devon, and these formed the main system of education for many generations. Nobody seems to have minded greatly whether a girl could read or spell, or whether, in fact, she could even write her own name, so long as she could make lace ; and this she would learn to do as soon as she was five.

It was at Beer that the lace was made for Queen Victoria's wedding dress, and the villagers still talk with pride of how Jane Bidney mustered together a hundred of the best craftswomen from all over the county, and executed the work at a cost of something like £1,000. So pleased with the result was the young queen that she at once sent word for the lace-maker to come to London to see her. But, alas, the ordeal proved too much for poor Jane, who was not used to such things; the story goes that she swooned while awaiting the audience.

Beer's link with royalty has not yet been wholly severed. A descendant of Jane Bidney still keeps the village lace-shop, and it is to her that Queen Mary sends her precious collection for periodic re-conditioning.

One old Devon lace-maker told me that she can remember the days when she and her kind were paid for their work in goods. As soon as an order was completed, she would traipse off to the village store to hand in her lace in exchange for her groceries or, maybe, such articles of drapery as she might be needing.

"Why, many of us used to buy almost all our household necessities in this way. Hardly ever put our hand in our purse for a penny, we didn't," she said.

The idea worked well, it seems, and everything went with a swing until, at last, the shopkeepers tried to palm off loaves of bread by way of payment. Since many of the women were faced with a journey of several miles, they, not unnaturally, revolted at having to carry back such heavy articles. Thereafter the practice stopped. The lace-makers were henceforth paid in cash, and their work was collected once a week and taken by carrier to Honiton.

The young girls of to-day prefer to visit the cinema rather than sit before their "pillows", but the Devon County Council are trying to bring about a revival in the re-establishment of the old-time lace-classes. A county organizer now travels from place to place superintending these classes, while many villages boast a salaried instructor whose duty it is to teach the art to children and adults alike.

The County Council is not unmindful of her heritage. Another craft to receive her blessing is thatching, for which Devon has long been famous. Here, too, a county instructor has been appointed to help swell the dwindling ranks of craftsmen, not only by training more young men for the industry, but also by staging periodic thatching contests in various parts of the county. As a foretaste of things to come, such contests have already been held with encouraging results at Dunsford, Drewsteignton, Cheriton Bishop, and one or two other parishes.

One of the most interesting of Devon's local industries is that of the little colony of edge-tool makers at Sticklepath, near Okehampton, who work in an old wool-mill and use a wheel driven by water-power from the River Taw for making axes, saws, hammers, spades, reap-hooks, and many other articles for the rural workman, as well as " tatie-cutters " for the Devon housewife. I am told that there are probably no more than half-a-dozen such craftsmen left in England, yet their goods are sent all over the world. They are, in fact, the traditional descendants of the first men ever to make tools out of metal.

Even in the days before the Industrial Revolution, when tools had to be made by hand, it was only by the rivers that such colonies could be found. For, by choosing such sites, the craftsmen were able to make the water serve the double purpose of providing the power in the first place, and the transport facilities both for bringing in the metal and for sending away the finished goods afterwards. Along these rivers the tools would be taken to the nearest port for export, or to some important highway to complete their journey by road.

These craftsmen use special forges with the tops enclosed for heating their metal. By means of long-handled tongs they hold their metal in the fire through an opening in the side. In the case of flat-surface tools, such as hooks, the hot metal is beaten into shape by an obsolete kind of drop hammer. An extraordinary business : the craftsman holds his piece in position over the anvil while a small boy, several yards away, solemnly raises and lowers an enormous hammer on to it by means of ropes and pulleys. Such articles as shovels, which have to be shaped, are beaten out hot over specially designed anvils.

One of the most interesting and most skilled stages is the " cutting " of the first edge. For this the craftsman lies flat on his stomach on a platform suspended above a huge grindstone, which is revolved at considerable speed by means of the water-wheel in the river. Only in this position can he get complete control and withstand the tremendous vibration—a job, as the craftsman pointed out, not to be recommended to anyone with false teeth !

There is still a great demand for these hand-made tools, many farmers refusing to use any others. In the old days they were taken off by cart and sold at stalls at the country fairs of both Devon and Cornwall.

" Why," said one of the men, " an ancestor of mine once walked twenty miles or more to Tavistock Fair with a load of billhooks on 'er back. Sold the lot, and returned home same night, 'er did."

" You mean she *walked* back ? "

" Why, bless me soul, yes ! What's more, a few days later she gave birth to a strapping son. Those were the days, I tell 'ee. A man knew what it was to work for his living then."

" You mean a *woman* did ? "

The tool-maker laughed : " Aye, and a woman."

Tools made at Sticklepath are still sold in the Devon markets, though, happily, modern transport makes it no longer necessary to go to such extremes to get them there.

Hardly less interesting is the little carpet factory at Axminster, where six grades of carpet—the Torquay, Super Seaton, Seaton, Super Devonian, Devonian, and Axe—are turned out in enormous quantities by power-driven looms before being examined and finished by hand. Incidentally, if you want to be certain of buying a carpet that has actually been *made* at Axminster, look at the underside of it ; you will see a red line running down the entire length one inch from the selvedge seam.

It was at Axminster and at Wilton in Wiltshire that carpet-making first sprang into prominence in England in the seventeenth century. The Axminster factory, however, closed for a hundred and six years, to open again with power-driven looms only as recently as 1937, so that it is to Wilton, where the work is still done as of old, that we shall turn for the romantic story of carpets.

Not far from Axminster, at the church at Axmouth, we may find a " Lord's Measure "—a relic of the days when, as a safeguard against possible cheating, corn used to be brought to the church porch to be weighed —while at Seaton, nearby, where the ancient Fosse Way is said to have started its long but remarkably straight course to Lincoln, we shall come upon the remains of a Roman villa.

Devon is, indeed, as rich as Cornwall in places of interest. At Lew Trenchard, where Baring-Gould lived and died, we shall be shown an avenue of trees that is said to be haunted by one of his ancestors, the " White Lady ", while at Combe Martin, once a great centre of silver-mining, we may see a " hanging stone ".

Ask a villager how the stone came to get its strange name, and he will tell you that a thief once rested here when making off with a stolen sheep. The sheep, it seems, was tied about the man's neck, and while struggling to free itself tumbled over to the other side of the stone, thereby tightening the rope and throttling the thief.

While at Brixham we shall find what is probably the only underground lighthouse in the world. At Bigbury-on-Sea we may cross to Burgh Island in the weirdest contraption imaginable—a kind of open-work, single-decker bus, mounted on caterpillar wheels, like those of a tank, which plies its leisured way through varying depths of water according to the state of the tide. A strange affair ; as strange as the cliff railway that passes through yards of solid rock to link together Lynton and Lynmouth, those lovely places on the edge of Exmoor, set amidst some of the most magnificent scenery in England, with nearby Countisbury and Hollerday providing probably the finest view-points.

Even Paignton, for all her " progress ", is not entirely without interest, and can still show us the remains of the old Palace where Miles Coverdale first translated the Bible in 1535 ; and at Buckfastleigh, up the River Dart, is the famous abbey that the monks of our time have re-built with their own hands, with a devotion reminiscent of the days before Henry VIII's Dissolution of the Monasteries, when the monks were among our finest craftsmen.

Hardly less interesting are the old bridge at Bideford, and the post office at Belstone. Though Bideford's bridge is mounted on no less than twenty-four arches, each is a different size. The explanation given is that, when it came to be built, the powers-that-be decided to get up a " round robin " to pay for its construction.

Instead of the money's being pooled, however, each subscriber paid for one arch, which was then made of a size commensurate with the value of his contribution. A precarious system one would have thought ; still, it has survived the test of some six centuries.

Should you at any time have occasion to seek the post office at Belstone, the native will point a directing finger and tell you that " what 'ee wants is the chapel ". And thereon hangs a story. Early last century, a villager told me, a Congregational chapel was built. Later it was handed over to the Wesleyans ; later still it became a village hall. During this time, the postal service was carried out by a certain stalwart, William Ellis by name, whose duties, however, also included those of telegraph messenger, watch-and-clock-repairer, seed-merchant, insurance-agent, church organist, church warden, bell-ringer, Dartmoor guide, and port-reeve to the Manor of Dartmoor.

By the time he reached the age of eighty, William, as might be expected, had become somewhat " browned off ", so to speak, with all this work. So that at last it was decided that Belstone really must have a post office of her own. Since, however, the chapel was the only building available, the pews were turned into shelves for postcards and telegraph forms, and a counter made of the original panelling. It is a queer feeling, going into a chapel to post a parcel, especially as the pulpit steps still remain to remind us of its old-time reverence ; queerer still to hear the village prattle where once there had been a hushed silence.

It is surprising how many inns in Devon carry the name of " Church House ". A clergyman with whom I discussed this point explained the fact as being a survival of the ancient practice of holding annual " church ales ". On such occasions an entire village would club together to act as hosts and hostesses to several neighbouring districts. The housewives would attend to the catering generally, while the farmers provided the malt, which was then brewed in the house adjoining the churchyard ; a house invariably known as the " Church House ". Such " ales " would be followed, more often than not, by a fair, games, dancing, and general merry-making, the money raised in this way—often amounting to quite large sums—being devoted to the upkeep of the church and to helping the poor of the village.

When one remembers that even as late as last century fives and other ball games were still being played against the church walls, one can readily appreciate that some form of repairing-fund must have been a stern necessity. It was the north wall that invariably suffered the most, for it was in this part of the graveyard that the murderers, felons, and still-borns were buried, and nobody minded much what went on here.

Not all the villages did their catering in a separate house ; many kept their vast stock of provisions in the church itself. At Chudleigh, for instance, an entire floor of the tower was given up to this, while the first large pew on the right is still referred to as the " bacon hatch ". This practice had one unfortunate consequence. The food brought rats to the churches, and they, in turn, attracted the dogs ; a state of affairs that was only rendered the more insufferable by the insistence of the rat-catchers on nailing their victims to the church doors as proof of their day's work. Indeed, so acute did the situation become in some parishes that many churches, like Exeter Cathedral itself, were compelled to appoint an official " dog-whipper " to keep them free of livestock.

Though the " ales " are now virtually a thing of the past, the fairs and markets still prosper in many parts

"The letters come along in the end"—an Exmoor postman doing a part of his round the only way he can.

" The forerunners of the market halls "—the old yarn market at Dunster.

"'Withes', as the natives prefer to call them"—basket-making from locally grown willows at Stoke St. Gregory.

"We shall find brushes of many kinds taking shape in these workshops"—making dairy brushes by hand at Wells.

of Devon. Geese are yet sold annually at Tavistock, and Exmoor ponies at Bampton, as in Henry III's time, and at both Modbury and Honiton the town crier, dressed in traditional costume, even now opens the day's festivities—as has been the practice at least since the thirteenth century—by hoisting a gilded glove above the heads of the crowds as a sign that the stage is set and the way clear for the merchants outside to enter the town and set about their business. For it was only at the fairs that outsiders were permitted to transact business in the streets, and it was a punishable offence for any merchant to enter a town or village for this purpose unless the glove was displayed to show that such restrictions had been temporarily lifted.

Okehampton still holds its " giglet " market, when the local farmhands may demand a kiss from any girl they can catch, while at Barnstaple—where Gay was educated at the Grammar School and where the famous Barum pottery ware is made—the ancient pannier market even yet takes place in the Market House.

But the greatest of all these festivities, surely, is the September fair at Widecombe-in-the-Moor, that unique little village clustered around its church and green. It was in the forge here that Tom Pearse's grey mare is said to have been shod. The blacksmith was busily making a shoe when I looked in.

" For Tom Pearse ? " I asked.

The smith smiled.

" Nay, I reckon 'ee won't need this where 'ee be noo. Noo more will the grey mare, neither."

Gone are the days of Tom Pearse, but Widecombe forge is still a busy place. For in this lonely, yet lovely, corner, men and women still prefer to move from place to place on their trusted steeds rather than in the fastest of cars. Not only do they find it the most convenient way of getting about ; there are plenty who still regard it as the nicest. Long may they continue to think so, for to be at Widecombe is to recapture a fragment of bygone England at her most charming.

I asked the smith whether he believed the story of Uncle Tom Cobley. To my surprise he answered in the negative.

" 'Tis said that the metal for the old mare's shoes was heated in this fire and beaten out on this very anvil. But 'tis a queer story, me thinks."

" Why queer ? There *was* an Uncle Tom Cobley, wasn't there ? "

" Yes, there was an Uncle Tom Cobley, right enough. An eighteenth-century yeoman. Lived to the age of ninety-six, and is buried up Spreyton way, they do say. Still, there's nothing in the old song to show that he ever *reached* Widecombe."

Be that as it may, there are plenty who still like to think he did, and every year people journey in their hundreds from far and wide to this little Devon village to watch the scene re-enacted by the villagers, and to sing to the lasting memory of the old Devon yeoman. Though there is nothing to prove that Widecombe was, in fact, ever granted a charter, we may still watch the cattle and sheep being sold, and join in the games, dancing, and old-time revelry.

But the Devonian by no means keeps his customs to the fairs. At Moreton Hampstead the villagers dress up in the strangest of costumes and lead a " camel " through the streets as part of their annual gymkhana, while at both Bishop's Teignton and Ilfracombe, every May, dolls are carried round the town in representation of the Virgin Mary, a custom which, doubtless, owes its origin to May's being her month.

At Okehampton the school children still hold

whortleberry parties when the berries are gathered and sent to the Lancashire mills for dyeing purposes as of old, while on November 5 we may yet find them "holloahing for stiffs" within the precincts of more than one village church. Here, at the end of a special service, three cheers will be called for the King, after which the stiffs will be thrown into the air, and the children allowed to scramble for them. Strangely enough, this ceremony appears to have no religious significance whatever; nor is it connected with Guy Fawkes. Though its origin is not known for certain, it is believed to relate to the landing of William of Orange—an event which also took place on November 5—when many towns and villages in this part openly showed their support for him at a time when the success or failure of his mission largely depended upon the reception he received as he passed through Exeter on his long and hazardous journey to London.

More than anywhere is the Good Friday hot-cross-bun made the object of customs and superstitions in Devon. It is said that it was in the little village bakery at Ridgeway, just out of Plympton, that the idea of the bun, and its recipe of tempting spices, originated. Every year before the war crowds would come from far and wide—in cars, on bicycles, on foot, or on horseback—to this bakery, many of them arriving soon after midnight. Long before first light they would be shouting for the buns, and by the time the bakers eventually opened the doors and emerged with their trays, police were needed to keep an eye on things.

Many a Devon housewife to this day will hang one of her buns from the kitchen ceiling until it becomes green with mould, faithful to the old tradition that, broken up in this state and mixed with water, it will prove the last word as a cure for her tired eyes.

Good Friday, incidentally, is a busy day in the gardens around these parts. It is the day on which the cottagers all like to get in as many as possible of their potatoes, believing the ground to enjoy a special blessing at this season. And on this day at Torrington we shall see the children dancing round the Maypole, their white frocks making a picturesque contrast with the many coloured ribbons that are draped around the two poles.

Strangest of all, though, is the Whit Tuesday ceremony at Kingsteignton, when the carcase of a ram is paraded through the streets and roasted in the open, while the entire town indulges in sports, dancing, and other gaieties. Pagan in origin, it is believed that this custom dates back to the time when the Devil got loose in the area, and caused the local stream to dry up. Only by making an offering to him could the spell be removed and the inhabitants once more allowed to drink of their water.

Old beliefs die hard in the West, and there are many who would even yet hesitate to cease their annual offering, for fear of what might happen as a result. Memories of the Devil are, indeed, as green in Devon as in Cornwall, even though at Northlew they will show you the place where they buried him, and so, one would have imagined, put an end to his evil deeds! For it was at Northlew, so the native will tell you, that he finally succumbed to a cold, and a monument marks the spot where he died.

Nowhere is superstition more rife than on Dartmoor and in the surrounding towns and villages. Every year thousands of people will trek for miles to a unique cork oak tree which grows in the garden of a house at Combe-in-Teignhead, firm in the belief that to carry away a piece of its bark will bring them all that they could wish for in the coming year and make life just perfect.

The owner told me that portions of the cork have been sent all over the world, and many people have written at various times to tell of the good fortune it has brought them. One man, for instance, found work within two days, having previously been unemployed for months ; another won a substantial sweepstake.

" Here, take a piece yourself," he added.

I did. So far, however, I have not been as lucky as the others. But then, admittedly, I never walked three times round the tree ; a condition which apparently improves your chances.

Still, there are plenty who would not be without their precious cork for the world, for many a Devonian will tell you with all seriousness that you need all the luck you can lay hands on when crossing the lonely moor at night. Not only may you at any time bump into a coach of bones, driven by a ghost with a sinister black hound lolloping along beside, but there are also the pixies to lure you into the bogs with their lights—bogs into which you may easily become completely submerged, leaving no single trace of your whereabouts. Whole parties have disappeared for ever in this way. Dartmoor must have been a grand spot for highwaymen and robbers of olden days. Indeed, it was.

To be lost on Dartmoor in the darkness of the night is a sorry plight. For there is nothing to guide one ; on the other hand, to diverge from the roadway is to court disaster. Even those who know the district well have often been compelled to spend the entire night on the moor, not daring to move too far before first light.

I once asked a native of these parts how he felt about it all. He at once looked grim :

" 'Tis terrible dangerous, I tell 'ee. There's only one thing to do if you come upon them pixies—take off your coat and turn it inside out. That *may* break the spell. But, mind 'ee, I don't say it will. Better not risk the moor at night."

No, the pixies' lights are no mere flight of the imagination ; they are there for all to see, beckoning us into the bogs. No one knows for certain what they are, for, naturally, no one can reach them to find out. Maybe they are glow-worms ; more likely the " will-o-the-wisp ".

But for all its eeriness, Dartmoor, with its 80,000-odd acres, is also a place of no mean beauty, many of the villages grouped around it dating back to Anglo-Saxon times. If Lydford—the largest parish in England—with its wooded gorge and " Devil's bridge " over it, and its memories of tin-mining days, is one of the loveliest and most romantic spots in England, Dartmoor can also boast Brentor, Widecombe, Bridestowe, and Buckland-in-the-Moor.

What more beautiful than that quaint little cluster of stone-built thatched cottages at Buckland, surrounded on all sides by trees, and with a stream rippling leisurely down the middle of them ? In this peaceful corner we can well imagine the inhabitants of these little cottage homes seated happily by the fireside on a cold winter's evening, singing their traditional folk song, *A Cottage Well Thatched with Straw*, while those without are pursuing their tortuous wanderings around the moor.

A strange mixture is Dartmoor : a land of rivers and springs, of cromlechs, and of hills and plateaux. While no less than five rivers—the Dart, Tavy, Okment, Taw, and Teign—rise in the neighbourhood of Cranmere Pool, farther south we shall find the source of the Yealm, Avon, Plym, and Erme. And, by contrast to the vast tracts of bog land, we have Hey Tor, Great Mis Tor, and Yes Tor, the last being the highest hill south of Cumberland.

Nor is Dartmoor Devon's only barren stretch ; part of Exmoor, too, is hers ; and it is along the lonely roads and trackways of this ancient " forest " that we shall make our way into Somerset.

Three *The Land of the Grail*

LESS forbidding than Dartmoor, perhaps, Exmoor is, nevertheless, every bit as lonely. For all its thirty or so square miles of wild and rugged beauty—relieved only by deep wooded valleys where, as at Haddon, Horner, Hawkcombe, and Badgworthy, a little stream adds to the tranquillity of the scene—we shall find probably less than a thousand people living there.

Cut off to a great extent from the rest of the world all the year round, many of them sometimes become in winter a " forgotten tribe " for days on end, possibly even for weeks. A horse or pony provides the only practical means of approach to some of the more remote hamlets, and it is by these means that the postman, the baker, and the like elect to make their rounds of delivery at regular, or irregular, intervals, according to conditions and their mood of the moment.

No one who lives on Exmoor can ever quite rely on anything ; it is unwise to expect too much. Independence, even if sometimes tantamount to downright inconvenience, is a first essential of life in these wilds of Somerset and Devon. But that, to the native, makes it all the more worth while.

One man, for instance, told me quite triumphantly that, weather permitting, he could usually expect to get his bread delivered once a week, or, if the elements were particularly favourable and the baker was feeling unusually energetic, twice. I asked him what happened when conditions were not so good—when Exmoor was snow-bound, for example. He confessed that there were occasions when all forms of movement were out of the question, but, at such times, the difficulty was overcome by his " old woman ", who would then bake her own bread. Very often, he explained, it happened that the baker was able to go so far but no farther, or, at least, did not *feel* like going any farther.

" What then ? " I asked.

" Quite simple. There's a stone by the roadside not above two miles from here. He leaves the loaves on that, and I just jump on to Sally's back, and quietly hack off after them."

The old cromlechs certainly seem to have their uses on Exmoor.

" What about the post ? " I went on.

" Never bother about it. The letters come along in the end, and that's all that really matters. Anyhow, it's a grand life."

I suppose it must be. It is certainly a grand country ; grandest of all, perhaps, in the beautiful Doone Valley, with its memories of Lorna, of Jan Ridd, and of Carver Doone and his tribe of wild outlaws who once spread terror and dismay around the countryside.

On Exmoor they will tell you that the Doones were descended from one of Monmouth's soldiers who escaped after the Battle of Sedgemoor. It was while his grandfather was rector of Charles, just over the Devon border, that young Richard Blackmore first became intrigued by the exploits of the Doones, spending hours at a time with the lonely moorsmen as they recounted—as only a moorsman knows now—the long and hair-raising list of the deeds of those evil men. It was at the Royal Oak Inn at Withypool, but a few miles away, that Blackmore, now a grown man, turned fact into fiction and wrote the greater part of *Lorna Doone*.

We may still see the quaint little church with its battlemented tower at Oare, where the author worshipped as a boy and where Lorna Doone and Jan Ridd were married. We may still see the window through which, alas, poor Lorna was shot at the altar by the treacherous Carver. We can picture, too, the life-and-death chase that followed when Jan pursued the outlaw on horseback across Exmoor to Cloven Rocks near Simonsbath ; a chase that was to see Carver swallowed up in a black bog and the end brought to a reign of terror. Certainly a more peaceful and beautiful spot than Oare to-day is hard to imagine.

Once a favourite hunting-ground of Saxon kings and noblemen, the same species of red deer that was so eagerly sought in the days before the Conquest still finds shelter on the wooded slopes of Exmoor. Indeed, stag-hunting is still a popular pastime of this wild countryside. Gone are the days when a freeman who chased a stag would be divested of his liberties, or a villein have his right hand severed above the wrist if it were his first offence, or be put to death if it were his second. Even so, the nomenclature devised by the Norman huntsmen still persists. On Exmoor the male of a red deer will even yet be known variously as a " knobber ", " bricket ", " spayard ", and " staggard " before becoming a stag in his fifth year and a hart in his sixth, by which time he will have his full horns and be deemed to be " chasable ".

Nor are the deer the only survivors of an age that is

past. The ponies, too, with their big eyes—known by the moorsmen as the "toad eye"—and measuring little more than twelve hands, are said to have roamed the "forest" for at least two thousand years. Then, too, there are the moorland sheep with their remarkable horns. Exmoor is, indeed, Nature's paradise, teeming with wild life of every description, from the fowls of the air and the beasts of the field to the salmon and trout of the streams and rivers which make the district a favourite retreat for anglers.

But the native is not idle on Exmoor. Here, as on Sedgemoor, peat-cutting has formed an important local industry since the days before Christianity. Before the discovery of coal, peat provided one of the main forms of fuel, and in many a Somerset home to-day we shall still find a fire of this type smouldering in the hearth as of old.

An interesting business. One old cutter, who told me that he had been at the work "all his life", explained that peat gradually forms below the ground as various plants—particularly heather—decompose to provide a seed bed for fresh vegetation above. Although it can be found at varying depths, it is the black peat, deep down in the bogs, that is the most valuable.

Throughout the spring and summer, especially from April to June, little groups of men and women will be hard at work on these moors, cutting, carting, and stacking. Once the top surface has been removed, the exposed peat, known as the "mumps", is cut with a sharp-edged tool which the moorsman delights to call his "scythe". These "mumps" are then stacked into "isles", all carefully arranged so as to allow the wind to blow freely around each. After some two to three weeks, each of the mumps will be turned, and then, later, the isles are taken down for the peat to be re-stacked into "ruccles", strange-looking piles, not unlike beehives in appearance, with a wider base than top. Finally, towards the end of summer, when the peat is comparatively dry, it is loaded into wagons, or specially-constructed boats, to be taken over land or by water to some central storage point in readiness for the coming winter.

But if Exmoor and Sedgemoor have given Somerset peat, the Mendips have likewise given her lead, the Athelney Marshes willows—or " withes ", as the natives prefer to call them—Radstock coal, and the Brendons iron ore, while quarries abound in many parts. At Bridgwater, too, Bath brick is made for scouring purposes, from special deposits found in the estuary of the River Parret, by a process patented by a Mr. Bath. Natural resources play a big part in framing the life of her people. As far back as the time of the Romans, the Mendips were a hive of industrial activity. After excavating by means of " grove holes ", and washing the ore in the local streams, they would laboriously cart the lead to Uphill, then the principal port, for shipment to Italy. As time went on and lead mines became more and more essential to our own needs, the Cornish miners were called in to sink deep shafts and devise a new system of furnaces, just as they were called to Radstock to develop the coal mines.

Though the lead mines of Somerset, like the tin mines of Cornwall, have dwindled in recent years, the " Mindry " is still a household word of the Mendips. At Priddy, moreover, high above Cheddar Gorge with its famous Wookey Hole and its relics of perhaps thirty thousand years ago, we shall meet with a people who still cling to the old lore and customs that were laid down in the fourteenth century by Lord Chief Justice Coke, when ten thousand people attended a mass meeting at Forge-on-Mendip ; and who still dance the weird traditional dances of their ancestors. A secretive people, many of them have never been out of their village.

A strange place is Priddy—it would not really be surprising if the inhabitants still behaved like primitives. A mass of caves and rocks, the ground is so hard that it is said that the only way to dig a grave up on the hill is to blast one ! From these rocks there issues a spring which never runs dry, and it is the stream from this spring that has helped to eat away the rocks below and give us Wookey Hole.

Incidentally, not far from Wookey Hole is one of the last mills in England, dating back at least to 1610, where high-grade paper of many kinds—from bank notes to drawing blocks, from vellum (imitation parchment) to papers with especially designed water marks —is still made by hand as in the seventeenth century. Here we may see the whole process through, from the arrival of the rags to the departure of the finished article. It is fascinating, indeed, to watch all the old curtains, shirts, and sundry other articles being carefully cut up and sorted by little groups of women, and then to follow them through the various tanks and see them steadily growing whiter and whiter as they are gradually rendered down to pulp. From tank to tank the pulp will slowly make its way through the mill, to reach the " vatman " below in the form of a thickish milky stream, not unlike half-cooked porridge in appearance.

It is the " vatman " and the " coucher " who are the all-important craftsmen in this industry. Here, the former takes up his " mould "—a kind of wire sieve (the same size as the paper he is to make) with detachable sides, known as the " deckle "—and dips it into the vat. Always careful to take out rather more pulp than he will require, he gives it a shake to enable it to run along his mould, from end to end. After allowing the surplus to run back into the vat, he proceeds to " nurse " his mould by gently shaking it this way and that, a process known as " spreading the fibres ".

" But for that, the paper would be a mass of holes," he explained.

When he has spread his fibres to his complete satisfaction, he removes the deckle and passes the mould to the coucher, who gently presses it on to a layer of felt before covering the sheet with a second layer. Thus with both men—each assisted by boys—working as fast as they can go, they gradually form a " post " of alternate paper and felt which is then clamped down into a press to drive out the water.

" Look at the post now," remarked the craftsman after a few minutes. The pile had shrunk to a fraction of its original thickness.

" Mind you, the paper is by no means finished," he went on. " There's a good two to three months' work ahead of us in that lot yet."

Before this consignment was ready to leave the mill, he explained, it would go through something like a hundred handlings. It must be pack-pressed, parted, dried and finished, sized, size-parted, re-sized, picked and glazed, and finally sorted.

But if Wookey's hand-worked paper mill is, as it were, almost an isolated survival, and if the Mendip lead mines have dwindled to comparative obscurity, on the Athelney Marshes we shall find whole colonies of men and women still growing willows and making baskets as have their ancestors on this very same land since the days before Christianity. We shall find them cutting the willows in the marshes ; peeling them in their cottage homes ; making them up in the little village workshops. We shall find old men and grandmothers, young men and maidens, all hard at work. We shall come upon them in villages far and wide, all over the marshes, and here and there, as at Borough Bridge, we may even see them sitting by the roadside making both baskets and chairs.

For the dweller by the marshes will tell you—and quite rightly—that nowhere in the world are better "withes" to be found than on Athelney, especially round the districts of Langport, Kingsbury, and Stoke St. Gregory.

"Why, don't 'ee know, zur, that Zummerzet withes were being sent all over the world before ever William the Conqueror was thought of?" one willow-grower, with whom I got chatting, asked me proudly.

I asked him why it was that the Somerset willows were so good.

"'Tis the zoil, zur. Withes won't grow on any old land, you know, zur. They don't like chalk, and they don't like the ground too warm, no more."

Every year, he explained, cuttings are taken from the crops, and are pushed into the well-cleaned and ploughed land between December and March, as many as twenty thousand cuttings being required to plant a single acre. Continual hoeing and spraying are necessary before the withes can be cut by hook in due time; a job entrusted only to the old stagers. After cutting, the withes are sorted into lengths, graded, and boiled in large tanks for several hours before being peeled.

There seems no end to the types of basket made by these Somerset craftsmen. There are the fruit and vegetable varieties, the potato hampers, sieves, strikes, and cucumber flats for the agricultural workers; the carrier-bicycle baskets for the delivery of goods, the crates, and the laundry baskets, all necessary for trade; while for home use the list is almost unending, ranging from the shopping-basket to the needlework variety.

As I say, natural resources are certainly made the

most of in Somerset. Flax is still grown for the manufacture of linen in parts where the soil is particularly favourable, while in a few districts, such as Curry Mallet, Curry Rivel, and Ilminster, we shall find the womenfolk carrying out an industry that is almost entirely peculiar to the county—the growing and harvesting of teazles. Vicious-looking things, these teazles I am told are sent to the weaving-mills of the north for raising the nap of the cloths. Wearing special gloves as a protection against the spikey leaves and stems, the harvesters—or " knappers ", as they call themselves—can be found every summer cutting off the heads by means of short, curved knives, especially designed for the purpose. After drying the heads in the sun, they do them up in bundles of perhaps twenty thousand at a time, ready for despatch to the mills—an altogether unenviable job in my opinion.

As varied as her industries is her scenery, and it is this very variation that gives Somerset her character. Whereas at one point we may find ourselves surrounded by low-lying swamps, or standing in the midst of flat, verdant meadows with a flock of sheep as our only companions—reminding us of the days when Somerset, like the Cotswolds to her north-east and Wiltshire to her east, was a flourishing wool centre—at another we may be perhaps a thousand feet or more above sea level, enjoying an uninterrupted vista of many miles of gentle, wooded slopes dropping down to the Bristol Channel beyond. To stand on the top of the Quantocks, the Brendons, the Poldens, the Mendips, or the seventeen-hundred-foot Dunkery Beacon on a clear summer's day, or in springtime, when the orchards are in blossom, is to look down upon the English countryside at its best.

More than in any other county in England, perhaps, shall we find the architecture varying with every few

“ Here plum puddings are carried in triumphal procession ”—“ Harvest Home ” at East Brent.

" Guns will be fired through the orchard "—
Somerset Wassailing.

Roman Somerset—the Roman Baths at Bath.

Elizabethan Somerset—the village pond at East Quantoxhead

miles of roadway. Whereas in the west we shall still come upon cob and thatch to remind us of our close proximity to Devon, as we make our way eastwards towards the Wiltshire and Dorset borders, or northwards towards Gloucester, we shall notice the cob giving place to stone. And if the homesteads of the east are more forbidding in appearance than those of the west—than those of, say, Porlock (where Southey once stayed at the *Old Ship*), Dunster, or Selworthy—they are, at least, in keeping with their natural surroundings, built, as they have been, of local materials. The Mendips, with their twenty miles' stretch of carboniferous limestone and their myriad caves, are never so kindly as the more gentle Quantocks, and it is only right that the architecture should differ accordingly.

And just as the villages keep in tune with their landscape, so do the people themselves likewise vary with the villages, not only in their life and outlook but also in their very words and phrases. So will you notice a difference in their many customs and superstitions.

Since time immemorial the Somerset yeoman, like the village blacksmith, has been held as the very symbol of English country life at its most glorious. At Watchet, Wellington, and Winscombe, and at East Brent, Cannington, and West Huntspill, we shall meet with men —and, on occasion, women—who even yet cannot forego the traditions that served their ancestors so well ; traditions that once meant so much to those whose whole life depended upon the fertility of the soil.

At Watchet, Wellington, and Winscombe, we shall see them holding their Court Baron, Court Leet and Moot respectively, just as their ancestors had done in feudal times. In those days, when several villages often came under one manor, each lord had his own court which, in time, became divided into two quite distinct sections—the Court Leet for the inquiry into cases of felony and the like, and the Court Baron for the general administration of the manor as a whole.

Though all lords varied in their views as to how a court should be run and as to how far they might go with their powers, it was not uncommon practice to form a jury of men from each village in the manor and for the lord himself to preside. As soon as he had taken his place on the dais, his clerk by his side, the beadle would call for silence, and shout " Oyez " either once or three times according to whether the court was to sit as Baron or Leet. Between them these two courts appear to have passed judgment on every conceivable subject, from minor criminal offences to disputes between parties, and even to clashes with the lord himself; from slander, trespass, and infringements of the highways to the harbouring of strangers, cheating, the haunting of low taverns by night, and adultery. In the main the courts were as fair to the " unfree " as the " free ", and were a genuine attempt at sound management of the land and its people. The over-crowding of commons, the control of the open fields, and the transfer of land held in villeinage all came under the jurisdiction of these courts. True, a man who wished to leave the district, marry, or take Holy Orders had to apply to the Court for permission to do so, but he could also ask to be allowed to exchange his holdings if he had any cause for grievance. On such occasions the jury would often go so far as to view the site and make a report at the next sitting, when, if they approved the application, they would give him a white wand, through the medium of the " cellarer ", and enter the transfer in the Records as a safeguard against possible future dispute.

I suppose it is no exaggeration to say that it is upon the old Manor Courts that the whole system of British democracy has been founded. If we visit the old Bell Inn at Watchet in October when the court is sitting, we may well imagine ourselves to be back in Tudor times as we hear the " presentments " being made and watch this age-old formality being followed by the appointment of the various " officials " who are to serve the community for the ensuing year, from the bailiff and the crier to the portreeve and the stock-drover ; from the ale-taster to the inspector of weights and measures. These, together with the beadle, constable, hayward, messor, shepherd, swineherd, waggoner, ploughman, woodward, and one or two others, all had a place in the scheme of things. Together they ensured the smooth running of the manor, and the appointment of suitable men for the jobs was a matter of paramount importance to all.

At Watchet, where it is thought that the court may have been held annually ever since the time of William the Conqueror, some of these officials still enjoy certain privileges by virtue of their exalted positions ; the portreeve, for instance, may to this day demand a royalty on every cargo of coal brought into the town. This, however, cuts both ways, for at Watchet I believe that strictly they can, if they wish, even yet enforce certain of the old feudal penalties ; there would not, it seems, be anything to stop their outlawing or imprisoning a man, or, if it comes to that, from condemning him to the ducking-stool, stocks, or whipping-post.

Though I am assured that it has not been found necessary to resort to such measures in recent times, it is perhaps as well to beware, and to remember that such punishments have been meted out in the past ! Still, the court is by no means only bent on business. At the end of the proceedings all will adjourn for lunch to drink each other's toasts in ale-punch : special punch, made, I am told, from a secret recipe at the inn that has been handed down from landlord to landlord for something like three hundred years now.

Although the Moot at Winscombe is, I believe, a revival rather than a survival, the villagers are finding in this old-style gathering of the people an excellent means of maintaining unity. Here, at their Moot, all the various parish organizations, such as we may find in any rural community, delight to get together to discuss their various plans and achievements. At Winscombe there is no such thing as bickering, petty squabbling, or jealousy. The Moot has seen to that, for by meeting regularly in this way the various units, while maintaining their individuality and independence, are able to plan in harmony, to the well-being of all concerned and of the community as a whole. Like the Devonians, they, too, are finding that there is much to be said for the old ways of life.

While at these three places—Watchet, Wellington, and Winscombe—we may find living links with the old-time system of administration, at West Huntspill, Cannington, and East Brent we shall watch customs relating to the actual work on the manor, customs that carry us back to mediæval times when the four church festivals, Plough Monday, Rogation-tide, Lammas, and Harvest-tide, formed an integral part in the life of all. On Plough Monday the ploughs would be brought to the village church to be blessed before being towed round the streets, and this would be followed at Rogation-tide by the blessing of the fields. Then, at Lammas, after the first sheaf of corn had been cut, the first loaf to be made from the new crop would be brought to the church as an offering. Finally, when all the crops had been safely gathered in, would come the thanksgiving.

At West Huntspill the plough and milk-churns are still blessed at the village church every January, while at Cannington a similar service is held in the fields in Rogation week. Likewise at East Brent, near Bridgwater, the " Harvest Home " is yet kept up—ever since its revival in 1857—in memory of the days when the long weeks of sweat and toil in the fields were brought to a happy conclusion with feasting and merrymaking. Here plum-puddings are carried in triumphal procession from the vicarage kitchen to a special marquee by the village maidens, headed by a band composed of the best that East Brent can muster in the way of local talent.

Though many of the other customs that once formed part of the rural calendar have long since died out, in many parts of Somerset we shall frequently come upon material links of one kind or another to help us complete the story of life on the English manor ; links such as are now admired only for their æsthetic merit, or are gazed upon for the strangeness of their design, and whose past purpose and importance is usually overlooked except by the more inquiring.

Among the most interesting of these links—apart, of course, from the manor houses themselves, of which fine examples are to be seen at Clevedon (where Thackeray once stayed and where Tennyson's friend, Arthur Hallam, lived), Cadbury, and Chard (where Judge Jeffreys held his Bloody Assizes in one of the rooms)—are the crosses. Richer in these than any other county in England—those of Cornwall falling into a different category—Somerset possesses something like two hundred. Set up for many and varying purposes, they stand as living testimonies of the part the Cross played in the lives of the people.

Deeply superstitious and always fearful of the unknown, the people of mediæval and Tudor England, when in doubt, invariably erected a cross to set their minds at rest. Thus, not only do we find the " preaching " crosses around which so many of the villages and towns grew in the first place, but we also meet with the " boundary " type—set up, like Ralegh's Cross on Brendon Hill, to mark the limits of a manor—and the " market " crosses.

Most interesting of all in many ways are the market crosses, of which perhaps the finest examples are those at Cheddar, Shepton Mallet, Bridgwater, Dunster, Somerton, and Taunton. In days when travel was all but unknown, it became customary for the king to give his consent for a regular market to be held in the largest of a group of nearby villages, so that the inhabitants of each could exchange their surplus goods with the minimum inconvenience. At such meeting-places an area of land would be earmarked for the market, and a cross erected to remind the merchants of their religion and of the desirability of honest dealing. For the " Black Market " was by no means unknown even in those days.

Thither to these crosses, then, would the merchants trek from far and wide, rounding off the day's business with singing, dancing, cock-fighting, bull-baiting, and general merry-making. While some of the crosses were used for the sale of all types of merchandise, others became associated with just one particular article, such as wool, yarn, butter, poultry, or pigs. At first these rendezvous comprised simply a cross surmounting a number of steps, upon which the merchants would display their goods. Later these gave place to covered-in affairs, designed, like the yarn market cross at Dunster, to give protection against the weather to merchants and merchandise alike. They were the forerunners of the market halls.

As I say, the people found in the crosses a good way of salving their consciences when in doubt, and this was so for many centuries. Even at the preaching crosses, farcical trials would often be held and punishments, such as the cutting-off of a man's ears, be meted out. Witches seem to have been particularly unfortunate. Securely bound, a suspect woman would be thrown into a nearby pond or river as a test of her guilt or innocence. If she was guilty she floated, and was hanged from the cross ; if innocent . . . well, she simply sank, and that was the end of it. Good enough !

Perhaps it was a certain feeling of guilt that prompted Charles II's bastard son, the Duke of Monmouth, to proclaim himself king from the cross at Bridgwater, and for Judge Jeffreys afterwards to hang one of the Duke's followers from that at Wedmore.

In contrast with these crosses are links of a less honourable variety. In a village street at Castle Cary, for instance, is a weird round stone object with a roof not unlike a policeman's helmet. This, the native will tell you, was used in days gone by for locking up all children above the age of seven who played truant from school. Judging by its size, it is to be hoped, for their sake, that not too many elected to do this at the same time ! At Monckton Combe, Pensford, and Kilmersden are similar lock-ups where the parish beadle used to detain his man overnight before taking him to court for trial next morning.

"Better than one of 'em modern prisons, don't 'ee think, zur ?" An old road sweeper seemed amused at my curiosity.

I assured him that I was not really in a position to judge.

The old man laughed.

"Well, zur, I doubt as though they gets drink in prison these days. Think 'ee so, zur ?"

"Drink ?"

"Aye, zur, that they did. Smokes too, I tell 'ee."

And he pointed to a slit in the wall. Through that

slit the prisoner's friends would solemnly pour quantities of home-brewed ale down a special tube straight into the man's mouth. Then, when he had had his fill, they would produce a long pipe and leave him to smoke away the evening in peaceful meditation on his deeds of the day and his prospects of the morrow. Given a long enough pipe, he could keep the bowl outside and so minimize the amount of smoke in the confined space within and avoid too much choking.

"Those were the days!" I remarked.

"Aye, zur, they were and all."

It is, perhaps, not inappropriate that Somerset should boast more crosses than any other county. For it was to Glastonbury—the lonely Isle of Avalon, entirely surrounded by marshes—that Joseph of Arimathea, tradition has it, set sail with the Holy Grail after burying Jesus.

It was to that enormously high hill which, to this day, stands out as a landmark throughout miles of Somerset, that hill we have long grown to love and revere as Glastonbury Tor, that Joseph and his companions, having been warned in a dream to watch for a hill resembling Tabor's Holy Mount, made their way up the Bristol Channel and across the marshes. On the spot where they landed, "weary-all" with their journey and their experiences—now known as Weary-All or Wirral Hill—it is said that Joseph struck the famous staff that was to take root and blossom forth into the Glastonbury Thorn; the thorn whose offshoots still flower in many a Somerset garden every Christmas. It is said, too, that it was upon the Tor that Joseph finally buried the sacred vessel, before building his little church of osiers to give us our first place of Christian worship.

Though the truth of the legend has never, alas, been ascertained, it is a story which few in Somerset would care to dispute. To the native the ground at Glastonbury will remain for ever holy, and to the disbelievers he will argue that not until cuttings from the first thorn had taken root could the original tree be destroyed. A Puritan fanatic who tried to hack it down severed his own leg before he could complete the job, and even then the top of the tree continued to flourish for some thirty years after being detached from the root. It is, indeed, a beautiful story.

But Glastonbury's story by no means ends with Joseph of Arimathea. After a while the little osier church gave place to an oratory of stone, and by the eighth century a monastery had been founded. That monastery was gradually to become the finest and richest in the land, largely through the efforts of a local man who, in the tenth century, became its abbot at the youthful age of twenty-one—St. Dunstan, later to become Archbishop of Canterbury.

For something like five centuries Glastonbury remained an important seat of learning and of religion, with its abbots meting out hospitality and tending the sick and poor, until the Dissolution brought about her downfall. So that all that is left to remind us to-day of Glastonbury's once noble place in the story of England are the ruins of the Abbey, Great Church and St. Mary's Chapel, the Abbots' Kitchen—a strange octagonal building containing four enormous fireplaces—the Monks' Cemetery, the Abbot's Tribunal House, tithe barn, and the Pilgrim's Inn in the High Street, a fine example of fifteenth century panelled stone work, built to accommodate the many pilgrims for whom the Abbot was unable to find room in the Abbey. Pilgrimages are still held periodically at Glastonbury, the last having taken place in 1937, when the organ of a nearby church was relayed to the Abbey ruins and the pilgrims were led by " servers at the altar ", draped in blue, red, and purple cassocks and white surplices and carrying candles and incense. On this occasion somewhere about a hundred choristers attended the ceremony of the purification of the altar.

In the Monks' Cemetery it is said that Joseph himself was buried and, after him, St. Dunstan, and at least three Saxon kings, Edmund the Elder, Edgar the Peaceable, and Edmund Ironside.

These are not her only relics, however. Close by are the remains of an ancient British lake village, a colony of wattle-and-daub huts where men plied their crafts, smelted their metals, and caught fish before ever Joseph was born ; a village dating back at least to the Iron Age.

But alas for the march of " progress ", Glastonbury's main interest to-day lies in her ancient past. She has failed to develop in harmony with her traditions, and Wells, with her Mayoral roll dating back to 1378, her fine Cathedral, Vicars' Close, Bishop's Palace and moat where the swans still ring their own dinner bell, has supplanted her, not only as the county's seat of religion but also as a place of beauty.

Incidentally, down a small side track, almost within the shade of the Cathedral, is a unique little craft centre where groups of men and women can be found daily making every conceivable article for the farm, from milk-filters and cheese-cloths to overalls, towels, and waterproof aprons ; from milking stools, draining boards, pails, coolers, cheese-moulds, and milk-recording apparatus, to sterilizing-chests, bottle-washers and fillers, and brushes of every type and description. From these small workshops—so small that it is easy to visit Wells without ever being aware of their existence—goods are made in enormous quantities not only for farms all over the British Isles, but for those of Sweden, Denmark, Holland, and the Empire as well.

A strange medley this centre, it provides a sharper distinction between the ancient and modern than I have yet seen within so confined a space. While in one room I found a group of women making overalls to the accompaniment of a blaring wireless set, in another, by direct contrast, I watched the brush-makers setting about their work in an atmosphere so still that one could almost have heard the proverbial pin drop.

With the greatest of difficulty I managed to make myself heard above the wireless and the mechanical sewing-machines, to ask the superintendent how he felt about all this noise.

"Why, O.K. ! Can't hear myself think without the wireless," came the reply.

"Doesn't it give you a headache ?" I pressed him.

"Headache ? I should say not. Why it's only when the music is on that I can work out my figures. Can't concentrate without it."

The introduction of the wireless, I was assured, had increased production enormously. The brush-makers could have had it too if they had wished, but they had chosen otherwise. But then they are handcraftsmen, and their outlook on life is invariably as different from those of the machine-workers as are their respective methods of production.

It is fascinating to watch these craftsmen at work. Here we may find a man wiring and glueing lengths of Bahia Bass, especially imported from Brazil, into strips of beech to make churn-brushes ; there we shall find another busy at the lathe, turning and grooving ash handles for bottle-brushes. His task completed, the ash will be taken to another craftsman to "fill" with South American mule hair, when the hair will be doubled over and wired into position by means of a hand-propelled tension machine before being trimmed by bench shears to a shape that will fit the inside of a specified type of bottle to perfection. We shall find brushes of many kinds taking shape in these workshops, from heavy scavenger brooms of West African bass and home-grown birch, alder, sycamore, or willow, for the stable yard, to soft brooms, made of more expensive fibres, for the farmhouse kitchen. But, no matter what the type, each, it is estimated, will have something like three times the life of similar articles made in other parts by machinery. Indeed, that is why the centre still thrives to-day : farmers, at any rate, continue to realize the advantages of hand-work, even in an age of industrialism.

It is surprising how often in Somerset one comes upon unusual centres of this kind, tucked away in unsuspected corners.

At Clevedon is a weaving-shed where ecclesiastical hangings are made in the traditional style, while at Henlade, Bridgwater, and Weston-super-Mare we shall stumble upon a few wood-carvers. At Yeovil, too, is an age-old glove-factory where much of the work is even now carried out by cottage women as in days gone by, while sail-cloth is yet made at Crewkerne.

More unusual still, though, is the hair factory at Castle Cary, said to be the only one left in England, where the work is done almost entirely by hand. To this small factory the hair of horses, oxen, and pigs is brought from Russia and South America in large coagulated lumps, to be prepared for use in the manufacture of furniture, upholstery, mattresses, tailors' linings, window blinds for the South African railways, brushes, fishing-lines, whips, sieves, and countless other articles.

It was in Somerset, they will tell you, that the idea of hair-seating originated, and it was here that much of the hair was prepared for stiffening the crinolines of Victorian days. At Castle Cary there are craftsmen who can remember those days as if they were yesterday. For age does not weary these Somerset stalwarts : no less than eight of the comparatively small band of employees have been with the firm for at least fifty years, while one man told me that he had been there for seventy.

" Seventy ! Quite the oldest inhabitant, what ? "

" No, zur, I can't rightly say as though I am. There's another chap that's been here six years more than me. Eighty-six he be if a day."

Great characters these country craftsmen ; truly Nature's gentlemen.

No easy job this preparation of hair. When it arrives at the factory in its raw state, every single strand from each of those vast, uninviting-looking masses has to be laboriously sorted into lengths by hand—the longer ones being set aside for weaving, and the shorter, which are then re-sorted into colours and weights, for curling—before being washed, pulled through bench combs, and " drawn ", a skilled business where the craftsman holds a bundle of hair in his left hand and pulls out strands to suit the various needs by means of a knife. It is a lengthy process demanding the highest degree of skill throughout.

But to return for a moment to Glastonbury : many a Somerset farmer will tell you in all sincerity that the orchards for which his county is famous—occupying, as they do, some nineteen hundred acres and giving an annual yield of one hundred thousand tons—were started by Joseph of Arimathea and his party when they carelessly threw down the cores of the goodly supply of apples which they brought with them on their mission. To the Devonian who is rash enough to hint that *his* orchards may be older and better, he will point out that it was from these cores that the first trees sprang up ; that Glastonbury derived its Celtic name,

Ynys Avallon (Apple Island) from this fact; and that, in any case, it was only through these trees' seeding themselves on Devon soil that Devon is able to boast any orchards at all. Be that as it may, the Devonian will have none of it. Rather, will he argue, was it the other way round. Dismissing all mention of Joseph, he will protest, in equally convincing tones, that it was the returning Crusaders who brought back the first seedlings, and that it was from the orchards of Devon that those of Somerset first sprang. But then, as I said, apples and cider are a touchy point in both these counties. They are matters on which each likes to be just a little individual, many a Somerset home even going to the extent of drinking cider with pork for breakfast.

In Somerset the cider falls into three distinct categories: "woman's", sweet and only suitable for women and "sissies"; "Good drinking", something with a bit of a kick, such as might well be served at weddings and such-like ceremonies where a certain flip is called for without, however, being overdone; and "Harvest", made of "Kingston Black" apples from Taunton way, for choice—far more potent and guaranteed to give something of a "hang-over" to those who wish it.

Incidentally, don't be alarmed if ever you should happen upon a weird, lumbering contraption with an antiquated-looking engine, enormous press and grinding machine, and seemingly a mass of cogs and belts, making its leisured, and somewhat noisy, way down some narrow country lane. They make cider on the highways in Somerset as well as at the farms, and this is simply the travelling press. I believe that its home is at Pensford, but you may happen upon it anywhere.

As much of a ritual in Somerset as in Devon, the autumn cider-making is still followed in various districts by the New Year wassailing of the trees. If, on the night of January 17—the night once celebrated as twelfth night—we proceed to the orchard of some Carhampton farmer and wait in the darkness among the trees, we shall soon find ourselves taking part in a ceremony dating back to time immemorial.

After a while the wassail parties will arrive, to be joined shortly afterwards by the farmers themselves. A ring will be formed around the trees, and then some burly local, whose voice, perhaps, is the lustiest of all, will start up the old traditional song. A good, rollicking song, we shall join with the others in the chorus, singing with gusto as though the trees were our own :

Old apple tree, old apple tree,
We've come to wassail thee,
To bear and to bow apples enow,
Hats full, caps full, three bushel bags full,
Barn floors full, and a little heap under the stairs.

Scarcely has the music died away, when the tankards are brought out and we all drink the toast of the trees. Again and again shall we raise our tankards to their good fortunes in the coming season, stopping only when we feel that we have really done them proud and have had as much as we ourselves can comfortably manage. But the ceremony is not complete. A piece of toast, suitably saturated in the precious drink, must be placed in the fork of the most magnificent of the many trees, while, just to make sure of things, guns will be fired through the orchard to drive away any evil spirits that might, perchance, still be hovering about in the background.

You can never entirely rid the West Countryman of his old beliefs and superstitions ; nor, I imagine, would you wish to, for they are part and parcel of his character.

Rejoice in the sun on Candlemas Day, and the Somerset farmer will turn on you in a flash, telling you that the sun never did any good on *that* day ; rather would he see a strong west wind to fill the buds with fruit. Let it shine if it likes the next day, or even the day before, but *not* at Candlemas. Ask him why a myrtle tree is often to be found growing in even the smallest of gardens, and he will tell you, simply, that it is because such trees bring luck, especially if the myrtle is cut when in flower and taken into the home. And he really believes it.

Talk of the Devil, and there is no end to the tales you may be told or the things you may be shown. While at Staple Fitzpaine they will point to a large stone on the Chard road, and tell you that it was thrown there by the Devil in an attempt to hit the church ; at Williton they will go one better by pointing to two stones, the remains of a cromlech, declaring that they landed there one day when the Devil elected to while away some of his evil hours in a game of hurling high up on the Quantocks. Nor is Somerset to be outdone by Cornwall in the " pillar of salt " stories : Stanton Drew folk have stones that are *definitely*, they declare, the remains of those who danced on the Sabbath.

Even the famous prehistoric bridge over the river at Barle, near Dulverton, stretching for some hundred-and-eighty feet, and known as the Tarr Steps, is credited to the Devil, built, it is said, in the course of a night.

Try moving a certain stone in the grounds of the ruined Manor House at Ilton, where Nicholas and Dorothy Wadham, founders of the Oxford College bearing their name, once lived, and if there is a Somerset man anywhere in sight, he will come running up, bidding you stop before it is too late.

" 'Ee mustn't do that, zur, or 'ee will be accursed. 'As 'ee never 'eard tell of the hidden treasure that lies buried beneath that stone ? "

Whereupon he will talk for as long as you like of the

" The days when towns and villages everywhere were built of local materials "—Lacock.

" With its wide main street, the widest in England "—Marlborough.

" Its tithe barn, church, and manor all clustered together "—Cherhill.

" The focal point of the ancient hill-tracks "—Avebury, with its stone circle.

" The highest artificial mound in Europe "—Silbury.

many attempts to find the treasure, and of the misfortunes that have befallen the curious, becoming particularly heated as he recounts the case of the man who even went so far as to harness his horses to the stone—only to lose both his animals, through death, within a few hours, and himself be rendered a cripple for life. And, as if to prove the stone enchanted, he will round off his story by pointing to a cavity which has never been known to run dry of dew in even the severest of droughts.

In many parts of Somerset, as, for instance, at the *Luttrell Arms* at Dunster, it is still considered more reverent to burn bundles of ashen faggots, neatly bound with withes, in place of the Yule log on Christmas Eve. For in parts of the West Country it is firmly believed that when the shepherds reached the Holy Family at that first Christmas, they at once gathered sticks of ash and kindled a fire to keep away the terrible chill.

In many a cottage home to-day we shall find little family groups standing around the hearth, ready to make their silent wish as the withes burst into flame, while, here and there, in some odd village " pub ", we may yet see the ceremony rounded off in time-honoured fashion by the ordering of a quantity of cider all round as the withes break.

Intriguing, these old customs. At both Hinton St. George and Lopen they still carry out a ceremony relating to the far-off days of Chiselborough Fair, when the men of these two villages, having successfully packed their wives off home, went off the rails a bit and proceeded to make a night of it. The story goes that the womenfolk went to the fair to buy red cloth for their cloaks, and, wearying of hanging about waiting for their husbands, they returned home on their own. Once left to their own devices, the men soon found plenty to interest them, and forgot to watch the clock.

Hour after hour slipped by without any sign of their return, until at last the women, doubtless feeling a little suspicious, decided to set off in a bunch to see what it was all about. But the night was dark, and the way to Chiselborough long and rough. There was a bit of a wind, too, and their candles kept blowing out. Indeed, at one time it seemed that to attempt such a trip was to undergo a fool's errand ; then someone hit upon the happy idea of pulling up the mangolds from the field and hollowing them out into lanterns.

How the women fared after that, or what sort of reception their husbands received, is not recorded, but Punkie Night is still kept up on the last Thursday in October, when the village children make lanterns of mangolds and call from house to house demanding fresh candles and chanting their song :

Adam and Eve wouldn't believe
It's Punkie Night to-night.

As at Padstow, a hobby horse procession forms part of the May Day celebrations at Minehead, though here it is said to commemorate an eighteenth-century wreck off Dunster, when a cow was the only survivor.

Likewise does Frome continue to hold its cheese-fair, to remind us that the making of cheese is still an important county industry. If we wander up to Cheap Street as the time of the fair draws near, we shall see the cheeses being christened, one after the other, in the little stream that flows down one side, and will be told that this is done to bring luck to the exhibitors. The fact that all can achieve luck in this way is, apparently, of little consequence.

Frome has another unusual custom. Here, every Whitsun, the children will dress up in their " Sunday-bests " and, carrying the largest handkerchiefs that their fathers have been able to lay hands on, will congregate at their respective Sunday schools. From each of these schools they will then proceed to the village church, headed by a band, choir, and clergy, where, at the end of a short service, they will be given enormous spicy currant buns in the churchyard to wrap up in their handkerchiefs and take home to share among their families.

Certainly there is no need for anyone to be bored in Somerset. There is altogether too much to see and hear.

If we pass along to Burrington Combe, with the Mendips rising almost sheer above us on either side, we shall soon find ourselves involuntarily gazing upon a huge rock which has long been celebrated the world over by men, women, and children of every race and creed, of every class and clime. For it was under this rock that a young curate from Blagdon found shelter when caught in a storm on his way home one evening in the early 1770's.

The lightning flashed down the valley ; the thunder cracked with terrifying nearness over the hill-tops above ; the rain beat down the gorge in torrents. It was a typical Mendip storm. As he sat crouched under the rock, the curate began to ponder his plight. After a while he put his hand in his pocket and took out a pencil. He began writing :

Rock of Ages, cleft for me,
Let me hide myself in Thee.

The curate's name was the Rev. Augustus Toplady, and it is said that he wrote the famous words on the back of a playing card. Every year crowds foregather in thousands from every corner of England to hold a commemoration service at the foot of this rock, and it is a stirring experience to hear the words of the old hymn echoing down the gorge. Nowhere in all

England are they sung with such fervour as at Burrington.

As I say, no one need ever be bored in Somerset. While on the Athelney Marshes they will talk for hours on end about the deeds of King Alfred, of his mishap with the cakes when posing as a poor minstrel, and will tell you that it was at Wedmore that he signed his treaty with Guthrun, round Sedgemoor way they will wax almost as enthusiastic about the Duke of Monmouth. For it was here that the last battle to take place on English soil was fought, Charles's luckless son having put up the night before at the George Inn at Norton St. Philip, a fine half-timbered building, once a wool centre and said to be the oldest licensed hostelry in the country.

While at Limington we shall remember that here Cardinal Wolsey was granted his first living at the age of seventeen, but was later relieved of his living through his indiscretion in building the tower of Magdalen College, Oxford, out of the bursarship. At Ilchester we shall instinctively turn our attention to Roger Bacon and Richard Sheridan, just as at Nether Stowey we shall look for Coleridge's cottage, imagining him to be still seated at work on the *Rime of the Ancient Mariner* or *Christabel*, or entertaining Southey, Charles Lamb, Hazlitt, and De Quincey, or preparing to walk on the Quantocks with William and Dorothy Wordsworth when the devoted brother and sister were renting Alfoxden in the beautiful woods near Holford.

Wherever we turn, almost, we shall find something of interest, whether it be to the quarries on Combe Down, where mushrooms are cultivated in the disused workings and where, in the course of centuries, men have dug so deep that the stone now has to be mined; or to the little island church at Orchardleigh, hidden away in vast parkland, unseen and all but unknown;

or to the packhorse bridges at Allerford and Bruton Bow ; or to the cockpit at Woolavington ; or to Montacute House, that fine Elizabethan mansion with its legend of the flint cross that gave its name to the Abbey at Waltham Cross ; or to the railway station at Farrington Gurney, where the booking office is likewise the village pub ; or to Odcombe, to find where table manners first took a turn for the better with the introduction of the fork in place of the hand.

But wherever we do decide to turn, there is one name that we shall for ever be reading on the finger-posts . . . Bath. Bath, the *Aquæ Sulis* of the Romans, the monastic centre of the Middle Ages, the most perfect specimen of a Georgian town left to us in England to-day, built entirely of local stone, most of it from the Combe Down quarries.

Let all whose lot it is to plan our towns and cities of the future look long and lovingly on Bath, mindful of the days of Ralph Allen and John Wood, when architecture and fine craftsmanship went hand in hand, and when good taste, both in design and execution, was a matter of greater moment than cheap labour and shoddy materials. Almost every building in every street, either great or mean, is an architectural gem in itself, and the gutting of the Assembly Rooms is one of the greater material tragedies of the war.

According to legend, Bath, it seems, was destined from earliest times to become the " City Beautiful ". A certain prince of the name of Bladud—son of King Hudibras, and later to become King himself—was unfortunate enough to fall a victim to leprosy, so that he was compelled to leave his father's court and seek a job as swineherd at the little village at Keynsham. All went well until Bladud realized to his consternation that he was passing on the dreaded disease to the pigs, then, fearful of his master's anger, he took the course of driving the animals to the other side of the river, arguing, as his reason, that the acorns were more plentiful there.

As luck would have it, the pigs wandered off and proceeded to wallow to their hearts' content in a quagmire that had formed around some health-giving springs, so that when the young swineherd came to wash them down he found to his surprise and joy that they had all been cleansed of their leprosy. Whereupon Bladud at once decided to follow the example of the pigs. And when he, too, emerged cured and fit to return to the Court, he declared that he would clean the springs and build around them the finest city in England, laying the foundations in 863 B.C.

Whether or not the story of Bladud is true, it was around these springs that Bath grew up, and it is said that it was largely this legend that inspired the Woods to their great work ; a fact which they acknowledged by introducing acorns into much of their stone work.

What a world of romance envelops this truly noble city. One moment we shall wander among the amazing labyrinth of Roman baths, watching the hot springs bubbling up water at a temperature of 170° F. and at a rate of five hundred thousand gallons a day, and imagining the Romans to be with us throwing in their offerings of coins ; the next, we shall skip many centuries to see the ladies of Georgian England, dressed in yellow linen and carrying trays of handkerchiefs, nosegays and snuff about their bosoms, paddling about in the more modern baths, which are still fed, however, by the same springs.

What a world of romance—Sally Lunn baking her famous cakes in the little bow-fronted shop (later made more attractive still by the addition of a Chippendale fanlight) in Lilliput Alley ; pork butchers in Cheap Street curing pigs' faces galore by their secret process that was to give us Bath Chaps ; the cream of the aristocracy arriving from far and wide to " take the waters "—three glasses of them, with intervals of music and wit between each—bathe, sip coffee, listen to concerts, lunch, walk (or take their exercise in Sedan chairs, according to their condition and general outlook on life), dine, and, finally, dance or gamble, or both.

And behind it all Beau Nash, uncrowned King of Bath, a bit of a snob but always a kindly Master of Ceremonies, even if his rules for the Pump Room never could be relaxed ; not even for the Princess Amelia, daughter of the King of England.

It was in 1707 that he framed these rules, and they make amusing reading :

I

That a visit of ceremony at coming to Bath, and another going away, is all that is expected or desired by Ladies of Quality and Fashion—except Impertinents.

II

That Ladies coming to the Ball appoint a Time for their Footmens coming to wait on them Home, to prevent Disturbances and Inconveniences to Themselves and Others.

III

That Gentlemen of Fashion never appearing in a Morning before the Ladies in Gowns and Caps shew Breeding and Respect.

IV

That no Person take it ill that anyone goes to another's Play or Breakfast and not to theirs—except Captious by Nature.

V

That no Gentleman give his Tickets for the Balls to any but Gentlewomen.—N.B. Unless he has none of his Acquaintance.

VI

That Gentlemen crowding before the Ladies at the Ball, shew ill Manners; and that none do so for the Future—except such as respect nobody but Themselves.

VII

That no Gentleman or Lady take it ill that another Dances before them—except such as have no Pretence to dance at all.

VIII

That the Elder Ladies and Children be contented with a Second Bench at the Ball, as being past, or not come to Perfection.

IX

That the younger Ladies take notice how many Eyes observe them—This don't extend to the Have-at-All's.

X

That all whispers of Lies and Scandal be taken for their Authors.

XI

That all Repeaters of such Lies and Scandal be shun'd by all Company—except such as have been guilty of the same Crime.

N.B.—Several Men of no Character, Old Women and Young Ones, of Questioned Reputation, are great Authors of Lies in this Place, being of the sect of LEVELLERS.

Throughout the greater part of the eighteenth century, Bath remained the great mecca of the "fancy" with the Bath Road a highway of phætons, curricles, coaches, tilburies, and the like during "the Season".

Though fast cars have long taken their place, we can still feel the ghosts of the "Men of Polite Society" around us as we make our way from the city on towards Wiltshire. On this same road, too, we shall still occasionally bump into some old "character" who would appear to have been more suited to Georgian days than to those of our own time. Just such a character was the bearded carrier with whom I got into conversation. The sky was clouding over after a long, bright period, and I asked him whether he thought the weather was breaking. Pushing his hat a little further back on his head, he looked up at the sky and said : " Yes, zur, I reckon it's now settling down to being roight unsettled." Rather delightful !

Four — *Where Shepherds Watch*

IF the "fancy" in their phætons now frequent the Bath Road only as ghosts, and if such characters as the weather-wise carrier are now, unhappily, few and far between, we shall still find men working below ground on either side of the road, excavating, cutting, and preparing Bath stone for the building needs of both East Somerset and West Wiltshire, just as did their forefathers in the days of the Woods.

Since earliest times the men of Wiltshire, with Corsham as one of their principal centres, have been cleaving stone from the very bowels of the earth and passing it on to others to replace on the surface in the form of houses. Working with a devotion born only of tradition, it is these quarrymen—and, of course, those in other parts of the county—who have given Wiltshire much of her character.

Down these mines we can, to this day, see how many of our old-world villages were started off on their path to loveliness, and, on account of that loveliness, world-wide fame. Down these mines we can readily hark back to the days when towns and villages everywhere were built of local materials and by the hands of local craftsmen ; the days when those three priceless gems, Castle Combe, Lacock, and Corsham itself, slowly and methodically rose from the ground.

Here you will meet with no machinery ; no explosives even. Instead, you will find men so steeped in their tradition that they can detect even the tiniest flaw in a layer of stone simply by tapping it with a small pebble ; men, moreover, who are every bit as particular about cutting away such flaws as were their forefathers, ever faithful to their creed that perfect houses require perfect stone and that only the best is good enough. Here you may find a man picking away at the chalk, while another cuts along the face of the rock at ground level ; there you will watch a third laboriously sawing a massive boulder into neat slabs, wielding his enormous saw entirely by hand. There, again, you may notice yet another group of craftsmen trimming and smoothing these slabs into the many and various shapes required by the builders and masons.

When their work is complete, the finished stone will be left for months to " sweat ", when the moisture will gradually seep through to the surface to form a weatherproof crust that will help to preserve the stone, keep the houses dry, and, incidentally, add charm to the general appearance.

As I say, it is these quarrymen who have given Wiltshire much of her character. For it is the delightful little stone-built towns and villages—each so different from the next, and yet all bearing a distinct regional similarity—that help to make her quite unlike her neighbours : such places as Castle Combe, Fonthill, Teffont Magna—sweetest of all, to my mind—Steeple Ashton, Compton Bassett, or Cherhill, with its tithe barn, church, and manor house all clustered together at the end of the lane ; Mere, with its squatters' huts that were built between sunset and sunrise ; East Knoyle, where Sir Christopher Wren was born, or Coate with the farmhouse where that strangely lonely naturalist, Richard Jefferies, first saw the light of day ; Garsdon with its sixteenth-century manor house that once was the home of the Washingtons ; Tilshead, with its memories of floods ; or Woodford, where Charles II hid in Heale House ; or Stratford and its manor house links with William Pitt ; or Milston, the birthplace of Joseph Addison.

Few counties can boast such pleasing places. The list seems unending, for we must not forget Boscombe or Hindon ; Bradford-on-Avon with its magnificent Jacobean house and perhaps even finer Saxon church ; Warminster, where Dr. Arnold was educated at the local grammar school before himself bringing about one of the greatest educational reforms of all time ; or Ramsbury, the county's former See, with nearby Littlecote and its stately mansion where William of Orange once stayed. Its haunted room is still there to tell the tale of the evil deeds of " Wild Darrell ", an unsavoury gentleman who lived in Tudor times and whose family came over with the Conqueror. The story—already made famous by Sir Walter Scott—goes that this Darrell, at his wit's end on discovering that he had given one of his wife's attendants a child, proceeded, on the night of the confinement, to a village across the Berkshire border to fetch a midwife, whom he blindfolded and brought to Littlecote on horseback. No sooner had the baby been born than he snatched it from the woman and hurled it on to the fire. As luck would have it, the child rolled out in its struggles, whereupon Darrell threw it back again and furiously heaped more coals on top. Finally, satisfied that all traces of his crime had been removed, he paid the midwife, and took her home again in the same way as he had fetched her. But crime will out! The midwife tracked him down, and Darrell was brought to trial. Things were not, however, quite the same then as now, it seems. The judge was open to be "squared", and agreed to allow Darrell his life in exchange for his house—a convenient arrangement! In any event it was one that certainly worked out well for the judge, who at once went on to make Littlecote the scene of extravagant entertainment.

We must not forget, moreover, Marlborough with its wide main street—the widest in England, I believe—and its fine Georgian architecture to remind us of its past importance as a stopping-place on the high road to Bath; or Salisbury with its lovely cathedral, unique close, poultry cross, and sundry buildings of historic interest—the city that once was Old Sarum but was later moved down the hill, largely, it seems, for purposes of convenience.

As unique as the towns and villages themselves is the scenery that provides both their setting and the inspiration of their people. While in the north we shall find ourselves in the centre of vast rolling downland—bolder in parts than even that of Berkshire or Sussex—with, here and there, an odd village nestling in a hollow around the bend of a hill, and perhaps a river valley or trickling stream to add to the beauty and general grandeur of the scene. In the south we may stand upon Salisbury Plain amidst country so barren in places that one writer was prompted to say of it:

No hedges, no ditches, no gates, no stiles,
Much less a house or a cottage for miles;
It's a very sad thing to be caught in the rain
When night's coming on upon Salisbury Plain.

It certainly is. And yet, in spite of it all, its many ancient relics, the quaintness of its few villages, and the fact that it is a haven for many unusual forms of wild life—notably the bustard—all help to atone for the monotony of the terrain.

Then again, South Wiltshire is not all like this. The Plain itself is almost entirely surrounded by a network of delightful rivers which, rising in the hills to the north or west, wend their way across or around it to link up by Salisbury to form the Nadder, and so continue their way through further downs.

Whether on rolling down or open plain, we may often, as in Somerset, wander for miles with the grazing sheep as our only companions and an odd cottage or farmstead as the sole proof that there must surely be human beings about somewhere. It is in these isolated parts, however, among the scattered barrows and burial mounds of the primitive dead that we shall learn the spirit of Wiltshire. For the downs and the plains, and the sheep that graze upon them, have been the county's lifeblood for countless ages ; the very seeds from which those lovely villages have sprung.

For Wiltshire, with the Cotswolds and parts of East Anglia, was once the principal wool and cloth centre in the days when these commodities were sent all over the world and provided one of our main sources of revenue. Though the north-west corner, in a triangle formed by Malmesbury, Devizes, and Bradford, proved always the main area of activity, we shall find evidence of the past importance of this industry to the county as a whole in town and village architecture far and wide. Indeed, many of Wiltshire's most charming houses might well never have been built—and certainly not in such splendour—had not the original owners succeeded in lining their pockets extremely satisfactorily out of the industry, while quite a number of the imposing Perpendicular churches with which the county is so richly endowed are said to have been paid for by the woolstaplers of long ago.

While the ruined Malmesbury Abbey once served, in Tudor times, as the factory of William Stumpe, finest clothier of all, at Chippenham, with its fifteenth-century Maud Heath causeway, Corsham, Trowbridge —where Crabbe was once rector, and where weaving is still an important industry—Devizes, and in many of the fascinating little villages along the beautiful Wylye Valley to Salisbury, are houses that once served as home and workshop alike for some of the " lesser fry ". At Devizes, too, is the old wool hall.

Most interesting of all these old clothiers' houses, in some respects, is the row of cottages reputed to have been built by Flemish weavers at Corsham. Humble in outward appearance, they are, nevertheless, quite unlike the average cottage home. Moreover, each differs slightly from the next. Only in two respects, as far as I can see, are they completely similar—all were constructed with remarkably high ceilings for the convenience of the looms, and with wine cellars for the convenience of those that worked them.

In the centre of this delightful row I noticed one with a church door and arch. In this cottage, I was told, the Flemings used to pray and hold Divine Service in early morning and again at the end of their long and strenuous day at their looms, ever faithful to the religion whose persecution had, in fact, brought them to England in the first place.

Though Wiltshire was always the greatest of the wool counties of the south west, the sheep-breeders, spinners, and weavers of both Devon and Somerset were hardly less active. Thus there gradually developed a certain rivalry between the farmers and craftsmen of the three counties. It was through that rivalry that Wilton and Axminster eventually came to the fore as carpet-making centres, and through them that the cleanliness of the English home began to take a turn for the better.

For centuries the floors of our homes—of castles, no less than of cottages—were simply strewn with herbs or rushes, or covered with animal hides, which were cleaned out and replaced from time to time according to the respectability or otherwise of the household. In the Middle Ages, however, it became increasingly fashionable for the foreign merchants, visiting the Wiltshire and Devon fairs to buy our wool and cloth, to bring with them the most exquisite Eastern rugs to barter in exchange. These rugs found a ready market among the more wealthy members of mediæval society, not as floor coverings—for that would have been a shocking and quite unnecessary waste in their opinion—but as wall-drapings or as runners for the massive oak tables of the halls and such like.

In course of time certain of our own master craftsmen, impressed with the superb workmanship, began to try their hand at making rugs of tapestry, embroidery, and petit-point, blending the various foreign influences into a new and quite original motif. So it was that, in their little cottage homes in the sheep-farming areas, the men and women gradually paid less and less attention to making cloths, but, instead, devoted their energies to weaving rugs. True, at first they made them mainly for themselves and for such of their friends as were less gifted than they, but since, unlike the noblemen, they used them on the floors rather than the walls, it was not long before their fame spread and they found themselves weaving rugs for the local gentry as well. Soon they were working for people all over the country. Nor did they confine themselves to what we should regard as rugs ; now that they were serving the needs of really large houses, they began to make correspondingly larger floor coverings.

A certain competition developed among the various towns and villages until, by the beginning of the eigh-

" The wind-swept Egdon Heath, with the little thatched cottage where he was born "—Thomas Hardy's birthplace.

" The smallest pub in England "—the *Smith's Arms* at Godmanstone.

" The lonely hamlets in the wooded hollows"
—Milton Abbas.

" That strange bank of pebbles out at sea "—Chesil Beach, under storm clouds.

teenth century, Wilton and Axminster had emerged as the principal centres, with the Wilton craftsmen boasting a royal charter. Indeed, by now the competition had become so hot that the ninth Earl of Pembroke, not to be outdone by the King of France's embargo on the export of craftsmen from his country, went to the extreme of smuggling over two leading carpet-makers in wine barrels to teach the Continental secrets at Wilton ; a move to which Axminster retaliated later by introducing a new idea from Brussels.

So the two distinctive styles took shape—the Wilton " cut-pile " and the Axminster " hand-tufted " or " loop-pile ", the entire plant of the latter workshops being moved to Wilton just over a hundred years ago —where, to this day, we may still watch carpets being made on the traditional lines of both counties.

Here we shall find men and women still adopting some of the very same technique that was employed in making those early Eastern rugs. As an instance of the splendid workmanship that goes into their making, I am told that it sometimes takes as much as a week to weave nine inches, and that so elaborate are many of the patterns that the women may have to knot as many as three million different pieces of wool to their warp before ever they can proceed with the rest of the work. Such carpets are woven in one piece, and are known as *real* Axminsters to distinguish them from the cheaper varieties which, like the Wilton pile, are made on power-looms at the rate of something like two hundred yards a week.

An interesting place, Wilton : it was here, in the great house, that Sir Philip Sidney wrote the greater part of his *Arcadia*, and entertained Queen Elizabeth after escorting her with considerable pomp and ceremony from Salisbury Plain ; here, too, that Shakespeare is supposed to have produced *As You Like*

It for the first time, and to have acted in various of his plays ; here that James I, and his son Charles after him, delighted to come every summer, though largely, it seems, to taste of the delicious salmon from the local streams and rivers. Wilton House, where they and so many others stayed, with its Holbein, Inigo Jones, and Webb influences, and its priceless collection of pictures by Vandyck, Reynolds, Rubens, and others, still stands in part.

There are one or two lovely old houses in the neighbourhood of Wilton and Salisbury—Hyde's House, Dinton, and Little Clarendon at Dinton, for instance, and Trafalgar House at Standlynch. It was at either Hyde's House or Little Clarendon that the famous Lord Chancellor Clarendon was born, while Trafalgar House, built in 1733, with wings added later by the younger Wood, was bought by the Nation in 1814 for the descendants of Lord Nelson.

But to return to the wool question : it is a strange sensation to pass straight from the busy little workshops at Wilton, where as many as seven or eight women may be lined up together along a forty-feet-wide loom—the widest in the world, I believe—all hard at work on the same carpet, to the tranquillity of the downs, in search of the shepherd, with his crook and cloak and his long-coated dog, whose sheep supply their wool. Strange but *so* peaceful ! Here, high up on the downs, life at once assumes altogether different proportions. The busy little towns below us seem far away, and, though we can often see the stream of traffic tearing its mad course along the main roads in the lower distance, the sound of the engines is drowned by the song of the birds in the clumps of trees about us. So peaceful, that we begin to envy the shepherd in his apparent loneliness, and can almost imagine ourselves listening to him singing his old time pastorals—those pastorals with which, in days gone by, he would welcome all strangers, from kings and princes downwards—as he wanders over the hills and dales and along the old drove roads. Certainly in such a setting we can readily appreciate why it is that he still has so little use for things modern. Here I always recall the story of the man who, asked what he thought of aeroplanes, looked up at the sky, and replied simply, but with feeling :

" If God had meant us to fly, He'd have given us wings ! "

Isolated he may be, but never really *lonely*. In the simple things of life he finds more than ample consolation for the absence of mere people ; to him Nature is ever the finest companion of all. Not that he is averse to meeting people. Far from it ; the downland sheep fairs, said to be the oldest of the kind in England, are the heyday of his year ; the day on which he emerges from his seclusion, mainly to meet others of his kith and kind. For as isolated as the shepherds are the fairs themselves, many of which—like the famous one on Tan Hill, high above Devizes, where salt beef and beans once formed the staple diet of the traditional feast—take place in spots so remote that their only approach may lie along trackways long neglected and forsaken at any other time.

To talk with a Wiltshire countryman is by no means always easy. What with his misplacing of pronouns, his use of the letter " z " for " s ", his total omission of vowels on occasion and " h's " always, and his queer way of rolling his " r's "—to say nothing of his many strange words and phrases—conversation is sometimes wellnigh impossible. Still, if you can manage to muddle along somehow, you will find that, for all his apparent detachment, he is well versed in all that is going on around him. He will tell you many a yarn of hill and dale : of highwaymen lying in wait on

Salisbury Plain ; of the Martinsell Festival on the Marlborough Downs, when schoolboys used to slide down the hillside on the jawbones of horses, and when neighbouring villagers climbed the slopes to settle their disputes in deadly combat ; of the famous huntsman, Thomas Assheton Smith, riding the Tedworth country and dumbfounding the local gentry by chasing hell for leather after his hounds down the steepest hill of all ; of the eccentric Captain Budd who, setting himself up as " Dictator of the Downs ", was among the first to introduce machinery to the Wiltshire farms, and who, in his enthusiasm, threw anyone who dared voice disapproval neck-and-crop into the pond at Winterbourne Bassett without more ado.

He will refer to the old sarsen stones about him as " grey wethers ", seeing in them a certain likeness to his sheep, and will tell of the Devil arriving with a team of white oxen at midnight, bent on pulling down one particular stone at Clatford Bottom. He will talk too of Palm Sunday feasts of figs and cider on Silbury Hill, by the Bath Road, and, if you ask him for his views about this strange eminence—the highest artificial mound in Europe, dating back to the days before the Romans—he will smile and say :

" Well, zar, they do zay it were built by the Devil."

Whereupon he will proceed to describe the old feud that once persisted between the people of Devizes and those of Marlborough, when matters reached such a pitch that the latter went so far as to enlist the help of the Devil in what was to have been one final round-up of their opponents. Unhappily for Marlborough, however, the inhabitants of Devizes got wind of the plan just in time, and, as a counter measure, sent the local cobbler with all the old boots and shoes they could lay hands on to meet him on his journey. Thus, when the two met at Silbury, and the Devil asked the cobbler the distance to Devizes, the latter, looking tired and weary, was able to point to his bundle and declare that all these boots and shoes had he worn out coming from there, and that it was, indeed, a long way. A bright idea, for the Devil, it seems, at once became demoralized, dashed the cobbler's pile to the ground, and made off back again in the same direction. So that Silbury Hill, he will assure you, is founded on no more than footwear.

But perhaps he is most at home when talking of the moonrakers, those smugglers who hid their kegs of contraband liquor in the ponds by day, and raked them out again by the light of the moon; those simpletons from Bishop's Cannings who, when caught in the act by a passing Preventive Man, pretended that they were trying to rescue a cheese that had fallen in! The Excise man was a simpleton himself, and advised them that their work was in vain, for that what they thought was a cheese was really but the reflection of the moon!

Delightful characters, these Wiltshire farm folk. I always remember one old shepherd pulling a tuft of sheep's wool out of his pocket and telling me, in so many words, that that was his passport into Heaven.

"Us allays likes to be buried with a lock of wool on our chest, 'ee know, zar," he explained. "You zee, zar, without it we might well end up in the wrong place. We might go down yonder instead of up aloft."

"But how does the wool help?" I pressed him.

"Well, zar, don't 'ee zee, that's the proof of our calling. Us carn't harrdly nevver go to church with our flocks to look arfter, so we must show the reason somehow."

"You mean that the wool will help to excuse your absence and prove your case on Judgment Day?"

"Yes, zar, thank 'ee kindly, us thinks it should."

This seems to be a pretty general way of working

things out in downland country, for the same idea, I find, is practised in both Berkshire and Sussex. Indeed, in Sussex they sometimes like to make doubly sure of things by placing the head of the old man's crook in the coffin as well.

While I was talking to this old shepherd, I noticed a number of sheep drinking from a dewpond. Knowing full well the mystery that is so often made of these ponds, I decided to tackle him on the question.

" Why, zar, they do zay they was making them ponds in Wiltshire afore ever Christ was born." And he looked proudly in the direction of the sheep.

In olden days, he explained, such ponds often provided the only water supply for cattle in dry parts, and they are still all-important in remote areas. They are made in spring, when a hollow of considerable circumference is dug to a depth of perhaps five or six feet. The earth is then stamped down hard and covered with straw, which, in turn, is afterwards coated with some six inches of puddled clay, the greatest care being taken to ensure that not a strand of straw is left exposed. With the straw acting as an insulator against the heat of the earth beneath, the night air at once becomes chilled above the cooler surface of the clay, vaporizes, and drops in the form of dew to form a pond which, in even the most severe of droughts, will never run dry, but will be maintained at a more or less constant level.

But if Wiltshire is founded on wool and cloth, her sheep are by no means her only mainstay. Ever since the Middle Ages—and, doubtless, long before that—the pig has figured prominently in the life of the native. As in other parts of the country, it was largely upon his pigs that the peasant depended for his very existence, and he would butcher, salt, and smoke the animals in his cottage home with a skill and pride almost amounting to devotion.

These Wiltshire hogs were no ordinary beasts, however; like those of Berkshire, they were altogether more succulent than the average. Among the first to realize this was a certain Thomas Harris, who, in 1770, decided to set up a centre at Calne to which farmers all over the county might send their pigs to be cured and turned into bacon. Thus the keeping of pigs gradually developed from a peasant occupation into an industry that has brought fame to Wiltshire bacon the world over.

The centre flourished from the start. But there were difficulties to contend with. All went well in the autumn and winter—and even in the spring, for that matter—but in the heat of the summer work virtually came to a standstill. This was not good enough for the enterprising Harris family, who could always be certain of a constant supply of hogs at any time of the year. Experiments were soon under way for finding a means of reducing the temperature to a sufficiently low level to enable work to proceed in even the hottest weather without the meat's going bad in the process. Thus was evolved the idea of packing blocks of ice in large chambers above and around the curing rooms, the ice being prevented from melting by the erection of non-conducting walls. Thus, in 1856, was set up at Calne the first ice-house of the kind in England, an idea that was soon to be adopted, under licence, by bacon-curers all over Great Britain and Ireland.

Wiltshire bacon at once became more famous than ever. Queen Victoria ordered it for the Royal Household; the Prince of Wales (later Edward VII) ordered it. Members of Parliament devoured it with gusto in the House of Commons, and declared it to be good. Hostesses everywhere numbered it among their principal catering needs. It went to the Continent, to India, China, New Zealand, the Cape of Good Hope, and countless other places. So great was the demand that a railway branch line had to be brought to Calne from nearby Chippenham, to take the place of the old road-carriers who could no longer cope with it all.

This new ice-house not only brought added prosperity to the farmer, but it also created an unusual winter industry. Whenever the winter turned cruel, those whose work ceased with the coming of the frosts at once found their salvation in the harvesting of ice. All along the rivers and canals, and by the ponds, streams and brooks, little groups of men and women, often accompanied by their children, would be seen breaking up and gathering ice to take to Calne; indeed, in some respects, a hard winter was almost something to which to look forward, for, when there were no frosts, the ice had to be especially imported from the Scandinavian countries.

Though modern refrigerators have long since taken the place of the old ice-chambers at Calne, bacon is still cured there by much the same methods, and I am told that, in normal times, something like three thousand pigs are handled every week by these workers, many of whom even yet cling to their traditional blue smocks and clogs.

Here the pig is first put painlessly to death by an electrical process, before being dropped into scalding water to loosen the hair, which is afterwards removed by machinery. Then, after being burnt to remove all final traces of hair, and scraped, it is sent to the "hanging room" to be examined by a veterinary surgeon, to the "chill room", and thence to the cutting table to be converted into bacon. Finally it passes to the curing cellars and the smoke stoves.

The bacon industry has certainly more than atoned for the falling-off of the wool and cloth trade. All over the county the farmers of to-day are taking their place in maintaining their world-famous tradition, just as did the woolstaplers and weavers of old bring fame upon their heads. An interesting business this pig question ; nowhere is the maximum made of the minimum to quite such an extent as here. While the farmers in the fields are able to use the by-products of the dairy for feeding the hogs, in the curing shops they are equally careful to see that every portion of the pig is put to some useful purpose. Here such of the meat as does not form part of a " side " will be made into pies, rolls, sausages, tongues, or galantines—real " Willsheere " and all very delicious. *Nothing*, it seems, is wasted. Surplus fat becomes lard, grease is treated by a benzine process to start life afresh as soap, the bones going back to the farmer as bone meal ; while even the blood is dried and returned to the fields in the form of fertilizers.

It is certainly a very different business from what it was in the days of the swineherd, when Wiltshire was almost all woodland except on the highest of the heights ; impenetrable jungle in many parts, with wild boars, wolves, and the like roaming at large to make life just a little difficult. But Wiltshire still has the *descendants* of the same hogs, though more " bacon-worthy " than ever—just as she still has Savernake, with its wonderful Grand Avenue of beeches, its King and Queen oaks, and its " Duke's Vaunt " ; Cranborne Chase, which she shares with Dorset ; Aldbourne Chase ; and Grovely Wood, to remind us of the time when kings and princes would cross her borders from London to hunt the stag with all the splendour typical of their age.

Most important of all was Savernake, for this was a forest in the true sense, and in Norman times there was a world of difference between a forest and a chase. While the king's hunting ground was always known as a forest, a chase was the term given to that of a nobleman, although if that nobleman elected to fence or wall in his land it at once became a " park ". The very beasts were different, too. While those of the forest comprised the hart, hind, wild boar, wolf, and hare, those of the chase were restricted to the buck, doe, fox, marten, and roe. Actually hunting fell into three categories, for below the forest and chase came the " warren ", where men of less noble birth might hunt the hare, rabbit, partridge, pheasant, woodcock, and, maybe, the badger, wild-cat, or otter.

Different tactics were, of course, adopted for hunting these various beasts, and at Shrewton, on Salisbury Plain, we may meet with men and women who even yet prefer to go after the " fowls of the air " with hawks rather than with modern sporting guns. To watch them at sport is to step back into the Middle Ages or the days of Elizabeth. For they are among the last remaining links with an age when hawking was held in such high esteem that a man was allowed to own a certain species of hawk entirely according to his position in the social scale, from a gerfalcon for a king to a miserable " musket " for the Holy Water Clerk; an age when owners, inseparable from their birds, would carry the creatures on their wrists even when going into battle, and have perches arranged in their bedrooms with, sometimes, a special attendant detailed to watch over them during the long hours of darkness.

As I say, Savernake was the more important, but Cranborne was also a forest before ever it passed into private ownership to become a chase, and at Tollard Royal we may still see the beautiful old house that once served as a hunting box for King John, just as at Upper Upham we shall find the one used by John of Gaunt when hunting Aldbourne.

If Savernake and Cranborne are among the oldest and noblest venues of the kind in the land, the latter has shrunk to but a fraction of its earlier size, so that to-day the magnificent Grovely Wood, high on the hills to the west of the Wylye Valley, is in many ways the most beautiful of all. From various points along its eastern fringe we may look down upon one of the most perfect panoramic views in all Wiltshire, with the trout-filled river—one of the most popular resorts for anglers in the country—woods, downs, and plain all merging into each other to form a single whole ; a perfect set-piece of Wiltshire landscape in all its moods and tenses.

Below these woods, at the foot of the downs, lies Wishford, whose church, it is said, was built by a group of grateful people in thankfulness at having crossed the treacherous marshes with which the district was once surrounded. Here, every May, we shall watch the villagers still celebrating a custom designed to ensure the continuance of their rights in the woods ; the right to collect such green timber as they can carry back with them.

In the old days it was customary for all to dress up in white, and, carrying boughs of oak, to proceed to Salisbury Cathedral, where, in a close filled with side-shows of every description, they would dance their traditional dances, while two of their number went inside to lay boughs upon the High Altar. Times change, however : the Victorian clergy considered such revelry unsuitable, so that the ceremony shifted to Wishford itself. There, then, on Oak Apple Day, if we rise from our beds at first light, we may tag on behind the triumphal procession as it makes its way slowly up the village street to the accompaniment of a brass band, headed by a Union Jack and two men carrying a banner bearing the words GROVELY ! GROVELY ! GROVELY ! AND ALL GROVELY ! UNITY IS STRENGTH. A somewhat slow procession, we shall stop outside every house to shout the words, not moving on until the inhabitants within have opened their windows to wish us luck. When the round of calls is complete, we shall move more rapidly on up to the forest, there to gather all the timber we can lay hands on, remembering always, however, that, though we may cut growing branches, such wood may only be gathered " by strength of the people ", and that, while hand-carts and even bicycles are permitted—since they are propelled by our own power—on no account may we advance with horse-drawn wagons or mechanical saws.

Our job in the woods complete, we make our way back to the village where we set up the boughs before the houses (in the old days, we should have decked the best of these with ribbons and suspended it from the church tower), and, at noon, foregather under the tree to the south ready to take part in a second procession, when four women, each with faggots on their heads, will take their place behind the band, with children in fancy dress and men with boughs following after.

It is a great day, for after this will come the dinner at the local inn, and an afternoon and evening of sports and revelry. At Barford St. Martin they carry out a similar custom, but here their rights extend only to dead wood, the villagers having long since commuted part of their privileges in favour of an annual payment of £5 from the lord of the manor.

Incidentally, among the articles carried in the procession at Wishford is a sieve. Somewhat irrevelant to the occasion, this, it appears, is simply to perpetuate the memory of a certain Elizabeth Bonham who, some five hundred years ago, so upset her husband by giving birth to twins that he at once went off in a huff of some seven years' duration ; a huff which he decided to render the more impressive by refusing to cut either his nails or hair, and one that was only brought to an end when a witch warned him of his wife's intended re-marriage.

And so they came together again. But poor Edith got her own back : the year after the reunion, she made up for lost time by producing no less than seven children at a single birth—one for each year of separation. What happened to the unfortunate husband then is not recorded, but the babies were taken to the church in a sieve for their baptism. Or so the villager will have it. You can argue as much as you like about the improbability of the story, but the native will merely shake his head, and explain it all away in the fact that Edith Bonham was an exceptional woman. She certainly must have been !

The rights to Grovely Wood are not the only ones to be maintained in time-honoured fashion in Wiltshire. At Wishford itself the parish clerk may even yet be seen auctioning plots of grass on the evening of Rogation Monday ; a survival of the Sale of Midsummer Tithes. As the cottagers busily bid for the land, he will keep a constant eye upon the horizon for the last of the setting sun. Not until it has disappeared will the strange auction end, when the clerk will strike the gate with the church key, and declare the plots to be the property of the last bidder until the following November.

At Cricklade, too, up in the north by Gloucester's border, they still hold their Court Leet in observance of the fact that, by ancient law, the residents may still, if they wish, graze nine head of cattle each on North Meadow throughout the autumn and winter, and thirty sheep in spring and summer.

Such rights as these survive not only on grounds of mere sentiment ; to the cottagers they are privileges that still serve a useful purpose, and ones which they would not willingly give up. For the cottager, with his cow, sheep, pig, or poultry, once an important feature of rural England, has not yet been entirely forsaken, and in these courts and other like customs we have the story of a life-and-death struggle of the common man for the rights of man ; the story of his victory over the feudal lords of long ago.

Indeed, in most of our surviving country customs we may, if we seek diligently, trace back some past importance. The June town-criers' contest at Pewsey, when men with the lustiest voices don their traditional costumes and travel from counties far and wide to prove that theirs is the loudest and best voice of all is, of course, no more than a timely reminder that once there were no such things as wireless sets, telephones, or fast moving despatch riders. Less convenient, perhaps, but how infinitely more leisurely and beautiful must the days of our grandfathers have been, when individuality and private enterprise were still held in higher esteem than standardization and nationalization.

So, too, in the making of Simnel cakes at Devizes shall we recall that the Sabbath was the one day to be exempted from the Lenten fast. Here, at Devizes, the many and various ingredients will all be kneaded together and moulded into the shape of the star, to be eaten in stately mansion and humble cottage alike on Mothering Sunday. Such cakes as these are sent every year to the Dominions and Colonies, to the descendants of Wiltshire men who emigrated many decades back, and, to make certain of their reaching their destinations in time, baking starts at Devizes soon after Christmas.

Most unusual of all Wiltshire's customs and ceremonies is the June service at Stonehenge, when the Druids, draped in white robes and scarlet hoods, give salutation to the rising sun, and hold a service around the altar—the altar where Tess of the D'Urbervilles spent her last night of freedom—just as did primitive man at the very same place and time.

Nowhere in England shall we witness a sight quite so moving ; for nowhere shall we find like monuments comparable with those of Stonehenge, or of the rather older Avebury to her north. All over this lovely down-land country we shall come upon burial mounds and barrows, earthworks, hill forts and camps—the most famous being on Windmill Hill—sarsen stones (these are to be seen in the very structure of some of the village homes and churches) that were left behind by the palæozoic seas, and numerous other relics to recall the early struggles of man in a county once overrun with forest and teeming with wild beasts ; struggles wherein the antlers of reindeer, the shoulder-blades of oxen, and crudely-shaped pieces of flint did service for picks, shovels, and sundry other necessary tools. Small wonder that in the midst of these struggles these early inhabitants of our island should have found need to seek the blessing of the sun, even deeming it worth-while to move—perhaps by some form of slide—the finest sarsens they could find to build themselves temples, first at Avebury and later at Stonehenge ; two places which, to this day, remain the capitals of North and South Wiltshire respectively.

Nowhere in Europe shall we find a stone circle to equal that at Avebury—a fascinating village in itself—with its sarsens, standing on twenty-nine acres of land, almost entirely surrounded and protected by a wide and deep prehistoric ditch and outer earth bank, the latter something like three-quarters of a mile in diameter.

Doubtless it was its position that prompted the primitives to pick upon Avebury for so magnificent a temple, for Avebury is the focal point of the ancient hill tracks from the Chilterns, the Cotswolds, the North and South Downs, and the hills of Dorset. Along these trackways and ridge roads we may still wander far and wide in almost any direction we choose. Let us this time choose the direction of Dorset with its many hill camps all leading us down to the greatest fort of all—Maiden Castle.

" The peculiar handcart "—village carpenters at Puncknowle, making a " dung-putt."

" Every conceivable type of net "—a Dorset cottage net-maker.

" Where every building almost is an architectural gem "—
Corfe Castle.

" Birthplace of modern cricket "—the *Bat and Ball* at Hambledon.

Five *The Cinderella of the South*

TO gaze upon Maiden Castle with its hundred acres or so of earth and chalk ramparts—some of them as much as ninety feet high—and its fragmentary foundations of chambers and other living rooms ; to think back upon the many earthworks and prehistoric camps we passed in getting there, Castle Rings, Winklebury, Tollard Royal, Hambledon Hill, Bulbarrow, Rawlsbury, Poundbury, Maumbury Rings, and many others ; and then to drop down into Dorchester to see the remains of people and animals, flint implements, fragments of pottery, and the like, all neatly displayed in the county museum ; to think of, and gaze upon, these things is to bring home to us the importance of downland country to primitive man.

If unalike in other respects, Dorset, Wiltshire, Berkshire, and Sussex at least have this in common : the highness of their hills gave hope and comfort to the inhabitants of our island thousands of years before Christ, when this, in the main, was impossible in the dense forests of the lower levels.

At Maiden Castle men and women worked and

toiled; plied their crafts; farmed; slaughtered beasts with stones or flint-headed spears, or ate one another when times were bad; lived, loved, and lost; brought up their children, and jabbered their incoherent speech—all more than four thousand years ago. Here, after them, settled the metal workers and others of the Iron Age; here, later still, came the Roman Vespasian with his mighty hordes to drive them out again, to set up his temple and build, at the foot of the hill—where once had lived the Durotriges, or "dwellers by the water"—Dorchester itself; planning its lay-out, like that of Wareham to the south (where Peter the Hermit was hanged by King John for falsely predicting the latter's deposition) and Chichester in Sussex, so that its main streets followed the four points of the compass.

All over Dorset we shall come upon relics of one kind or another to help us piece together the long story of strife and struggle that took place in our island for centuries before the Conqueror was ever thought of. Maumbury Rings itself, hardly less interesting than Maiden Castle, was, as Thomas Hardy says, the county's coliseum. Here, in their vast amphitheatre—capable of holding five times as many people as the Cornish one near Perranporth, and comparable only with that at Silchester in Hampshire—the Roman gladiators, splendidly attired with plumed helmets and gaudily-decorated shields, would hold those life-and-death contests that formed such an integral part of their lives; contests wherein a defeated man would often be finished off with a dagger where he lay, unless he had fought well enough to be pardoned, and then be carried off on a bier amidst the excitement and general applause of the spectators. Bloodthirsty days! When the Romans went, Maumbury Rings lost none of its importance but, instead, became the scene of tournaments and jousting, and, later, of May Day revels ; the scene of chivalry and merriment.

Dorset then, with Dorchester as her focal point, was one of the earliest centres of life and work in our island. Much water has flowed under the bridges since the departure of the Romans and the arrival of the Normans, however. Dorset has seen much coming and going. Charles II has hidden in the chimney of the *Queen's Arms* at Charmouth—once a Roman station—after narrowly avoiding capture at Lyme Regis ; his unfortunate son has landed where he himself had tried to embark ; civil war has raged far and wide over the countryside with the Parliamentary troops covering the Weymouth Road from the heights of Maumbury ; Judge Jeffreys has held his " Bloody Assizes " at Dorchester, putting-up for the occasion in a house that is still standing ; and the sports of the amphitheatre have given place to the " hanging fairs ".

As I say, there has been much coming and going. But times change. Dorset has become the " Cinderella " county of the south ; the forgotten land through which the people of to-day drive fast and furiously, but, more often than not, only to reach some destination beyond. The twentieth-century traveller has, in the main, no eyes, it seems, for the rolling hills—more gentle than those of Wiltshire—and lush meadowlands ; the little winding streams that trickle so peacefully through the fields ; the snug thatched cottages, built of Dorset stone, that go to make up the villages ; the lonely hamlets in the wooded hollows ; or the many fascinating coves to the south, not, as yet, " discovered " ; the modern traveller has no eyes for all these things which, together, are Dorset.

But then, that, to my mind, is one of her main charms. Little known, inconvenient of approach and, as a result, frequently by-passed, she has avoided being swallowed up in the maelstrom of modernity. Never was a land so well portrayed as in Hardy's words " Far from the Madding Crowd ". The windswept Egdon Heath, with the little thatched cottage where he was born, standing on its fringe at Higher Bockhampton ; Lower Bockhampton, where he was taught and where stands his famous " greenwood tree " in Yellowham Wood ; Stinsford, where his heart lies buried and where his grandfather and uncles, dressed in blue coats with brass buttons, and buckled shoes, made music in the church with 'cellos and fiddles—all, indeed, are far from the madding crowd.

Untouched by the hand of *man*, yet skilfully kept in trim by the hand of the *craftsman*—always a very different person—her beauty lies in her natural simplicity more than in anything else. In Dorset you will find few places to take your breath away, as do Buckland-in-the-Moor, St. Just-in-Roseland, Oare, Dunster, or Lacock ; you will find few corners upon which you will gaze spellbound. On the other hand, except in one or two black spots—and there are remarkably few of these—you will seldom see a house, either old or modern, that does not tone perfectly with its setting.

Only by living in Dorset—or, at any rate, staying there for some time—and mixing with her charming people, can one learn her inner secrets, and see her in her true perspective. Do this, and, after a while, you may well find yourself answering to her call. Traverse the hills and valleys—not by car, but on foot—and get talking to the natives as they set about their work ; explore the towns and villages, and you will soon see what I mean. Dorset grows on you in quite a mystical way, as you will readily appreciate after you have several times visited, say, Corfe Castle, Burton Bradstock, Sturminster Newton—where, incidentally, a strange notice on the bridge warns anyone contemplating damaging it that they run the risk of being transported for life—Portisham, Spettisbury, Bridport, East Lulworth, with its beautiful land-locked bay close by, or Milton Abbas, with its fine rows of chestnuts—the first " model " village in England.

Apart from anything else, there is hardly a town or village that has not some interesting story to tell or relic to show ; Blandford, the town that was pawned to a Lincoln Jew in the time of Richard I, and that has since been twice burnt almost entirely to the ground ; Wimborne with its fine old minster ; Swanage with its quaint little harbour. Or Sherborne where Sir Walter Raleigh is said to have smoked his famous pipe and so caused an anxious cottager to throw a pail of water over him, imagining him to be on fire ; or Tolpuddle, where the famous martyrs met in 1831, under a tree still standing, to protest against their low agricultural wages of seven shillings a week—a meeting that was to end in their deportation in chains to Australia to work as slaves.

At Godmanstone you may drink a tankard of beer in the smallest pub in England. Once the village forge, and now known as the *Smith's Arms*, it is only some twenty feet long, and yet contains no less than three types of building material—wattle-and-daub, cob, and Dorset stone. And if you like small things you may worship in a church at Oborne that is only one foot longer.

At Cerne Abbas, where the famous giant, cut in the downland chalk, looks threateningly down upon the cluster of cottages, you will find men who are down on their luck still being befriended and fitted for the outside world by monks whose abbey was founded by another order more than a thousand years ago. Here, too, you may be shown a well that is said to have sprung up in a waterless area when the people flocked here, far back in the dim and distant ages, to be baptised by St. Austin on his arrival from converting the people of Kent. Unlike his Cornish counterparts, this saint, I gather, had no need to resort to his staff: the water obligingly arrived of its own free will . . .

Cerne Abbas was not, it seems, the only place in Dorset to lack water. At Shaftesbury, high above the lovely Blackmore Vale, where King Alfred is said to have founded the abbey and appointed his daughter first abbess, the position was once so acute that, as recently as the eighteenth century, many of the more humble folk earned their livings by collecting rain water in pits and carrying it in pails to the homes of the gentry. Indeed, at one time the water had to be fetched from as far afield as Gillingham—now the home of the National Stud—when, by way of acknowledgement of their indebtedness, it was customary for the mayor and burgesses of Shaftesbury to present the lord of the manor, through the medium of his steward, with a raw calf's head and a pair of gloves every year on the Monday before Holy Thursday.

Sherborne, too, one of the oldest towns in England, with its famous public school occupying the site of the old monastery, is said to derive its name from having grown up around a clear water spring—the old "bourn", which has become "burn" in Scotland.

As I say, most Dorset places have a story to tell. If Weymouth will ever be linked with George III—the town that was so loyal to this monarch that the band invariably played "God Save the King" whenever His Majesty plunged headlong into the waves from his bathing machine—Beaminster can scarce forget Joanna Croppen, the worsted-spinner, who lay buried six days in four feet of snow at Chardstock, keeping herself alive by eating her clothes.

Yes, Dorset grows on you. Indeed, a county containing such extraordinary place-names as Piddletrenthide, Piddlehinton, Puddletown, Woodcutts, Tolpuddle, Mappowder, Godmanstone, Melplash, and others equally intriguing, could hardly do anything else.

Such names as these are by no means without their meaning, however. They date back, very often, to mediæval or Saxon times, and form a close link with the old three-field system of communal farming when an entire village would club together to till the soil to the mutual advantage of all. Take the case of Piddletrenthide. This, simply, means the scene of thirty hides of land in a marsh, a hide being a measure of ground that could be ploughed by one team of oxen in the course of a single year, "piddle" being the old word for marshland, and "trent" coming from the French for thirty. So, too, I imagine, does Woodcutts date back to the old practice of "assarting", a system whereby, when a community outgrew itself, or a man married and wanted to bring up a family, permission could be obtained from the court to make a clearing in the nearby woods to start a fresh community. And this, incidentally, is why one so frequently meets with villages of the same name that are prefixed with a "Higher" or "Lower" or an "East" or "West".

It is not only in the place-names that we come upon links with the mediæval manor. The "open-field" system still maintains on a reduced scale at Portland, while at Wareham there is even yet a hayward to superintend the pasturage. Here, as in Somerset and Wiltshire, the Court Leet and Court Baron still sit in November, when the beadle opens the proceedings by calling upon all who owe service to the lord to come forward, and when the constables, as of old, stand on either side of the court table bearing the arms of their master during the swearing-in of the chimney-sweeps, haywards, reeves, ale-tasters, and sundry other characters. And these ale-tasters are no sinecure figures; they may yet go round the district sampling the beer! The toast at Wareham remains, as ever, " God Save the King and the Lord of the Manor ".

Essentially a farming county, we may still watch the natives of some of the more outlying villages dancing and singing the traditional dances and songs that once were such a feature of their Harvest Homes. Great days, those!

How Hone loved them! When the last load had been ricked, all who had taken part in the harvesting—" labourers, male and female, the swarthy reaper, the sun-burnt haymaker, the saucy boy who had not seen twelve summers, and the stiff horny-handed old mower who had borne the toil of fifty "—all would assemble at the farmhouse to be greeted by the beaming-faced farmer's wife in her quilted petticoat, apron of linsey-woolsey and silver-buckled shoes, there to feast from wooden trenchers on good old English beef, bacon, and, if the season had been a good one, perhaps a fowl or two, or even a turkey. Great days! There would be beer and cider in plenty to wash it all down, served in cups of horn, and the better for that. There would be toasts in plenty, too, and, after them, joking, singing, and dancing, the ball being set rolling by the most stalwart of the farmhands—a man with a hand " like the gauntlet of an armed knight ", a " pair of legs which had long outgrown the largest holes of the village stocks ", and a voice that might well be thought to be issuing from " the deep-seated lungs of a lion ".

The Harvest Home, though never the same since mechanized implements eased the toil and so robbed

earing strange costumes, comprising strips of coloured paper"—the "Mummers" at Freefolk.

"Half a gallon to every woman"—the Tichborne dole.

" The distribution is carried out by the vicar "—the Munstead dole.

" Life-like models of more than two hundred different animals "—a Brockenhurst toy-maker at work.

the occasion of much of its significance, is still kept up, and, at these Dorset suppers we may yet hear the "lion-throated" voices singing their old time song :—

Here's a health unto our maister
The founder of the feast,
And I hope to God wi' all my heart
His soul in Heaven mid rest.

That everything mid prosper
That ever he take in hand
For we be all his sarvants,
And all at his command.

So, also, may we sometimes see them dancing the "Broomstick", the "Bricks and Mortar", the "Heel and Toe", or the "Ring" at such places as Marnhull, Piddlehinton, Burton Bradstock, and elsewhere.

At Marnhull, too, they still remain faithful to their time-honoured "feast", when the inhabitants, wearing rosettes, proceed through the village to the accompaniment of pealing bells for their "club day" church service, dinner, and sports.

Everybody knows everybody else's business in these Dorset villages, of course. But why worry? It is only healthy gossip; a lingering survival of the old community spirit which, taken in the right way, all helps to make life sweet. In the village pub or the post office —which is often also the general store, where anything from a toothbrush to a lawn-mower may be sold—you will hear chatter as good as anywhere. Words that would have no possible meaning anywhere else assume a quite definite significance here. When, for instance, Mrs. Jones, the postmistress—a kindly soul, she will always send her grandson with messages to those not fortunate enough to be on the telephone—tells you that your parcel is too heavy and advises you to take it to the "tranter", she means, simply, the carrier;

as also, when she asks you to count your " dibs ", will she mean coins.

Mrs. Jones—like a good many others of her kind—is not always entirely easy to follow in her meaning :

" Lundle, lundle, how can I car in such a caddle, whog away ! " she may exclaim heatedly, and the unfortunate individual to whom the remark is addressed will readily interpret her words as " Go away, go away, how can I carry on in such a muddle, get on ! "

Rather fascinating these old Dorset words ; pleasing to hear them still spoken. They all add to the spice of life—" glutch " to swallow, " clavy " a mantelpiece, with " tun " as the chimney-top, " smeech " a cloud of dust, or " spur " to spread rumours. You will hear them all over the county : in the fields as much as in the villages. The plough will ever remain a " zull " in Dorset, just as the peculiar handcart—once so popular in these parts, but now, I am told, made only by the carpenters at Puncknowle—will always be known as the " dung-putt ". The man who collects the eggs from the trap nests on the poultry farms is still a " higler ", while he who is unlucky enough to spring a leak in his gum boots will even yet be considered to be " wotshed ". They have a word for most things, these Dorset folk, and their language varies from west to east. Be cautious though : not all words are as they would seem. Take the case of " sock ". In the midst of any quite ordinary conversation the cottager may at any time shake her head and ask concernedly the reason for your " sock ". When you show your confusion, she will laugh good-naturedly and explain that you sighed and that she was merely inquiring the reason.

In this strange tongue of theirs, then, these Dorset men and women will tell you tales galore of their countryside ; of superstitions and beliefs, of ghosts that even yet *will* keep turning up on the highways—stories as deeply-rooted in their bosoms as the trees in the soil around them.

Once let your dog howl at night at Shipton, for instance, and the villagers will look sorrowfully upon you next morning, knowing full well that that means death within the year to yourself or one of your family, while if a single crow should elect to fly above your roof-top . . . well, that is the end of all things, unless, of course, by lucky chance, a couple of magpies should decide to cross your path soon afterwards to counter-balance it.

At Corscombe and Halstock they will readily agree with the Devonians in saying that a piece of raw meat will cure warts, but at Thorncombe and Marnhull they will shake their heads and say :

" Naw, that won't do't, never. What 'ee needs is a bean pod or half an apple, s'know you."

And even that will hardly meet with the approval of Horton folk, who will declare, equally emphatically, that what is really required is the blood of a mole, or, as they prefer to call it, a " vant ".

A poultice of chickweed is still regarded by some as good for reducing gatherings, just as by others an egg, dissolved in vinegar in its shell, and mixed with brown sugar, is held to be the only *reliable* cure for a cold. Snails have many uses, while the leaves of violets might be considered for anything from a sting or bite to cancer. Indeed, there is hardly a wild flower that cannot be made to serve some useful purpose. The cure I like best, though, is that of the gardener : should he be unfortunate enough to run the prong of his fork into his foot when digging, he will at once push the *fork* forcibly into the ground to remove all risk of poison and tetanus.

Try to trip them up on the everlasting question of the Devil, pointing out that his wanderings must surely have ceased with his death at Northlew, and they have you. On Studland Moor they will show you the massive Haggerstone Boulder which he had intended to hurl at Salisbury Cathedral, if only the weight had not proved too much for him ; and at the famous beauty spot at Thorncombe they will point high up to the three rows of trees, that stand out as a landmark for miles around, as being the landing-points of his three jumps when the inhabitants turned out to a man to drive him from the county. But, though he beat a hasty retreat, his connections with Dorset were not finally severed ; it appears that he left behind certain of his relatives to carry on on his behalf and so give further food for thought.

Headless bodies, it seems, roam the Dorset countryside far and wide, with nocturnal funerals in abundance to make it all more realistic, and just a little creepy. Though they may not have witnessed the spectacles themselves, at such places as Marnhull, Shipton Gorge, or Milborne St. Andrew, we shall experience but little difficulty in finding folks who have at least " heard tell " of them, and they will pass on the details with all the fervour they can muster ; of phantom pall-bearers, their heads tucked under their arms, arriving with phantom coffins at the churchyard as the clock strikes the hour of midnight. All very stirring, and, to make it more so, the villagers will go on with the lurid details of the many and fierce battles that once took place around these parts, when soldiers fell like ninepins, a fact borne out by the unearthing of numerous human remains near the Todber quarries.

These troops certainly make good ghosts ; when they are not too busy burying one another, they may perhaps be found guarding the woods above Corfe Mullen, or, maybe, blocking the way at Red Port, at the junction of Corscombe, Rampisham, and Chelborough. Nor are they the only ghosts—far from it! By Trent Barrow, in the neighbourhood of Sherborne, is a "bottomless pit", every bit as sinister as Tregeagle's. Here when the weather is rough, they will tell you, the clattering hoofs of horses, and the wailing voices of travellers who lost their lives when a coach plunged headlong into the pit one dark and stormy night, long years ago, can still be heard issuing forth.

There is certainly plenty to stir the imagination in Dorset. At Milborne St. Andrew they will tell you of a golden coffin that lies buried in Culgage churchyard, and of terrifying thunderstorms breaking out over the district, with lightning flashing through the graveyard, whenever anyone is inquisitive enough to try to dig it out. Many attempts to unearth it have been made, it seems, but always with the same disastrous results. Then again, at Winterborne Whitechurch they will lead you to a field where the hay can never be harvested dry; not even in times of drought. Tradition has it that, many centuries back, a farmer who failed to get in his crops in time, laid a curse on the field and that it has been bewitched ever since.

The curfew is still rung in many Dorset towns and villages in memory of the days when all and sundry lived in horror of finding themselves benighted, while at Lyme Regis—with its queer "cobb" harbour and its "umbrella cottage", the setting for a scene of Jane Austen's *Persuasion*—men with voices as carrying as the bells themselves still meet annually for their town crier's contest.

A great day—greater even than that at Pewsey. I am told that when a Dorset man really gets into his stride he may be heard anything from five to eight miles away. "Deep-throated lions" at Lyme Regis there certainly are; lion-hearted their proclamations too. Here is one of good pre-war vintage:

"Oyez, oyez, oyez!

"Despite the known goodwill of men and women of all nationalities; despite the warnings of the wise and the prayers of the earnest; despite sacrifice, endeavour, hope and fair intention;

"LOST: Our sense of security, but

"FOUND!—

"Not only within the confines of this ancient and honoured borough of Lyme Regis, but beyond our Dorset borders, over tideway and windswept seas, ever beyond to all those lands which have their being beneath the sway of Britain's Realm—

"This Empire's determination to guard our rightful place in this good old earth. To maintain steadfastly and with true endeavour, that liberty of thought and action for which our fathers fought, suffered and died; and in so maintaining bring once more to this heartsick world, the word of God and democracy. And so, in token of this, I do declare in the presence of you, my countrymen:

"GOD SAVE THE KING!"

Hardly less noisy is the scene at Sherborne, when, in the small hours of the morning of the day of the October Pack Monday Fair, we are awakened by an ear-splitting din as "Teddy Rowe's Band" clatters and crashes its way through the streets with the blowing of bugles, horns, and whistles, and the beating of trays, kettles, and other equally responsive objects. Strangely peaceful at other times, these Dorset folk are by no means averse to a bit of a shindy on occasion. And this is one of the occasions, for the "band" justify their behaviour in the thought that they are commemorating the day when the masons at work on the Abbey church in the fifteenth century were led in triumphal procession through the town by their foreman, one Teddy Rowe, on the completion of their task.

Pleasantly musical by contrast are the voices of the children of Durweston as they call from house to house on Shrove Tuesday, begging oranges, cakes, and sweets, and singing :

We be come a-shroving
For a piece of pancake,
Or a bit of bacon,
Or a little truckle of cheese
Of your own making.
Blow the fire and hot the pot
For we've come a-shroving.

This is not the children's only day. At Abbotsbury —famous for its swannery and gardens with sub-tropical plants—the village children still make garlands of a local design to lay on their war memorial. Until quite recently Garland Day was an occasion for games and merry-making both on the green and the beach. Pagan in origin, this custom is connected with the opening of the fishing season, and dates back to the time when the fishermen made sacrifices to the seas as surely as did the farmers offer their beasts to the flames. In olden days the garlands would be hung upon the bows of the boats, which then put to sea for prayers to be offered and the emblem surrendered to the waves.

Incidentally, Abbotsbury is the western terminal of the famous Chesil Beach, that strange bank of pebbles out at sea that stretches for some ten miles down to Portland. A fisherman once told me that the stones become steadily larger towards the east, and that he and his kind are able to judge their whereabouts by the size of the pebbles when homeward bound in their boats in a fog.

Then there is Poole. A strange place Poole, once a great centre for pickled oysters and noted for its pearl industry. Queen Elizabeth regarded it as so cut off from the mainland that she granted the town letters-patent to become a county on its own account, with the right to have its own sheriff, keep a court, hold pleas, and to enjoy " divers immunities ". It was on Brownsea Island, in the centre of the harbour, that the Boy Scout movement was born.

Undoubtedly the most interesting of all the surviving Dorset customs are those of the Ancient Company of Marblers, who work the Purbeck Quarries around Corfe Castle, that fascinating little village with its ruined castle standing on a high mound above it ; Corfe Castle, where every building almost is an architectural gem, built from stone taken from the Southern range of the Purbeck Hills around Worth Matravers, Langton Matravers, and Swanage ; Corfe Castle, one of the earliest strongholds of the Crown, where Edward the Martyr was murdered in 978.

A unique band, these quarrymen, it is said that their charter was already ages old when it was confirmed in 1567. An exclusive band, too ; only those whose fathers have worked the quarries before them are ever welcomed to this Company. Their laws and articles are as unbending as the stone they seek ; their tradition an unswerving guarantee of good craftsmanship.

Every Shrove Tuesday, then, men and boys of all ages will abandon their quarries and make their way to Corfe Castle for the holding of the annual " Court ". Here, after the appointment of the officers, such apprentices as have reached the age of twenty-one since the previous meeting will present themselves with a penny loaf—especially baked for the occasion—in one hand and a tankard of beer in the other ; their traditional offering on applying to be registered as " free boys ". It is a proud day in the life of a young quarryman as he watches the older men—his father, and, maybe, his grandfather, among them—devouring his bread and drinking the beer while the officers consider his case. Upon admittance to the company's rolls, he will be required to pay the sum of 6s. 8d., or,

"She had been making these gloves for seventy years"— Ringwood glove-maker at work.

"That crucifix saved many a murder from taking place"— the remains of the crucifix near Lyndhurst.

" Hampshire is, nevertheless, still rich in beauty "—a riding-party near Liphook.

“ The forest itself lies for ever in the shadow of a deadly menace : the menace of fire ”—a New Forest look-out tower.

if he has unwisely married one whose father is not a quarryman, 7s. 8d., the extra "marriage shilling" guaranteeing his widow the right to have an apprentice to work for her in the event of his death.

It is a proud day for all, and when the "Court" is over, young and old alike proceed to kick a football along the road to Owre Quay, taking with them a pound of pepper, in order to maintain an ancient right of way. For it was down this passage that the marble was drawn on sledges, from Wilkeswood and other places along the marble vein, for shipment abroad, the pepper—then a highly-treasured spice—being paid to the lord of the manor by way of quit-rent for the right to use the quay.

Though the passage has long been entirely valueless, it was once a busy centre. For the quarries of Purbeck "isle" have been worked at least since the time of the Romans. As far back as the twelfth century the marble was being exported, and it is said that every sizeable English church built between 1170 and 1350 had the stone introduced into its structure in some way or other—either in the form of solid lumps, or as polished dressings—so that to this day we may find examples of it in Westminster Abbey, Romsey Abbey, and the cathedrals of Ely, Chichester, Salisbury, Exeter, and Winchester, to name but a few.

But the Purbeck Hills are not the only quarries to bring fame to the men of Dorset: from Portland—once a sheep run, and so barren that even in Georgian days the inhabitants were compelled to burn ox- and cow-dung on their fires for lack of fuel—came the stone used by Sir Christopher Wren in the re-building of London after the Great Fire of 1666. It is of Portland stone that St. Paul's Cathedral and the Wren churches of the City were constructed, and, in our own time, modern Regent Street and the Cenotaph. More popular than ever, something like 100,000 tons of stone are quarried in this " isle " every year to serve our building needs.

Still, Dorset's reputation is by no means founded only on freestone. In their little cottage homes at Swyre, Burton Bradstock, Puncknowle, Loders, Bradpole, Hamworthy, and elsewhere to the west of the county, we shall find women of all ages making every conceivable type of net, from trammels for the fishing fleets to tennis, football, and hockey nets for sports clubs ; from camouflage nets to billiard pockets ; from " life-savers " to hammocks.

In these cottages we shall see old women of perhaps eighty or more working side by side with their grandchildren, or even, on occasion, their great-grandchildren, carrying out a work which they themselves had learnt in early childhood from their parents and grandparents. These " braiders " are following a tradition that is older than Domesday, and, just as Honiton is the " capital " of the Devon lace-makers, so has Bridport been their administrative centre since time immemorial. Indeed, it was on account of her part in providing nets and cables for the Navy that King John granted Bridport her charter in the first place.

It is fascinating to watch these women plying this age-old industry. Here we may see them at work within the snugness of their kitchen living-rooms on a cold winter's day ; there we shall find them working from their cottage doors in the warmth of the summer sun. There again, when the net to be made is a particularly large one, we may stumble upon a whole group of them working their way down a street or lane with a single net stretching from porch to porch. The craft is not only confined to the women, though. Sometimes we may meet with an old man, who has toiled perhaps sixty summers or more in the fields, lovingly endeavouring to help his "missus", and so increase their earnings.

One old "braider", who said that she had learnt the work from her mother at the age of eight, told me that every week representatives from the Bridport firms call on these cottagers with supplies of fresh materials and to collect the finished articles, which are then taken back, tarred, and packed for delivery all over the world, an important market being the Newfoundland fisheries.

"Do you make *all* kinds of nets?" I asked.

"Oh, no, sir, not *all*. Some o' we make one sort, and others another."

"So between you you manage to serve the entire market? Can you make much money at this business?"

"Well, sir, us don't do too badly on the whole. Us usually reckons to make about a shilling an hour."

A shilling an hour, and that for skilled labour! I thought at once of the 2s. 6d. an hour certain charwomen have suggested that I should pay for the privilege of having the last of my china broken, and asked her whether she would not find it more profitable to change her occupation.

"No, sir, thank 'ee. Anyone can scrub a floor, but not everyone can make a net." She laughed.

Such is the pride of these Dorset folk; pride of workmanship means more than riches. You will find men and women of this kind all over the county: "broom squires" making besoms in Cranborne Chase; potters at Verwood, who puddle their clay with their feet as in Tudor times; rush-workers who gather their materials from the banks of the River Stour for making into dog baskets, church kneelers, and the like; flax-workers round Shaftesbury; millers who still process their corn by the power of water wheels.

Along the highroads and down the narrow lanes, too,

you will meet with hedgers and ditchers in far greater abundance than elsewhere, while I am told that the number of thatchers in Dorset is higher than in any other county, with the possible exception of Norfolk.

It is the combination of the thatchers and stone-workers that helps to bring individuality to the Dorset countryside ; an individuality that becomes only the more noticeable as we pass on into Hampshire, and see the stone and thatch giving place to bricks and tiles.

Six Acorns and Wooden Walls

IF to many the brick and tile of Hampshire is a sorry exchange for the cob of Devon or the stone of Wiltshire or Dorset, and if the county's closer proximity to London has, admittedly, brought many angry gashes in the way of jerry-building, robbing her fair countryside of much of its old-time peace and quietude (not that it has by any means *always* been peaceful), Hampshire is, nevertheless, still rich in beauty.

She still has the incomparable New Forest, stretching over some sixty-five thousand acres, the verdant Meon Valley, the hardly less lovely valleys of the Test, Itchen, and Hamble, and the sandy heaths along her northern fringe.

Angry gashes there may be, yet she still has villages and small towns in plenty whose old-world charm has been little, if at all, affected by the march of time. In these villages we shall find as varied an assortment of architecture as anywhere else in England, with the possible exception of Kent and one or two of the eastern counties. Stone, timber, slate, weather-boarding, and tile-hung all make their appearance here and there, but brick houses with tiled or thatched roofs predominate throughout. In many cases the bricks have been skilfully fashioned by hand-craftsmen out of clay taken from some nearby seam, and the thatch prepared from home-grown straw ; and where this is so, the homes, both large and small, harmonize with the landscape every bit as effectively as do those of the stone areas.

Hampshire has, indeed, a wealth of picturesque spots : sleepy Lasham, with its pond decked with beds of yellow iris ; Southwick, where Charles I once stayed, or Milford, whence he set off for the scaffold ; Lepe, with its fine views across the Solent to the Isle of Wight which, too, belongs to Hampshire ; or Laverstoke, with nearby Freefolk sharing the same church, where the Bank of England notes have been made in the local papermill ever since a Huguenot refugee, Henri Fortal, escaped to Southampton after the Edict of Nantes and learnt the art of paper-making at South Stoneham more than two hundred years ago ; or Hurstbourne Tarrant, a favourite rendezvous for the illegal Georgian prize-fights when, in utmost secrecy, for fear of bumping up against the law, the " Fancy " would make their perilous trips along the rough by-roads of England, halting now and again, perhaps, to right some vehicle that had overturned, and often diverting their course to allay suspicion, but all converging in high spirits upon this one pre-arranged meeting-point, to witness a spectacle that ever held pride of place in their lives.

Then there are the Wallops—Nether, Middle, and Over—as fascinating as their names, and the Anns, Abbot's and Little, in the former of which it is still customary—the only place in England where it is so, I believe—to hang a white paper garland and gloves in the village church at the funeral of a young man or maiden, as a symbol of respect for virginity.

There are Hursley, where Richard Cromwell, a broken man—" Tumbledown Dick ", they called him —whiled away his time at bowls and was later buried in the churchyard ; Woodlands, where Monmouth was finally captured ; Broughton, where Robert Owen founded his socialist colony in 1842, and where Hazlitt lived and entertained Charles and Mary Lamb at the Pheasant Inn a mile away ; and, of course, Selborne, with its screen of beeches and its little green, spreading like a carpet as if to lure us from the main street, up the slight incline, and into the churchyard to seek the simple grave marked " G.W. 26 June 1793 ". Gilbert White would surely still love Selborne, and find plenty to interest him in the wild life round about.

Nor must we miss Wickham, with its wide main street and its flour mill that was built partially out of the embattled timbers of the early nineteenth-century frigate, *Shannon*, famous for her victory over the American, *Chesapeake ;* Stockbridge, the " Paradise " of anglers ; or Upper Froyle, where the statuette of a saint, presented by the lord of the manor, stands guardian over almost every cottage from an alcove above its porch or upper windows.

We must not miss the towns and villages where age-old customs still maintain : Chilbolton, where wafers are made for Mothering Sunday by means of special " irons " and according to a recipe that has been kept a carefully-guarded secret for several centuries ; Basingstoke, where a hymn is still sung from the church tower to herald the New Year ; Twyford, where the fields are blessed and bounds beaten once a year, and where the bell-ringers continue to peal their bells on October 7 and indulge in feasting in memory of a man whose life was saved when, in the darkness of the night, he diverted his course to follow their sound, and so was prevented from plunging headlong on his horse over a steep precipice ; or Overton, where, as at Longparish, Andover, and Freefolk, the "mummers", with blackened faces and wearing strange costumes, comprising strips of coloured paper, still perform the famous Christmas "plays" that were once such a feature of village life all over England, plays whose words were never recorded but were handed down by word of mouth from one generation to the next.

Incidentally, should you at any time have occasion to travel along the Andover-to-Winchester road, look out for a clump of three fir trees, known as Three Maids' Cross. At this spot, it is said, three maidens poisoned their father and left him to die by the roadside. When their crime was detected, angry villagers led them back to the scene, buried them side by side up to their necks, and put up notices warning travellers not to feed them. Only one man ignored the notice—a compassionate horseman, who threw one of the sisters an apple core upon which she subsisted for three days ! A fir tree was planted in each grave ; hence the group.

Intriguing, many of these places. What is more, around a great number of them hovers a world of romance. Indeed, as we pass from one to the other, the story that each has to tell seems yet more romantic than that of the one we have just left. If the Romans turned to Silchester, Winchester, deep in a hollow of the chalk downs, was already old when the Saxon kings made her England's first capital. And if London robbed Winchester of her greatness, Portsmouth rose to become the senior naval dockyard, and Southampton the principal passenger port, the berthing-place of the largest of all the great Atlantic liners.

What a fund of history envelops those two cities, Winchester and Portsmouth ! I once remarked to a native of Winchester on the fact that whenever I visited the place it invariably rained.

"Well, you must thank St. Swithin for that," he laughed.

"St. Swithin? But why should he affect Winchester more than anywhere else?"

"He was born here. Why, it is said that the whole legend of the forty days of rain arose when it was planned to remove his bones from their original grave to the cathedral in 971."

The saint, it seems, was not beyond displaying his angry grief even in death, and proceeded to weep copious tears. Whether he continued to weep for forty days, or whether, when his eyes grew weary, he sought the aid of the heavens to help him out with a steady downpour, seems doubtful. There are several versions of this legend, and each is as good as the others. At any rate, St. Swithin was definitely a native of Winchester, and he it was who taught Alfred the Great his lessons.

It was at Winchester that Alfred held his court and helped to compile the *Anglo-Saxon Chronicle*. Here William the Conqueror had his palace, and that most famous of bishops, William of Wykeham, founded the college upon which all other public schools, Eton included, were later to be modelled; here were buried the Saxon, Danish and Norman kings—Alfred among them—before ever Westminster and Windsor rose to their greatness; from here set off the pilgrims on their long treks over the North Downs to worship at the Canterbury shrine of Thomas à Becket.

We may explore the streets and buildings of Winchester for hours—for days, maybe—and still be left with much to see. If Bath is England's most perfect Georgian town, Winchester—the old part of Winchester that is—must always rank among the finest of the mediæval. Her magnificent cathedral alone, originally founded on bogland, but later set on concrete by means of a remarkable tunnelling operation, is of particular interest as having once been the longest in all Europe, much of the architecture having been inspired by William of Wykeham himself. Ancient relics abound everywhere : the Norman Castle with its Great Hall, where Parliament met of old and where Sir Walter Raleigh faced his trial ; the ruins of Wolversley Castle ; the butter cross ; the Pent House in High Street, under whose projecting upper story dairy produce was once sold ; and West Gate ; to say nothing of the college itself.

Hardly less interesting than the buildings are some of the customs still practised in this one-time capital. Every year the boys of Winchester College make a pilgrimage to the Iron Age fortress of St. Catherine's Hill—once famous for its fair—in memory of one of their number who wrote their well-known song, *Dulce Domum.* The story goes that he wrote the words when, by way of punishment, he was ordered by the headmaster to be chained to a stone pillar on the hill at a time when the rest of the school were going home for their Whitsuntide exeat. When, on their return, certain of the pupils went to release him, they found him dead, with the stirring verses, composed in Latin, beside him.

To this day we may still, if we are feeling hungry and thirsty, knock at the door of the porter's lodge at the ancient Hospital of St. Cross and demand a horn of beer and a helping of bread-and-cheese, free of charge, just as did the weary wayfarers and others down on their luck some six hundred years or more ago. It is interesting to see the practice still kept up, for around these old " doles " is written the story of the influence of the mediæval Church upon the lives of the people, of her benevolence in an age of cruelty. As soon as Christianity really became established in England, the people grew more fervent in their religion than has generally been the case, unfortunately, in later times. Though the parsons were sometimes rogues to a degree and hypocrites in the extreme, and though their sermons were often wholly unintelligible, the Church was the be-all and end-all of their lives. So that not only did the villages spring up around the parish churches, and the cities around the cathedrals, but the people themselves equally moulded their whole thought in harmony with these sacred edifices, though, admittedly, very often largely through fear of the unknown.

And the Church responded by becoming the patrons of the poor and destitute. The more wealthy among the congregations would set aside sums of money or areas of land to be used to provide for the needy, in exchange for which they would—not unreasonably—expect to have their souls prayed for after they themselves had departed. Sometimes the money would be used for establishing monasteries, chantries, or almshouses; sometimes for the distribution of annual charities among the aged and other deserving cases in the district; sometimes for the setting up of regular doles from which all who cared to might benefit.

While the Church often acted as the trustees, as well as dispensers, of these gifts, many of the doles were administered directly by the heirs and descendants of the original benefactors. Such a dole is that still distributed at Tichborne, to the east of Winchester in the valley of the Itchen. Here, every Lady Day, a service is conducted in front of the great house, when, before an enormous bin of flour—made from wheat grown on an area of the estate known as "The Crawls", and processed in the mills at Fareham—a priest in colourful robes leads the villagers of Tichborne and Cheriton in prayers for the soul of Lady Mabella de Tichborne, who lived in the time of Henry I. At the end of the prayers the flour is sprinkled with Holy Water and blessed before being distributed at the rate of a gallon to every man, and half-a-gallon to every woman and child, by the holder of the Tichborne title ; a procedure which, I understand, may take anything up to two hours to complete.

A good story is told as to the origin of this dole. This Lady Mabella, it seems, was much loved by the Hampshire country folk on account of her manifold good deeds. Her husband, Sir Roger de Tichborne, on the other hand, was not so popular. Fearing, then, as to what would happen to the poor of the village after she was gone, Lady Mabella implored her husband on her death-bed to set aside some of the estate to grow food for the needy. To this the noble knight at once acquiesced—but on one condition. Taking a burning log from the hearth and handing it to his wife, he promised to devote as much land to growing grain for them as she could move around before the flame went out. Since Lady Mabella was in her last hours and was wellnigh prostrate, Sir Roger must have believed himself to be on a good thing. Lady Mabella, however, decided otherwise. Praying to God to give her strength, she ordered her maidservants to carry her into the park where, unable to stand, she nevertheless managed to crawl round some twenty-three acres before the fire went out—a tremendous feat.

Back in her bed again, she called her husband to her, and warned him that if his promise was not fulfilled to the letter—not only by himself but also by the generations to follow—a curse would be laid upon the house of Tichborne. A generation of seven sons, she told him, would be followed by one of seven daughters, whereafter the family would be no more. Strangely enough, in the last years of the eighteenth century, when the dole was modified on account of the disorderly nature it had grown to assume, the curse came true in part. Seven daughters followed seven sons, and the old house fell into uncannily bad repair. For a time nothing went right. But the curse was not to be allowed to run its full course—the dole was at once restored, and has, I believe, been held annually ever since.

These doles are not uncommon in Hampshire. At Minstead, too, some two hundred and fifty half-gallon loaves are distributed on New Year's Day under the will of a man named Brown who died more than three hundred years ago. Here the distribution is carried out by the vicar, who, after preaching a special sermon, leads the poor back to his vicarage for the purpose.

But to return to the cathedral cities : if the ghosts of kings and bishops accompany us on our explorations through Winchester, in Portsmouth we are for ever bumping into those of admirals and adventurers. At the street corners, by the dockyard gates, in the inns we meet them—Nelson, Howe, Byng, Rodney, Keppel, Franklin, and a whole host of others. For in Portsmouth memory of them is as green as if they had been alive but yesterday.

It was in 1212 that Portsmouth became our senior naval dockyard, when King John wrote to the Sheriff of Southampton :

> We order you without delay, by the view of lawful men, to cause our docks at Portsmouth to be enclosed with a good and strong wall for the preservation of our ships and galleys. You are also to cause penthouses to be made to these walls, in which all our ships' tackle may be safely kept. Be as quick as you can in order that the work may be completed this summer, so that in the coming winter our ships and galleys and their rigging may not receive any damage. When we know the cost you shall be paid.

" Red tape ", it seems, was not so common in those days. . . .

What a noble part has this city played in our island history since then! Foreign kings and queens have landed here to seize the British throne, and have been disappointed; three times during the fourteenth century the French invaded the town and destroyed large areas of it; battles and mutinies have taken place off Spithead; and on at least one occasion the harbour was blockaded by the French. Possibly she has seen more fighting than any other English town, while at Porchester Castle, at the head of the harbour, the troops of Agincourt were mustered, and the kings of long ago decided upon their invasion tactics and formulated their plans for the defence of this realm. It was here that many of the prisoners of the Napoleonic and Crimean wars were encamped.

It was at the Old George Hotel in High Street—unhappily destroyed in the blitzes—that Nelson spent his last few hours before setting sail to defeat Napoleon at Trafalgar; to meet his own death, but to bring peace to Britain. At half-past ten on the evening of September 13, 1805, he had left his home at Merton and driven in his chaise to Portsmouth to join his flagship, *Victory*. Arriving at sunrise next morning, he made straight for the *George*—always a favourite haunt of his—hopeful of snatching a few hours' sleep. But news of his arrival soon spread and before long dense crowds had gathered in the street outside the inn. As their voices rose to a great crescendo of "Save us, Lord Nelson, save us!" the admiral put aside all thought of rest and appeared at the open bay window of the first floor to give them words of encouragement.

Has anyone, I wonder, ever been given such a send-off as when he left the inn a few hours later? So vast was the crowd that he was forced to make his escape by way of the back stairs, through the courtyard, down Penny Street, and across Southsea Common to the beach instead of setting off from Sally Port as had originally been intended. But even this ruse was of no avail ; as he passed across the common, men, women, and children fell to their knees in tears, blessing him and wishing him God-speed. Never was a sight so stirring.

Though bombs have robbed Portsmouth of many of her most precious relics, we may still visit the spot on Southsea beach from which Nelson sailed, as we may also yet see his famous flagship. And if, alas, the *George* is no more, the Elizabethan hostelry, known as the *Star and Garter*, remains. In the old days it was customary for the " middies " to drink at the *Blue Posts*, farther down the street, and to move on to the *Star and Garter* as soon as they gained their promotion.

Here, then, have foregathered at various times the most notable in the land, from kings and princes—George III, William IV, Edward VII, the Duke of Clarence, George V, Edward VIII, and George VI among them—to painters, actors, and other celebrities. Inside is a window on which many of them scratched their name with a diamond. Once the window of the old bar parlour, it has now been removed to a safer spot.

I remember once, some years ago, reading these names—Nelson, Lady Hamilton, Lord Charles Beresford, Montgolfier, Judd Green, and so on—while leisurely munching a sandwich and gulping down a tankard of beer, when a veteran naval officer sidled up to me and, with a nudge and a wink, asked me if there was a £5 note in my sandwich.

" A five-pound note ? Why should there be ? " and I involuntarily began to peel apart the slices of bread. At this the captain laughed.

" All right—don't bother. I was only pulling your leg. Still, I remember watching the wags eating sandwiches made of five-pound notes in the old days. Ate them in settlement of wagers. A grand lot they were; more money than they knew what to do with."

"How long ago was that?" I asked him.

"Oh, about the time I got my second ring—towards the end of last century. Astounding quantities of liquor they drank, too. I remember that one particularly potent concoction of rum gloried in the name of 'Nelson's Blood'."

What a wealth of fascinating stories are woven around the life of Portsmouth! On another occasion I came upon a woman carrying a massive bundle of nettles under her arm, only to be told that she had gathered them from the grounds of Southsea Castle and was taking them home to cook for lunch.

"They do say the nettles were planted three hundred years ago to make beer for the sailors," she went on.

Though she could tell me no more, after searching through a number of ancient city documents I found her story to be quite correct.

In 1628, when the country's finances were in a bad way, the supply of beer for the Navy nearly petered out. The Governor of Portsmouth, the Earl of Pembroke—who was responsible for the supply of drink both to the dockyard and to the ships entering and leaving—found himself in a tight corner. Since he already owed more than £700 for past supplies, the brewers refused to grant further credit until the account was settled. The stopping of the beer might well cause a mutiny, but that was no concern of theirs.

So it was that the Governor, beside himself with worry, decided to start a special brewery of his own. Seeds of a particular type of nettle were obtained, and these were sown in the grounds of Southsea Castle. Premises were taken over, brewing plant installed, and, within a short time, the Navy was in receipt of its

"These birds, it is believed, may well have come over with the Vikings"—swans on the Thames. (*Farmer and Stockbreeder* photograph.)

" Scattered villages along its noble banks "—looking across the river from Pangbourne.

" Afterwards will come the scramble for oranges "
—Hocktide at Hungerford.

special beer. Few were let into the secret, but it is recorded that when it found its way into the messes, officers and ratings alike remarked on its excellent quality, and demanded to know the name of the brewers!

That was three hundred years ago, but the nettles still flourish despite all efforts to put them down. Maybe it is a portent of further troubles to come!

Famous men have been legion in Portsmouth (Charles Dickens, and others hardly less great, were born here too), and, lest ever we should forget those admirals who have trod her streets, drunk her drink, and then set off from Spithead to do battle for their country—perhaps never to return—their names are ever before us in the great battleships, called after them, that pass majestically in and out of this ancient harbour. It is, perhaps, fitting that a whole aisle of the Cathedral—where officers appointed to ships at Portsmouth were once required to produce a certificate every Sunday, confirming that they had attended Holy Communion—should have been dedicated to the entire Royal Navy.

But "great names" are not confined to Portsmouth. In towns, villages, and hamlets far and wide, we may visit the spots where great men and women were born, lived, laughed, worked, or died, and gaze upon scenes they once knew; scenes which, in some instances, proved the very inspiration of their work.

Southampton, with its famous Bar Gate, was a mecca of fashion in Georgian times, surpassed perhaps only by Bath, Cheltenham, and Tunbridge Wells. A town of bow windows, stately pillars, and cobbled streets, it presented a very different spectacle from the busy industrial place we know to-day.

Here, in a house still standing in French Street, Isaac Watts was born, in 1674, at a time when his father, a clothier, was serving a term of imprisonment for conducting illegal religious services in the Independent Meeting House. Strange to think that the son of one whose views were so decried by law should have written the words of the hymn sung every year at the Cenotaph—*O God Our Help In Ages Past.* Stranger still, perhaps, that it should first have been sung in the very building that brought discredit to the family.

But it was not until after Watts's time that Southampton really blossomed forth, when, in the months of summer, wealth and beauty would flock to the Assembly Rooms, and, in those of winter, to the *Dolphin.* A favourite haunt was the *Dolphin.* Edward Gibbon, the historian, would frequently drop in when serving with the Hampshire Militia ; Thackeray, who spent much of his boyhood at Fareham, wrote part of *Pendennis* under its roof ; Jane Austen attended as many of the balls as possible that she " might have a good bargain " on her subscription. Here, we are told, would assemble all the " bepatched and bepowdered dames and duchesses, bewigged and beruffled gallants " from miles around the Hampshire countryside to hold nightly revel. Here, in later times, would be stabled Queen Victoria's horses whenever she crossed to her beloved Isle of Wight.

Among the patrons of the *Dolphin* was Mary, Lady Palmerston, who made the journey from Romsey, a little to the north-west. Here, at Romsey, standing in some four hundred acres of land overlooking the river, we may still see the stately home, Broadlands, with its impressive porticos, where her Prime Minister son played as a child, learnt as a boy, and studied as a young man ; the home where, too, in earlier days, James I had once stayed.

Still an attractive town, Romsey boasts many ancient relics, of which the most interesting are the abbey that was founded by Alfred's son and the flint-built hunting lodge where King John sent his daughter, Joanna, under the care of a governess, and charged the Mayor of Winchester two pence a day for her keep.

Great names seem almost commonplace in Hampshire ; more so perhaps than in any other county. While Alton—once an important archery centre and a stepping-stone on the Pilgrims' Way—talks of the poet Spenser, and leads us to his Tudor cottage in Amery Street, Alresford turns with pride to the birthplaces of Mary Mitford and Sir Frank Benson, or the nearby Grange, once occupied by the Prince Regent, or Old Alresford Place, the stately mansion which a grateful nation presented to Lord Rodney. Nor was this the only Hampshire home to be given to a hero. At Strathfieldsaye is the Queen Anne house which Wellington found too costly in its maintenance to be enjoyable. It was in the great park here that his famous charger, Copenhagen, who carried him to victory at Waterloo, was buried with full military honours.

While that pleasing little market town, Bishop's Waltham, boasts the burial place of William of Wykeham, and recalls the time when Henry II held council there before setting off on one of his crusades, Eversley can show us the delightful rectory where Kingsley was rector, a place dignified in its graceful simplicity and well suited to the character of its famous incumbent.

The Isle of Wight will boast of visits by Millais and George Morland, and of the great poet laureate, Tennyson, making his home at Freshwater. But perhaps the proudest boast of all is that of little Steventon. For here was born, and lived for some twenty-five years while her father was rector, Jane Austen. And Jane Austen is to the Hampshire man what Thomas Hardy is to Dorset ; the very epitome of his countryside and of the people who live and work upon or by it, and who love it for what it is.

But we must not forget Hambledon with its Broadhalfpenny and Windmill Downs and its *Bat and Ball* inn, close by the former ; Hambledon, home of a famous hunt and birthplace of modern cricket, where dukes and blacksmiths, earls and ploughmen, would foregather of an eighteenth-century summer's day to do battle with curved bats and bowl against two lone stumps, set so far apart that often the ball would pass between them without removing the single bail. What a world of high-feasting, laughter, and general conviviality has little Hambledon seen ; what a host of personalities has she welcomed to her downs ! We can picture them still making their leisured way up the hill of approach in their numerous assortment of carriages, some of them, like Lord Palmerston, the statesman's father, coming from near, others from far away ; some of them coming to play, others merely to watch. We can see them still : Lord Winchelsea, the Duke of Dorset, Sir Horace Mann, Lords Darnley, Tankerville, and Nottingham, the Duke of Chandos, the Earl of Albermarle, Lord John Russell, the Duke of Richmond. But the list is too long to tell. What other village in England has welcomed such aristocracy to her midst for such a purpose ?

Democratic meetings they were, too. Here comes Noah Mann, who has ridden some twenty-seven miles from Northchapel, over the Sussex border, where he is both inn-keeper and cobbler, and who will ride the distance back again in the evening. And there stands William Beldham, the greatest bat of all, talking to Lumpy Stevens, Lord Tankerville's gardener and no less notable for his bowling. Lumpy, perhaps, is chaffing him about his thirty-nine children. Who knows ? Then over there is William Hogsflesh, and, beside him, Tom Sueter and David Harris. But it is hard to pick them out in such a crowd, for there may well be twenty thousand or more congregated around this noble green.

Match-day at Hambledon, especially when there were stakes of £500 or more hanging on the result, was a day of days : the day when their " general ", Richard Nyren—landlord at various times of the *Bat and Ball* and the *George*—would bring out his refreshment-booths and prove that good eating and drinking went hand in hand with good cricket. How his son, John, loved those days :

> Oh ! It was a heart-stirring sight to witness the multitude forming a complete and dense circle round that noble green. Half the county would be present, and all their hearts with us. Little Hambledon pitted against All-England was a proud thought for the Hampshire men. Defeat was glory in such a struggle. . . . How these fine, brawn-faced fellows of farmers would drink to our success ! And then what stuff they had to drink ! Punch !—not your modern cat-lap milk punch . . . but good, unsophisticated John Bull stuff—stark !—that would stand on end—punch that would make a cat speak ! Sixpence a bottle. . . . The ale too ! . . . barley-corn such as would put the souls of three butchers into one weaver. Ale that would flare like turpentine . . . vended at twopence per pint.
>
> Then the quantities the fellows would eat ! Two or three of them would strike dismay into a round of beef. . . . There would this company, consisting most likely of some thousands, remain patiently and anxiously watching every turn of fate in the game, as if the event had been the meeting of two armies to decide their liberty.

Yes, match-day was always a great event. And at the end of it there would be a concert when all would strive to prove themselves as fine musicians as they were cricketers.

Lord's and the Oval have long supplanted Hambledon, but by Broadhalfpenny Down we may still drink our tankard of ale in the *Bat and Ball*—not so " stark " as in Nyren's time, maybe, but good for all that. Moreover, we may still watch the men of Hambledon turning out in their high hats once a year, as of old, to do battle on the famous down against some neighbouring village.

"When the Australians are over here on a Test tour, we always reckon to give them a run for their money too," the landlord told me proudly.

"The Aussies? Do you ever beat them?"

"Never have yet. Still, no matter; we keep trying. We don't forget how our ancestors used to beat all comers."

Indeed, how could they ever forget? More likely are they to lose sight of the fact that Thomas Lord himself, who, so to speak, stole their thunder, lies buried at West Meon, uncomfortably close by.

Still, Hambledon is not the only Hampshire village to leave her mark on our island history. Nestling snugly up the beautiful Beaulieu River lies Buckler's Hard. A more peaceful spot than those two little rows of cottages, with their single street and an area of grassland stretching down to the river, along which an odd yacht or two may pass leisurely by from time to time, would be hard to find. Yet once the scene was very different. For here were built many of the "wooden walls of England" with which Nelson fought and won Trafalgar; here was constructed the good ship *Agamemnon* that brought him fame in the first place.

A busy place was Buckler's Hard in days gone by. As Napoleon's armies swarmed across the Continent, and the cry for ships, ships, and yet more ships echoed throughout the land, Henry Adams and his band of craftsmen would be busily felling, rinding, seasoning, and cleaving oak trees from the Manor of Beaulieu and the New Forest, and turning them into men-of-war. Perhaps a thousand oaks would go into the making of but a single ship. The woodlands grew barer as Adams grew busier. But no matter, there was always Admiral Collingwood behind them, walking round the countryside picking up acorns and planting them again in the more barren spots ; Collingwood *always* had a pocket full of these wherever he went, or so it is said.

Great craftsmen, these shipwrights : lords of the Admiralty, kings, and princes would journey to Hampshire to see them at work, inspect their vessels, and discuss the finer points of design. Many a secret must Henry Adams have been told as he entertained them all in the little banqueting hall—built especially for the occasion—in his home. Buckler's Hard was in her heyday, and might well have risen to still greater prosperity. But, alas, when the time came for Henry's sons to take over, they failed to deliver four ships to time. The Admiralty lords were furious ; and that was the end.

Sail has long since given place to steam, and timber to steel, but the home of Henry Adams remains to remind us of the noble part this little Georgian village once played in helping to maintain our destiny as guardians of the seas.

Yet if Buckler's Hard has gone into her decline, Hampshire is still an important ship-building centre. All along her seaboard are shipwrights' yards of varying sizes, some of them boasting immense buildings extending over vast acres of waterfront, others content with just one or two more humble wooden structures ; some of them at work on naval vessels or merchant ships, others making yachts for sportsmen frequenting such centres as Cowes, Ryde, or Lymington, or smacks for the fisherfolk.

The fishermen may not be so numerous here as in Devon or Cornwall, but they are hardly less superstitious. At Mudeford, for instance, they still like to see the padre put to sea to bless the waters once a year, and in the more lonely creeks, especially around the once prosperous oyster fisheries of the Emsworth area, you will meet with men who even yet can tell you tales of smuggling in their time.

One man told me quite proudly how his father had been a smuggler—a much "wanted" man from all accounts.

"But they never caught him, sir, not they! He were too sharp for them Excise Men," he added.

"How did he get away with it?"

"Why, bless me soul, sir, you'd never guess! He hid the bottles in the hollow tombs in the churchyards. Just lifted the lids, as bold as brass, and laid them down inside. No Customs Officer ever thought of looking in one of them, no more they didn't! Many a bottle did my old dad smuggle away like that."

But those days are passed. Such methods are too hazardous for these times, and those fishermen who are unable to make a sufficient living from the sea alone work part of their time on land as well. It is unusual to find men following such divergent occupations, yet in Hampshire I have met with many traditional fishermen who are no less skilled in the art of thatching, building, joinery, certain branches of farming, and the like. When conditions are unfavourable at sea they will find their salvation on the land; and vice versa. Sometimes they will toil in the fields by day, return home for their "tea"—more often than not quite a sumptuous spread—and then make straight for their boats. Thus, between sea and land they make sure of earning a steady livelihood.

I asked one of these "amphibians"—who, incidentally, is over eighty-five and yet still thinks nothing of rowing three miles or climbing the highest ladder—whether this combining of trades was a recent idea, designed to meet the changing times. He told me that, on the contrary, his father had been a fisherman and thatcher before him.

"Aye, and me grandfather, too. And you'll find plenty of others like us around these parts. My father always used to say: 'You never knows what the morrow will bring forth. Better be Jack of two trades than idle at one'. Why, I remember going out in the boats when I was only six, and my father carrying me round the fields on his back so that I shouldn't use up all my strength walking."

Certainly the idea works well; the fishermen of Hampshire, unlike those of other parts, are far from idle when the seas blow rough.

Though essentially local industries are few and far between in this county, here and there we shall come upon little colonies of men and women carrying on a work for which their districts have long achieved a certain reputation. Round Botley way strawberries are still grown on a prolific scale for the London markets, and in the thick chestnut woodlands men and boys are to be found daily felling, cleaving, splitting, or wiring together chestnut pales to make durable fencing for the farmers and for the country estates. Only in Hampshire, Sussex, Surrey, and Kent are such fences made, for it is only in these four counties that chestnuts grow in sufficient profusion.

In many a cottage home in the villages and hamlets around Ringwood you will find women and young girls knitting gloves by a secret stitch that has been handed down to them by word of mouth for more than a hundred years. At the outset their ancestors swore never to divulge their secret to any but a Ringwood woman, but, as more and more of the younger generation grew up and left the district, so it spread to other parts. Even so, Ringwood is still the administrative centre. From here the wool is sent by post to the cottagers, who, however, prefer to make the handing in of their finished articles an occasion for renewing old friendships, and so will travel many miles to deliver their gloves in person rather than cross the road to their local post office.

One old cottager told me that she had been making these gloves for seventy years and had won many prizes for her work.

" Many people have tried to find out the secret of our stitch by unravelling the gloves, but they never found the answer—not they ! " she told me proudly. " It's a fine old industry. There's not another like it in England."

More " local " still is the small colony of toy-makers at Brockenhurst, who fashion, in wood, life-like models of more than two hundred different animals that may be found in the New Forest and the Hampshire countryside—ponies, pigs, sheep, ducks, geese, cows, dogs, and so on—besides making replicas of coaches that once bore passengers precariously over the bumpy roads of this very same corner of England, of the men who work in the forest, and of the buildings that surround it.

Certainly few workmen have a more delightful setting for their activities. For the New Forest is surely Hampshire's greatest heritage.

What a story has this noble forest to tell, with its ponies (brought over from Spain after the Armada, some say) roaming among the oak, beech, holly, and yew—" Hampshire weed ". Preserved in all its magnificence to provide a hunting-ground for William the Conqueror and his privileged followers, it has probably seen as much brutality as any other corner of England—any other not visited by the wicked Jeffreys, that is. Here were sown the seeds of the Game Laws in all their harshness, as a result of which a commoner bowed and scraped to the will of his lord and master and lived in terror of his life. For even the most harmless misdemeanour he might well have his eyes plucked out or his feet chopped off. And William's son, Rufus, was still more cruel, preferring to hang than to chop. Small wonder that Sir Walter Tyrrell's arrow so mysteriously found its way into his bosom on one of those hunting expeditions—few, indeed, could have wished to pursue the noble knight as he made his way across the ford at Avon Tyrrell, bound for Poole to take ship for France. Much rather, I imagine, would they follow the charcoal burner, Purkiss—whose descendants still live in these parts—as he carted off the much-detested king for his humble burial at Winchester. Seldom can death have brought such joy to the countryside.

We may still see the pond near Canterton Glen where Sir Walter washed his blood-stained hands and where, it is said, the water turns red once a year in memory of the event ; so too may we visit the smithy where his horse is supposed to have been shod.

To the kings of the Middle Ages the forest was of greater moment than the palace ; hunting of more importance than affairs of state. Even so, those who lived within its confines were not to be wholly deprived of their age-old rights so long as they behaved themselves and did not interfere with the beasts. Thus, in course of time, there gradually came into being a whole team of officials to superintend the life and work of the forest, with a number of courts to enforce the laws, just as there were already courts and officers to control life on the English manor.

Under the supreme authority of the Lord Warden would come the foresters, rangers, woodwards, agisters, regarders, keepers, beadles, bow-bearers, verderers, and numerous others. While some of these would tend the "venison" (the term given to the game as a whole), others would be responsible for the "vert"—the timber and turf, that is—in as much as they affected the venison. It was a deep and carefully-laid plan, designed to ensure that the forest and its livestock were kept ever in a state of perfect readiness for the King, and that the commoners received their lawful dues, but no more.

Dead and buried are the brutal kings of long ago; reduced in number are the deer they loved to chase; but the commoners of the New Forest have not yet surrendered the rights to graze their cattle and their ponies, feed their pigs upon the beech mast and the fallen acorns, gather timber, and cut turves for their open fires. And the ancient Court of Swainmote—more often referred to as the Verderers' Court—freely elected by the forest people themselves, still sits at Lyndhurst as guardian over those cherished privileges; a firm bulwark against any who would deny them what has so long been theirs.

What tales, indeed, can this lovely forest recall: of bowstaves fashioned for the archers from the yews, and ships built from the massive oaks; of smugglers from Lymington hiding their casks of rum in Ambrose Cave; of life-and-death struggles between poachers and keepers; of Christmas-time squirrel-hunts with "squail" or "snogg", two obsolete weapons of the catapult type, comprising sticks and hard wooden balls, with which the local sportsmen would dislodge the squirrels from the branches of the highest trees with uncanny accuracy.

The urge to kill can never, it seems, be entirely banished. Just out of Lyndhurst stands a tree whereon is fixed the remains of a crucifix. And that crucifix saved many a murder from taking place in this quiet spot even in our own time.

At its base is a quaint sign, and a woodman who witnessed the scene of its past importance told me its unusual story. Here, in the war of 1914–18, were stationed a number of Portuguese lumberjacks. A somewhat rowdy lot, they were unable to " take their drink ". One night, after a particularly heavy bout at a local inn, knives were brought out and free fights developed on the grand scale.

" I was here at the time, and, believe me, it's a miracle the whole lot weren't murdered," my woodman friend assured me.

" Well, why weren't they ? " I pressed him.

" Because they were so religious."

Devout Catholics, their leader called them to order simply by reminding them of their faith. And to bring home to them the folly of their ways, and to prevent any further repetition of such a scene, he at once fashioned a crucifix from two strips of wood, nailed it to the tree, and wrote a warning sign at the base of the upright. Thereafter, every day, before starting their felling and sawing, the Portuguese would say their prayers around the tree and bow their heads to the crucifix, repeating the performance when they stopped work in the evening.

" It did the trick, sir. We never had no more trouble from them Portuguese after that," added the forester.

But if the commoners can now live in peace, the forest itself lies for ever in the shadow of a deadly menace ; the menace of fire. Dotted about the roadside and along the little trackways are racks of fire-brooms for all to seize should occasion demand ; and towering above them all, some sixty feet high, are the look-out towers with their watchers, maps, telephones, and communicating system, whereby the entire 65,000 acres can be kept under permanent surveillance throughout the twenty-four hours. For a forest fire is a terrifying thing, capable of bringing utter destruction to vast acres and causing thousands of pounds' worth of damage to trees within a matter of hours. Indeed, every year large areas of gorse and heather are deliberately and systematically burnt in order to reduce the risk and prevent the encroachment of gorse and scrub over the grazing lands.

If by far the largest, and undoubtedly the most glorious, the New Forest is not Hampshire's only one. She has, too, the remains of the forests of Bere, Wolmer, Alice Holt, and Harewood, in all of which kings and princes once chased the stag. Little more than pleasant woodlands now, they fell from grace when their deer were removed to Windsor across the borders of Berkshire.

Seven *In the Wake of Father Thames*

IF Windsor to-day is a park more than a forest, it was a hunting-ground as far back as the time of the Saxon kings. Ever since Edward the Confessor had his palace here, Windsor has been a royal residence, and the march of time has only increased her dignity.

When William the Conqueror came to build his motte-and-bailey castle here, as one of his chain of strongholds, how bitterly must the Anglo-Saxons have resented this sign of their vanishing freedom. And yet to-day this same castle, with its imposing round tower, built as a shell-keep by Henry II, and its many other additions, stands upon the hill-top as the very symbol of democracy, strength, and unity. And when the Royal Standard flutters at the mast-head to denote that the King is in residence, that sense of security strengthens noticeably.

Nowhere else—not even within the shades of Buckingham Palace—can one sense quite this atmosphere, I think. For around Royal Windsor is written the pageant of ages ; a pageant far older than that of any other royal home, and more enduring than that of

Winchester. And within the castle stands the great hall of St. George, built for the entertainment of the Knights of the Order of the Garter, the Chapel Royal, and the Garter Chapel, where kings and princes innumerable sleep their lasting sleep.

Then, too, at the bottom of the hill, across the river at the end of the narrow main street leading to Slough, just over the Buckinghamshire border, is Eton College, with its playing-fields around the bend beyond, where men of royal blood have mingled with the sons of noblemen since earliest times. Many a king has watched those young aristocrats being kicked down Salthill as part of the now defunct "montem" ceremony, or gazed upon his mud-spattered sons labouring at the "Field" or "Wall" game, or taking to the boats.

If the Castle above provides a home for the constitutional head of the State, the College below has produced more of his rulers and ambassadors than any other school in England. Many a Prime Minister has toiled at the classics within the class-rooms of Eton; Sir Robert Walpole, William Pitt and his adversary-turned-friend, Charles James Fox, Canning, the Duke of Wellington, and Gladstone, to mention but a few. From being fags at the College, these, and many others, have grown to become honoured guests at the Castle.

No public corner of England is quite so regal in its make-up, for through the Great Park, in the opposite direction, where George III once loved to hunt the stag, is Ascot, home of the world's most fashionable race meeting. Even those who, like myself, are never enamoured of racing, can hardly fail to find a certain glamour in such a field of grey top-hats and colourful dresses. How proud would Queen Anne be if she could but watch the kings and queens of nowadays

" Once a common feature of Cathedral cities and grammar schools alike "—the ceremony of the Boy Bishop at Addlestone.

" In parts she is enchanting "—near Abinger Hammer.

Left) : " Perhaps the oblest of these Surrey towns "—Farnham.

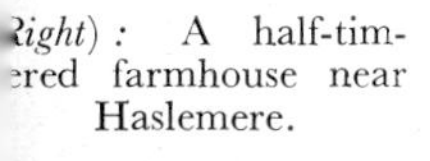

ight) : A half-tim-ered farmhouse near Haslemere.

" These stalwarts ' flipping their alleys ' "—the Marbles championship at Tinsley Green.

driving in the state landau down the course ; Anne who founded Ascot merely as a centre for private races between those who hunted regularly with her Royal Buck-Hounds in Windsor Forest. How the critics who predicted that Ascot could *never* become as fashionable as Cheltenham would turn in their graves at the thought of such a scene ! And well they might, for less than a hundred years ago the horses were still being weighed in canvas booths and stabled in tumbledown cowsheds, while the spectators contented themselves with watching from a few coloured tents and sitting on hired camp-stools, the cost of which, I gather, was a permanent bone of contention. Many a soaking did they receive when the driving force of the rain caused the tents to collapse on top of them !

But if Windsor, with Ascot, is Berkshire's greatest heritage, all along the winding course of the Thames we shall be reminded of the county's age-long link with royalty. Many of the very swans that glide so gracefully upon the peaceful waters, adding enchantment to the scene, are of royal stock. These birds, it is believed, may well have come over with the Vikings, and certainly the cygnets have been held in the highest esteem as a table delicacy at least since the days of King John. Indeed, so highly prized were they in olden times that the reigning monarch assumed overall proprietorship of the birds, granting licences to maintain their own cygnets to only his chosen few.

To-day they are the property of the King, the Worshipful Company of Vintners, and the Worshipful Company of Dyers, and every July the six-hundred-year-old custom of " Swan Upping " is carried out, when the cygnets are lifted from the water and marked with the signs of their respective owners ; a ceremony extending over many days.

How picturesque to see the boats making slowly

upstream, from Southwark to Henley, each bearing its distinctive flag of recognition, the King's with the " G.R. VI " surmounted by the Crown, the others decorated with different swan emblems ; the scarlet blazers of the King's men contrasting vividly with the blue-and-white striped jerseys of the Vintners, or the green-and-white of the Dyers. So regal, and yet so simple.

Slowly the procession passes on its way until within sight of Windsor Castle, when the boats owned by the two Companies, bowing subservience to the Crown, move away to either bank of the Thames to form a guard of honour. The Vintners' men and those of the Dyers are on their feet and holding their oars erect . . . the royal boat moves majestically along the lane between them . . . three cheers are called . . . three cheers for the King ! And so the little armada links up again and continues on its course.

As I say, the ceremony may extend over several days. For the marking of the cygnets is no quick or easy business. As soon as a brood is sighted the cry " All up, all up ! " is passed from boat to boat, when, under the direction of the three swan-wardens, the oarsmen skilfully manœuvre their craft around the brood and gradually drive the birds to one or other bank. Thus securely penned in, the work of " upping " proceeds. If the cygnets prove to be the property of the Crown, they will be left unmarked ; if of the Dyers, a single nick will be cut on the bill, or of the Vintners, two nicks. It is a tricky business, too. Every bird throughout that long stretch of water has to be lifted into the boats to be examined, and a full-grown swan can well break a man's arm unless handled correctly. Still, the " uppers " give little thought to this. I am told that some of them have been tending the swans and taking part in this ceremony for thirty years or more. But perhaps it is the idea of the cygnet banquet to follow that keeps them going.

If the motor road and the railway have robbed old Father Thames of some of its ancient glory, in scattered villages along its noble banks we may yet meet with men whose offices recall the days when the river was an important highway of London and when the nobility and the City companies all employed their own watermen.

Down by the water's edge at Wargrave, I talked to a boat-builder who has been one of the King's twelve watermen in no less than three reigns. Many a time, he told me, has he rowed in the royal barge down to the Tower of London to collect the Crown Jewels and deliver them to the Palace of Westminster for the State opening of Parliament.

"Nowadays both the Crown and the jewels are lodged overnight at St. James's Palace. But they are still in our charge on the day of the State Opening, and our responsibility ends only when the bargemaster hands them over to the Lord Chamberlain," he explained.

" I suppose you have actually handled the Crown, then ? " I asked.

" Lord, bless me soul, yes !—many a time."

" What's the betting it has been on your head many a time, too ? "

The waterman laughed, and I thought it best not to press him further.

Yes, Berkshire is truly a " royal " county. But then, she always has been. It was at Wantage—a place once notorious for the lawlessness of its citizens, and whose name, it is said, comes from the peculiar number of " wants " (the local term for moles) to be found there —that King Alfred was born. And Alfred owned land at Hambourne which, later, he left to his wife, and a palace at Faringdon upon the site of which now stands the Salutation Inn. At Chaddleworth is one of King John's many hunting-boxes, while at Shaw-cum-Donnington and Great Shefford are the manor houses where Charles I stayed before and after the Battle of Newbury, respectively. In a wall of the former of these, Shaw House, they will show you the hole through which the shot passed when an attempt was made on the King's life. Incidentally, the ruined Castle at Shaw-cum-Donnington, almost wholly destroyed in these battles, was once in the keeping of the Chaucer family, and some still contend, despite the difficulty of fitting in dates, that the poet used to sit and ruminate beneath the nearby oak tree ; the tree long known as " Chaucer's Oak ".

It was at Hurley that Richard Lovelace plotted William of Orange's invasion of England ; at the Bear Hotel at Hungerford, still a favourite rendezvous for travellers on the Bath Road, that Dutch William's councillors met the three commissioners of James II to negotiate the future of the Crown ; at Milton, during his march on Oxford with some twenty thousand picked men, that he received the news of James's flight to France, and felt himself able to breathe securely at last. A fine mansion is Milton House where he stayed : Inigo Jones at his best.

An interesting old hostelry, the *Bear*. Built as far back as 1297, it once formed part of the dowry of Anne of Cleves, and, later, of Catherine Howard. Queen Elizabeth, as might be expected, stayed there—in Room 17 for the benefit of the curious—and Charles I adopted the place as his headquarters during the Civil Wars. It was while journeying to Windsor from Salisbury that William of Orange decided to seek the hospitality of its walls, and the story goes that when James's Commissioners arrived, he refused to leave his room, and so entertained them in his bedchamber, a massive room (No. 14) with an extremely uneven floor. For the best part of a day the respective councillors continued to bicker and argue as to who was best suited to be king, until, at last, William, deciding that the inn was becoming a little " noisy ", called the meeting to an abrupt halt, and, without more ado, made off for Littlecote.

Still, William's, though memorable, was only a fleeting visit. Hungerford remembers better John of Gaunt, son of one king (Edward III) and father of another (Henry IV) but never to reign himself. He it was who granted the manorial and fishing rights which the commoners enjoy to this day, and his memory is kept ever green in the strange Hocktide ceremony that takes place here every year on the Tuesday following Easter week.

Unlike other boroughs, Hungerford has no mayor and corporation ; instead, she is governed, as of old, by a constable, portreeve, bailiff, and a Court of Feoffees. It is at this ancient ceremony that these and other officials are elected, and the time-honoured rights confirmed and administered.

Sharp at eight o'clock on the morning of Hockney Tuesday, the Town Crier, dressed in his traditional garb, will appear on the balcony of the Corn Exchange to blow the old hunting-horn which was made over three hundred years ago to take the place of the battered affair (still in the town's possession) presented by John of Gaunt himself. For close on an hour he will continue to blow it intermittently, until the Bellman or Assistant Bailiff, in his grey and scarlet coat with brass buttons and high hat with gold band, proceeds to add to the noise and general hubbub by clanging his bell around the streets, shouting as he goes :

" Oyez ! Oyez ! Oyez ! All ye Commoners of the Borough of Hungerford are requested to attend at your

Court House at nine o'clock this morning on pain of being fined. God Save the King ! "

And it is only the unwise who fail to obey the summons. For any who neglect to pay the " Commoner's Penny " must run the risk of losing their rights for the ensuing year. Even those who really have good reason for their absence are still always careful to come out into the streets and hand over their coin to the Bellman as he passes on his way.

Then, as the clock strikes the nine chimes, the Court assembles, the Constable seated in an old carved ebony chair with the horn on the table in front of him. The provisions of John of Gaunt's grant are now read by the Steward (the Town Clerk) ; a further proclamation is made ; and the lists of " free-suiters " (freeholders) and commoners are called out and the pennies collected. Now comes the election of the officers—the Constable ; the Portreeve, whose job will include the collecting of the " quit-rents " ; the Bailiff, in charge of the tolls due at the fairs and street markets ; the Assistant Bailiff, responsible for similar tolls elsewhere ; the Water Bailiffs, Overseers, Keepers of the Keys of the Common Coffer ; Hayward, Tithing or Tutti-men, Bellman and Ale-Tasters. In olden days, when tanning was an important local industry, there were also the Searchers and Sealers of Leather and the Tasters of Flesh and Fish.

It is an exacting day for the commoners, for while the Court of Feoffeement is busily arranging who is to do what, the Tutti-men, carrying nosegays on poles, accompanied by a man with a sack of oranges, will be wandering about, here, there and everywhere, calling from house to house collecting further pennies, kissing every female who seems worth while and giving her an orange in exchange—a reasonable enough bargain for both parties in these times, I should say—and visiting schools and other institutions, demanding that the day be kept as a holiday.

Not that anybody in Hungerford would think of doing anything else ; Hockney Tuesday is the day of days. When the business side of the proceedings has been completed, the new constable will preside at a civic luncheon, to be followed by the " Shoeing of the Colts ", when a " blacksmith " and his " apprentice " will proceed to drive horse nails into the soles of any visitors or new commoners who may be present ; an operation that will continue with increasing fury until each of the respective " colts " decides that he is now roadworthy and agrees to stand drinks all round. Yes, it is a great day, and afterwards will come the scramble for oranges, when such of the fruit as has not already gone in kisses will be thrown to the vast assembly of children outside.

The fisheries of the Kennet are still regarded as among the finest in the country, and the trout-fishing at Hungerford, which the commoners have enjoyed three days a week ever since John of Gaunt granted them his " free gift ", is famous in every corner of the world where fly fishermen delight to gather together. Appropriate is it, then, that at Hungerford is the largest and most modern trout farm in England. From this farm, I am told, something like three hundred thousand trout and several million eggs are sent away every year to stock the rivers far and wide. Probably there are less than a dozen such farms in the whole of England.

The proprietor told me that the trout are classified into various age groups—Ova, Alevins, " ready-to-feed " fry, one-to-three-months fry, yearlings, two-year-olds, and so on. On leaving the eggs, the fish spend the first two months in indoor tanks, before being moved to the first of the fifty-four outdoor ponds, each of which is graded according to age. Here, in these ponds, feeding is carried out on a scientific rationing basis, and the growth of every batch is systematically checked and recorded so as to ensure the most even development throughout.

" Although the trout are dispatched at all ages," he explained, " the two-year-olds are the most popular with the fisheries. At this age they are about ten inches long, and the risk of loss through floods or vermin less than with the yearlings. At the same time, they often make faster growth than the three-year-olds."

Still, everything depends upon conditions at the fisheries to which the trout are going, and they are sent in enormous enclosed tanks that are insulated and supplied with oxygen.

Hocktide is not Hungerford's only ceremony ; here the inhabitants are still expected to wade through the streams as part of the beating of the bounds.

Surprisingly rich in surviving customs is Berkshire. Gone are the days when the people of East Hampstead, near Bagshot, would carry the lord of the manor shoulder high on a chair to the top of a hill, hurl him to the ground, beat him soundly with twigs, and then dine with him at his expense ; gone are those days, but far and wide throughout the county we shall watch the people indulging in ceremonies far less painful and, in most instances, far more purposeful.

As at Winchester and Tichborne, doles are still paid out at Cumnor, Ufton Court, and Reading. At Ufton one hundred and sixty-nine loaves of bread, five yards of flannel, and eleven yards of calico are distributed to the poor every March under the terms of the will of a certain Lady Marvin, who left annual provision for ten bushels of wheat for making bread, twelve-and-a-half ells of canvas for shirts and smocks, and a length of blue cloth for the manufacture of coats and cassocks. To this day the gifts are distributed from a window of the house where she lived in the sixteenth century. At Reading the dole is paid in cash at the Town Hall to three maidservants who have served in the same household for at least five years and can prove themselves to be of good character.

At Winterbourne, too—where the natives will tell you that they can yet hear the ghost of a man, whose horse ran away with him with fatal results long years ago, riding down Bussock Hill—bread and money charities are periodically given away. Here also, as at Inkpen, may we watch the blessing of the fields at Rogationtide.

What a busy place must this pleasing little village of Inkpen and the surrounding hill country have been in days gone by. Here the Knights Templars had their first home, and, before them, the men of the Iron Age their fortified camps on Walbury Hill—highest chalk hill of the South—and by Bull Copse and Ham. But things were happening here even before that. The " Old Way ", which passes through Walbury Camp, was first trodden, it is said, by Neolithic man as he brought his herds from France and migrated along the highways in search of suitable pasturage. It was used by him before ever it became a trackway for the pilgrims and merchants, or a drove road along which to drive the cattle and sheep to market. The ancient dyke, too —known as the Wansdyke—which is still visible in parts, is believed to be the remains of a protective line that was constructed as far back as 800 B.C., and that once ran right across the downs from Cissbury Ring along to Winchester.

And not far off is Coombe Hill, from whose summit we may see some of the most magnificent views in Southern England, with grassy slopes all around us, falling away down to flat fields, chequered with hedgerows ; winding lanes and little clumps of woodland ;

fields that stretch like a patchwork from county to county in all directions as far as the eye can see to merge with the sky in the distant horizon. Here it was, on the top of Coombe Hill, that a local labourer, George Broomham, tiring of his wife—and falling in love with another, one Dorothy Newman—decided to waylay both her and his son and throw their bodies into a nearby pond ; a crime for which he and Dorothy alike were hanged upon that gibbet whose leaning remains still stand as a timely reminder to any who might even yet be possessed of a sudden urge to follow his example.

A strange place Inkpen : although the beacon stands some five hundred feet above sea level and is miles from any shore, it nevertheless contains a stratum of pebbles such as one would expect to find only in such places as the beaches of Sussex or Kent.

I remember once discussing this curious phenomenon with a native. He was quite unable to advance any sound reason, but seemed more concerned with the fact that it was going to rain.

" There goes the smoke from the old man's pipe. That means rain afore morning, sir, and the hay not cut yet. 'Tis terrible serious, I'm telling you."

" The smoke from *what* ? Where ? "

" Look, sir, athurt yonder ! See those puffs coming up from the copse ? When you see clouds like that it means rain, right enough."

And right enough it did. For two whole days it deluged. Indeed, the " smoke from the old man's pipe " is a thing that the " yellow-legs "—a name enjoyed by the villagers ever since pottery formed an important local industry, and all and sundry walked about with the yellow clay clinging to the bottoms of their trousers—wish to see only at times of drought.

But to return to the customs. The Mummers are still busy at Swallowfield, burial place of Mary Mitford ;

Northcourt, where Charles I is believed to have bid his last good-bye to Henrietta Maria ; Buckland, and Burghfield, at the last of which the " St. George and the Dragon " play is produced at the *Three Firs* inn as part of the proceedings of the Boxing Day meet of the South Berkshire Hunt. And at Abingdon, the residents of Ock street, after a lapse of something like fifty years, once more elect their Morris Dancers' Mayor. Here the voters drop their cards into a box set up in a side street, and after the election the successful candidate is " danced in ", when, for days on end, the " team " will lead him triumphantly through the streets, eventually rounding up the proceedings with a traditional supper and general merry-making.

Said to have been introduced from Spain by John of Gaunt, Morris-dancing, with its King and Queen of the May, Maid Marion, Festival Fool, and Sword-Bearer, took its place in mediæval country life with the mummers' plays and dancing round the Maypole as one of the great events of the year.

Feasts and fairs are still held far and wide in Berkshire : at Chilton, every spring ; East Challow, on Trinity Sunday ; at Kingston Lisle—where " primrose pudding ", made of chopped primrose petals, suet and flour, is considered a tasty dish—in cherry time ; at Yattendon, where their charter dates back to 1318, every Whit-Monday.

By the way, should ever you have occasion to attend the Yattendon feast, don't be put off if, perchance, you come upon a ghost-like figure wandering about the nearby meadows. This, the villagers will tell you, is but the spirit of a man who once lived here in style but was forced to beat a hasty retreat during the Civil Wars.

" Don't say he's looking for his head, too ? " I chided one old man.

"No, it's not his head he be wanting : it's his gold," he said.

"Gold ? Well, where did he hide it ?"

"Down a well, they do say. But," he added, and his wrinkled face broke into a smile, "damme if the bloomin' well ain't disappeared too !"

Most interesting of the Berkshire fairs, to my mind, is that of St. Bartholomew's at Newbury, for here is still held the Court of Pie-Poudre, or Pie Powder, which, by ancient right, lays down the regulations governing its conduct, and settles disputes between traders and merchants. No longer so necessary as in days gone by, these courts were once all-important as a means of preventing cheating and ensuring that the terms of the charter were not infringed.

At Aldermaston the hire of an acre of church land is auctioned every third year, when the vicar sticks a pin into a lighted candle and declares the man who makes the last bid before the burning wick causes the pin to fall to the ground to be its temporary possessor.

Every Sunday morning, at ten o'clock, we shall hear the church bells at Hinton Waldrist ringing out the hour just as they did in the days when there were no such things as clocks or watches. Nor is this entirely pointless to-day : at Hinton you will even yet find men who are as unable to tell the time as they are to write their own name.

In few counties so near to London shall we meet with people who cling quite so lovingly to the old ways as do these Berkshire folk. And it is not only in the matter of customs that they keep faith. Their speech, too, is hardly less strange than that of the Cornishman, or of the men of Devon, Somerset, or Dorset.

He who grows old in Berkshire is considered to be "arky", and when the time comes for him to move on to the next world he will be buried, not in a grave but a " pity hole ", which, in turn, will have been " hucked up " rather than dug. A shed to the Berkshireman is ever a " cart hovel ", just as a sparrow is a " spadger ". There is no such thing as a young man in these parts : " boy-chap " is preferred to " youth ". So, too, is an untidy person classed as a " shag-bag ", and a gypsy as a " diddycot ". Neither do you eat your lunch in these parts, but " quilt your nunchin ".

When the genial countryman asks you " How be ? " you will reply " featish " or " unked " according to your physical condition of the moment, and he will readily understand that you are feeling either " middling " or " rotten ".

Should, unhappily, the latter prove the case, he will at once inquire what it is that ails you. In which event it is as well to be on your guard ! For if your complaint is of the commonplace variety, he will, without doubt, recommend one of his many " cures ", and these are by no means always entirely palatable.

I shall not quickly forget being overcome with a bout of coughing when talking to an elderly hurdle-maker in the woods one day. To my horror he began searching in the undergrowth for a frog, telling me that if I would but swallow it alive and whole, my troubles would be ended. Believe me, they ended before ever he found his frog !

I asked him if he had any other such tempting remedies up his sleeve. He had. As an alternative to the frog, he assured me, bread from the Communion Table, powdered and taken with water, was usually reliable, while the verdigris scraped from the church bells was quite the last word as a cure for shingles.

" I suppose you don't often need to send for a doctor ? " I chaffed my friend.

" No, sir. Never been to one in my life. Of course the young 'uns go to him more than what we should.

Why, my old mother, she brought eight of us into the world, and never seed a doctor not once, she didn't. She always used to swear that the only time she'd call in one of them medicine men was when she was feeling fed up with life and wanted to hasten her end ! "

I assured him that doctors were really not so bad as his mother had painted them.

" No, sir, I don't suppose they are, no more. Still, *I* never needs 'em."

You will meet with plenty like him who even yet prefer to rely on the cures in which their fathers and grandfathers—and many generations before them—had such unswerving faith. You will find men and women who will yet solemnly declare that a cut finger should be bound with a cobweb ; that the white hairs of a donkey, if placed on the chest, will banish whooping-cough ; that sage tea and vinegar make an excellent gargle ; or that the juice of crushed snails, strained through muslin and mixed with milk, is good for seedy children ; or that lily leaves, soaked in brandy, will ease chapped hands ; or that the fat of bacon will remove the most stubborn of thorns within the batting of an eyelid.

Great characters these, they will hold their own against any but the West Countryman in the matter of beliefs. When the blackbird sings while the thrush is silent, the Berkshire countryman will shake his head concernedly and warn you to expect at least three days of bad weather. On the other hand, when he sees that the mulberry leaf has grown to the size of a mouse's ear, he will sigh with relief, confident in the thought that he has seen the last of the spring frosts for that year.

Ask him about the beautiful purple anemone to be found in so many parts of the county, and he will tell you that this rare species grows only on soil where the blood of a Dane has been shed ; as also will he tell you that the purple crocus was brought over by the Knights Templars, and the chives by the Roman legionaries. Question him about two particular acacia trees at Radley, and he will assure you that they are the mummified bodies of a gypsy and a married woman who let passion get the upper hand of them one moonlit night. Certainly *he* is not to be outdone in the " pillar of salt " technique ; nor, for that matter, will he allow the Cornishman to get away with his wells and mediæval springs unchallenged.

While at Sunninghill—where Scott wrote *Marmion*—they will talk proudly of the time when the Earl of Chatham drank of the magic waters ; at Frilsham they will lead you to a well on the common that has never yet been known to run dry. The story goes that a certain female saint, Frideswide by name, was being hounded down by one Ogar. Running hard for a swineherd's hut on the common, a spring issued forth from the ground with each step she took. How that eased her plight seems a little difficult to grasp—extremely uncomfortable for poor Frideswide, one would have thought ! But, no matter, the well is fed from these springs, and everybody is happy. Wittenham, too, has a well, as also have Finchampstead and Sunningwell, and the waters of some of them are still taken on occasion for various ailments.

Round Uffington way, in the beautiful Vale of the White Horse, they will assert with confidence that the famous hillside carving marks the spot where St. George slew the dragon, the blood of the latter killing the grass and making the work of carving somewhat easier. Here the local widows still go " mumping "—the Saxon for begging—on St Thomas's day before holding their annual feast ; a survival of the old " Pastimes ", when, for two whole days, the people of both Berkshire and

Wiltshire would indulge in all manner of games and merry-making on the downs. It was at Uffington that Thomas Hughes, author of *Tom Brown's Schooldays*, was born, and at Compton Beauchamp is the " moated grange " that figures in this work.

Nor is the Berkshireman lacking in his " stories " and " sights ". While at Cookham Dean they will show you the manger from which Black Bess munched her hay when her celebrated owner, Dick Turpin, was not too busy holding up coaches on the Bath Road, and will embark upon harrowing accounts of how the ghost of Hern the Hunter can still be heard blowing his horn as he rides with his hounds across the common at night, at White Waltham they will pooh-pooh this as nothing. They have *three* ghosts.

Get on to the subject of his church, and the native of Kintbury will wax enthusiastic as he recounts the sorrowful story of the tower—how it was destroyed by storm somewhere about a hundred and fifty years ago, how the bell was hurled into the river, and how, acting upon the advice of a wizard, a hook and chains were attached to it. It was then to have been drawn out in moonlight by twelve white heifers, led by twelve maidens wearing white dresses adorned with red sashes. All would have been well if only everyone had kept their mouths shut. As it was, a witch turned up at the crucial moment—as they invariably do—and sang a disparaging song. It was all up then : the spell was broken—so was the chain.

Most famous of these Berkshire stories, though, is that of Weyland Smithy, a cave near the Vale of the White Horse. The son of a giant, young Weyland was taught the art of metal work by the mountain dwarfs, and became so skilled that some mythical king took him into captivity, cut the tendons of his legs to prevent escape, and set him to fashion various articles for the

"Where King Canute's daughter was drowned in the moat"—Bosham.

"How picturesque and snug they nestle"—a typical Sussex village green.

" Essentially a farming county "—ploughs at work on the South Downs.

" The older folk take it in turns to baste the animal "—the Ebernoe Horn Fair.

" These plays are far older than Christianity "—the Sussex Tipteers.

royal household. Weyland, however, had ideas of his own. After murdering the King's sons, he proceeded to make drinking bowls out of their skulls, toys of their eye-balls, and necklaces of their teeth. Whereupon he fashioned a fine pair of wings for himself, flew to the palace with his " gifts ", told the King and Queen how he had made them, and then glided quietly off again. And that was that.

Not far from the cave is a stone, and tradition has it that anyone placing a coin upon it will return to find that his horse has been shod by some invisible smith. A pleasing story . . . but who, I wonder, gets the money ?

What a wealth of interesting places there are to visit in this rolling downland county ! If the talk at Newbury is still of the exploits of the poor clothier, Jack, who raised an " army " to help Henry VIII in his wars with the Scots, and ended up a rich man, the day is also remembered when, in 1811, in fulfilment of a bet by one Sir John Throckmorton, almost the entire district turned out by Greenham Mills to watch wool being shorn from the backs of two sheep and made into a tailored coat between the hours of sunrise and sunset. By tea time their wool had been washed, carded, dyed, spun, and woven into cloth. From the looms the material passed to nine tailors who, ready with their scissors and their needles threaded, at once set to work busily stitching for something like two hours. By six o'clock the coat was finished, whereupon Sir John, richer by one thousand pounds, saw fit to roast the sheep and provide a sumptuous feast for all present ; a feast washed down by a hundred and twenty gallons of strong beer.

Incidentally, talking of beer, I am told that this beverage is still sold by the pound at the inn at Waltham St. Lawrence.

While at East Hendred we shall still hear a four-hundred-year-old clock playing the Hymn of the Angels. At Chaddleworth we shall see the strange round house, with its central pole extending through three floors, which the local schoolmaster and his boys erected in their lunch hour as a " funk-hole " at the time of the Napoleonic troubles. Though, happily, never required for its intended purpose, it served as the county's first Wesleyan preaching place.

At Hagbourne there stands the mill where that careless workman accidentally dropped a measure of sulphuric acid on to a stack of paper, and, in doing so, gave us blotting paper ; and on Bucklebury Common we may watch the last of a colony of craftsmen that once flourished in these parts, still turning bowls in his rickety shed by means of a pole lathe.

Hardly a village is there that will not arouse our curiosity in some way or other. At Brimpton is the octagonal church that was built to allow James II's wife to follow her Catholic faith while staying at Hyde End House ; at Binfield is an off-shoot of the Glastonbury Thorn, to prove that this hallowed tree will bloom at Christmas time as readily in Berkshire soil as in that of Somerset ; on Rivar Down, close by Shalbourne, is the " British Ditch ", a tunnelled lane used for driving cattle from the high ground to the more protected hollows below in times of crisis.

Wokingham may talk of Swift, Gay, and Pope, but Ruscombe and Longworth will not readily let us forget that William Penn, founder of Pennsylvania, and Richard Blackmore, respectively, were their sons. While at Reading we shall be assured that that " merry old soul ", Old King Cole, was no other than Thomas Cole, a local weaver who lived in the time of Henry I. If we linger a while in that fascinating little village of Bray, we shall soon appreciate why it was the one ambition of her Tudor incumbent, whose fame has long been sung the world over, ever to remain her vicar.

But the one of whom I always think first in Berkshire is Jethro Tull, born at Basildon in 1674; the man who brought about one of England's first agricultural revolutions with the invention of the seed drill and his "horse-hoeing husbandry". Called to the Bar but abandoning the law courts for the fields in the same year, he returned at once to his native Basildon. Wandering over the bleak and barren downs, visiting farms both large and small, he found much to criticize: crops choked with weeds; crops in one part so thin and poor as to be hardly worth the harvesting, yet in another so thick as to be stifling; waste everywhere. From his visits to these farms he soon saw where lay the greatest mistakes, and on his own farm he proceeded to set them right. Here, derided by his neighbours and insulted by his labourers, Tull fought a lone battle for the fields of England; a battle rendered only the harder by his personal sufferings from "the Stone and other incurable diseases". Though Tull could prove to all, by his successful experiments, the wisdom of his methods, it was not until after his death that any would acknowledge his doctrine.

Berkshire may well be proud of Jethro Tull; his name, though forgotten by the "man in the street", will ever be linked with that of Tusser, of "Turnip" Townshend, Bakewell, and of Coke of Norfolk, as the great pioneers of farming England. We can think of him not only on the downs he knew and loved so well, but also at the great horse and cattle sales at Reading. For it is only by a visit to these famous sales that we can hope to appreciate what agriculture means to Berkshire.

Still, the downs belong not only to the farmer. To

many the breeding and training of racehorses is a matter of far greater moment. By them Newbury is thought of only in terms of its racecourse, Reading and Lambourne as centres for the manufacture of travelling " boxes ", and the grassy slopes as a site for the training gallops. Many a winner has been put through its paces on these downs ; many a horse—Felsted and Windsor Lad among them—has set off along the high road into Surrey, bound for Epsom and the Derby. Let us ourselves tag on behind this procession of horse-boxes and make for the scene of this Blue Riband of the Turf.

Eight *The Londoner's Countryside*

IT was in 1773 that the twelfth Earl of Derby bought himself a house at Epsom. Passionately fond of cock-fighting, he kept no less than three thousand birds on his estates, and it is said that it was his insistence upon staging "mains" and "battles royal" in the drawing-room of his home that finally drove his first wife, Lady Elizabeth Hamilton, to the Divorce Court.

A great sportsman, the Earl did not confine his attentions to the mains. No less devoted to the Turf, he looked as well to the downs as to his drawing-room, and, in doing so, brought Epsom to the pinnacle of her fame. In 1779 he gave the name of his house to one race, The Oaks, and, a year later, his own name to another—The Derby. Yet how little could the noble earl have guessed with what abiding solidarity his name was to be linked with that of Epsom as he spun the coin over the dinner table with his celebrated guest, Sir Charles Bunbury, that far-off evening. For had the coin but fallen the other way up, the race would have been known as the "Bunbury", or so it is said.

Still, what's in a name? The character of Epsom

would never have been different. There would still have been Tattenham Corner to add to the confusion and excitement of the race. The gypsies would have been on the downs to tell your fortune just the same ; the touts and tipsters would have been no less busy. Whether " Derby day " or " Bunbury day ", it would still have been *the* day.

If Berkshire can boast the world's most fashionable course, Surrey can claim the most popular race. Nowhere is such a scene to be witnessed as when almost every type in the land meet at Epsom on this one day in May. How strange the contrast between the ragtails of the gypsies, or the open-neck shirts or no-collar-or-tie-but-maybe-a-stud of the yokels, or the " Sunday-bests " of London's " cockneys "—how strange the contrast between these and the morning coats, top hats, and fine dresses of the chauffeur-driven rich. How truly democratic is the Derby !

But fame came to Epsom before ever the Earl bought " Lambert's Oaks ". As far back as the time of Queen Elizabeth, people had been coming here to benefit from her medicinal springs, and in Charles I's days thought nothing of paying as much as five shillings for but an ounce of the precious salts. At first they came to rid themselves of ulcers ; later they made the journey when they felt themselves in need of a purge. Pepys himself on one occasion " did drink four pints ", and feel the better for it. And here came Charles II, too, with poor Nell Gwynne.

Indeed, so famous did these springs, with their sulphate of magnesia and hydrochloride of lime, become, that the town of Epsom had to be enlarged to accommodate the vast concourse of visitors who would wend their way here, not only from all corners of England, but also from many foreign lands. And what with dancing and music, public luncheons, racing at odd intervals throughout the day on Banstead Downs, hawking, singlestick and foot races—to say nothing of the cock-fights—the programme was as full as the town itself. Busy days, and when energy inclined to lag there were always the waters to jerk one up a bit.

But Epsom's innings as a fashion centre was to draw to its close as Bath, Tunbridge Wells, and Cheltenham got into their stride, and as the dandies began to brave the sea at Weymouth, Brighton, and elsewhere. The salts lost none of their potency, but the " fancy " now preferred to receive them in packages and to travel farther afield for their " cures " and their round of night life.

For even in Georgian days Epsom was growing to be regarded as too near London. And Time has only worsened the issue. Alas, that is the whole tragedy of Surrey ! The angry gashes of Hampshire pale before the wholesale mass-murder of Surrey's northern borders. Vast areas that once were as beautiful as almost any in England have been buried under the bricks and mortar of the jerry-builder, to lose entirely and for ever their greenery, their woods, and their character. How pitiful is her plight as the desecration of Surrey goes on from year to year !—how truly pitiful we can judge only by exploring the highways and byways of that which is still left to us.

Compare the atrocious Kingston by-pass with the glorious Richmond Park to her north. And in Richmond herself—once known as Sheen, and a royal manor since 1126—look upon the Green with the remnants of the palace where Edward III, Henry VII, and Queen Elizabeth died, the tow-path by the river, and the scene from the Terrace on the hill, and then pass on into the noise and hubbub of the High Street. Visit Reigate with her still lovely common and Colley Hill, and afterwards move a few miles north to Purley and beyond—and if you would accentuate the difference still further, call in on that fascinating little village of Bletchingley which, too, is in the same neighbourhood.

Compare the dignity of Haslemere, Leatherhead and Dorking—where Disraeli lived at nearby Deepdene (now dreadful) and wandered, as we may still, over beautiful Leith Hill, and where Sam Weller ducked Mr. Stiggins in the horse trough at the *King's Head*—compare these two towns with, say, Croydon and Kingston. To think that Kingston was once the Coronation centre of Saxon kings and a Roman settlement ; to think that the inhabitants used to congregate in the parish church here every Michaelmas Eve to crack nuts during the sermon as part of the ceremony of electing her bailiffs ; and that the place was ever able to stage football contests through the streets with all the fury and excitement of the Cornish hurling game, the inflated bladder of a bullock sometimes serving as the ball. Dorking, too, played street football—" camping ", they called it—on Shrove Tuesdays in bygone days. Here the game, in which several hundred would compete, was preceded by a procession through the town, led by three men, each carrying a ball and singing :

Kick away, both Whig and Tory
Wind and water, Dorking's glory.

The town-crier would set the ball rolling, so to speak, and the match would last for four hours.

Still, the desecration has not yet proved entirely fatal. Where Surrey is still pretty she is enchanting—" where she is good she is very very good, but where she is bad she is horrid ". But even in her " good " parts her nearness to London has robbed her of much of that rustic charm that forms so essential a feature of the other counties through which we have passed. The country folk our ancestors knew and loved so well have, for the most part, made way for the City business men,

" Still the finest centre of the kind in the country "—the glasshouse industry in West Sussex.

A hurdle-maker at work in the Sussex woods.

Sussex children learning to cure rabbit-skins.

just as the ponies and traps that, even in my childhood, once moved so peacefully along the little wooded lanes, have been ousted by extravagant-looking cars. The pleasing breath of the horses has been exchanged for the fumes of petrol. Where Dorset gains through being somewhat off the beaten track, Surrey loses through being on it, so that to-day she is the Londoner's countryside more than the countryman's.

But, as I say, in parts she is enchanting. She still has Hindhead, with its Devil's Punchbowl, on the Portsmouth Road, a highway as famous as the Bath Road ; Newland's Corner, with its magnificent views and the " Silent Pool " a little way down the hill on the road to Dorking ; the Hog's Back ; and the western end of the beautiful North Downs that roll on to Kent, on, on right down to Folkestone, Dover, and a little beyond. She still has villages and small towns as good—or nearly so—as any : Friday Street, with its lake and pinewoods, Shere, Gomshall, Abinger Hammer, once a centre for the smelting of iron, Chiddingfold, with its fine old Crown Inn and its elegant period houses clustered around the picturesque green ; Godstone, Ewhurst, with its lych gate leading into the churchyard, Witley, Shamley Green, Cobham, where Matthew Arnold once lived close by, Wotton, the birthplace of John Evelyn, Worplesdon—as pretty as any—Elstead, Egham, and Runnymede, where King John signed Magna Carta, Cut Mill, Frensham with its ponds of a hundred acres, Peperharrow, and many others.

Nor are Dorking and Leatherhead the only of her larger towns to maintain a certain dignity. The development around her outer edge may be lamentable, but Guildford's steep high street, lined on either side with a wealth of fascinating old buildings like the *Lion* and the *Angel*, has not yet forsaken its character. Nor has Godalming, with the stately stone buildings of

Charterhouse School looking down upon her from the hill above. How often as a boy did I run the entire length of that exacting climb for fear of being "locked out" by my house butler! Curious to think that the rough-and-ready street football of such towns as Kingston and Dorking should have given place to Association Football largely through the medium of this school, the idea of "dribbling" the ball at the feet having been devised as a safety measure when the Carthusians, like the Westminsters, were forced to play within the confines of their cloisters. But that was before Charterhouse removed from London last century.

Taking it all round, though, perhaps the noblest of these Surrey towns is Farnham, if only on account of her mass of Georgian architecture and the *Jolly Farmer* inn where Cobbett was born. They still drink their pints at the *Jolly Farmer*, but what, I wonder, would Cobbett say of Surrey now if he could but have his "rural rides" all over again? Things have moved apace since his day.

One thing that, no doubt, would please him would be to see so many of the centuries-old inns he passed on his journeys still standing as survivors of a fast-vanishing past. For Surrey is rich indeed in such places, and we have only to glance at some of the names on their signboards—*The Plough*, *The Running Horse*, *The Sun*, *The Fleece*, *The Cock*, *The Marquis of Granby*, *The Saddler's Arms*, and, of course, *The Jolly Farmer* itself—to realize that the village pub was even more closely linked with bygone country life than with that of our own time.

In the Middle Ages most villages boasted an ale-house, and here the cottagers would drink, dance and make merry in the evening after a heavy day's work on the land. The beer was home-brewed and of a high quality, but the floors were strewn with rushes, and those who slept there usually slept naked. These alehouses achieved an evil reputation as being dirty and the scenes of drunken brawls.

The inns, on the other hand—or " guest houses " as they were termed—were very different. Set up by the Church, mainly in parishes frequented by pilgrims—as in the case of *The George* at Glastonbury—they were, by contrast, clean and comfortable, if few and far between.

As travel increased with the passage of time, so did the number of hostelries. Inns were built at strategic points along the highways, sometimes, as in the case of the crosses, at the junction of four roads ; sometimes along some lonely trackway as a safeguard against any unfortunate wayfarers' being benighted.

What an interesting story could these old inns tell if only their walls could speak—as fascinating as the story of the signs themselves, that beckon us to step into the warmth and comfort within. At first, it seems, this sign of the inn comprised merely a pole with a bundle of hay on the end. Then came the custom for an itinerant knight to have a shield bearing his coat of arms displayed on any house where he had spent a *comfortable* night—a friendly tip to any further gallants who might later seek hospitality on the same road. This practice led to the innkeepers' spending large sums on having the most elaborate signs painted, some of them even going so far as to commission great artists like Hogarth, Millais, or George Morland to carry out the designs, or Jean Tijou—who fashioned much of the magnificent wrought iron work at Hampton Court—to attend to the scrolls and hangings.

Though Surrey can boast no " guest houses " such as the pilgrims once used, we may still visit the little chapel of St. Martha, high on the hill above Chilworth, and the ruins of St. Catherine's, just off the Guildford-

Godalming road, where they stopped and prayed on their journeyings to and from Canterbury.

How delightfully quiet and peaceful stands St. Martha's to-day !—only a little less so than when the pilgrims passed this way. Here, indeed, we may well feel ourselves to be on top of the world as we stand by the little chapel and look down upon eight counties. Surrey, Berkshire, and Middlesex, Oxford and Buckinghamshire, Sussex, Hampshire, and Wiltshire—we can see them all from this fine vantage point. Here, high up on this hill, disturbed in our thoughts only by the song of the birds in the trees or by the soft tread upon the sandy soil of some other as curious as ourselves, here among the graves of men of countless ages the whole romance of the Pilgrim's Way unfolds.

We can picture the foot-sore pilgrims plodding their slow but steadfast course along the ancient track a little below us. All sorts and conditions of men there were : noblemen and peasants, rich visitors from overseas, who had landed at Southampton some days before, lepers from their various isolation colonies. We can picture them all. For the shrine of St. Thomas at Canterbury, towards which they wended, was to eclipse even that of St. Joseph at Glastonbury, attracting sometimes as many as one hundred thousand worshippers in the course of a single year.

As they drew up to the chapel, the lepers would make their way through a special doorway into a section of the building set aside for their exclusive use, so that they could be segregated from the normal congregation and thus minimize the risk of spreading their dreaded disease. The service over, we might, perhaps, have seen one of their number carve their quaint cross upon the masonry of the chapel, before all continued on their way, sustaining themselves, it has been said, with edible snails. And if we could but have awaited their return, we should have noticed that they each now proudly wore a brooch containing a likeness of the head of St. Thomas. Perhaps, too, we should have seen one of them cutting a second cross to link with the first as proof of a mission fulfilled.

It is a popular, though unfounded, belief that John Bunyan was inspired by this Surrey setting when writing *The Pilgrim's Progress*. Was it of Martyr's Hill that he was thinking when he wrote of the " Hill Difficulty " :

> *This hill, though high, I covet to ascend,*
> *The difficulty will not me offend ;*
> *For I perceive the way to life lies here ;*
> *Come, pluck up, Heart ; let's neither faint nor fear.*

Were the rolling hills to the south his " Delectable Mountains ", or the marshes of Shalford his " Slough of Despond " ? Was it the famous Guildford fair that prompted his " Vanity Fair ", or was he describing the one at Shalford ?

Certainly Bunyan would have found plenty to inspire him here, for fairs were once held far and wide in Surrey. Particularly interesting, apart from those of Guildford and Shalford, were the Holyrood Day Onion Fair at Chertsey, and that of Mitcham, which is still held every August when, instead of the glove, an enormous golden key, close on five feet in length, is displayed as the signal that all is well.

Feasts, too, there were in unending number, though perhaps none could ever quite equal that of St. Blase when, every February, solemn high mass would be conducted by the Dominican Friars at Guildford, alms distributed to the poor, and a chain of bonfires lit on every hill top. Guildford was then a wool-producing centre, and in all such places it was once customary for manual work of every description to be brought to a complete standstill on the third day of this month.

How gay and festive was Surrey once ! But, alas, the fine shadows of the past are fast receding under the clouds of modernity ; the old land customs that meant so much to the peasant of old are now no more. Customs of any kind, in fact, are all too rare, though at Addlestone a religious ceremony—that of the election of a Boy Bishop for Childermass—such as, since early Middle Ages, was once a common feature of cathedral cities and grammar schools alike throughout the land, may yet be witnessed.

A strange business : these pseudo-bishops would be chosen from among the choristers, and, throughout the greater part of December, were allowed to wear all the usual episcopal vestments, and, aided by the rest of the choir—each member of which assumed the rôle of another cathedral dignitary—to enjoy many of the rights of a bishop. They could, for instance, dispose of any prebends that fell vacant during their term of episcopacy, while in the event of their death during tenure their parents could claim the right for them to be buried in the cathedral with the full honours normally accorded to a bishop. On the north side of the nave of Salisbury Cathedral is the tomb of one of these youthful ecclesiastics who died " in office ".

One other old custom that is still kept up is the annual Good Friday marbles contest in the forecourt of the Greyhound Inn at Tinsley Green, on the border of Surrey and Sussex. Since time immemorial there has been close rivalry between the men of these two counties. To them Good Friday was ever " Marble Day ", and even before there were such things as marbles they would fight out their battles with stones within the precincts of the parish churches.

Here then, at Tinsley Green, within a stone's throw of Gatwick Airport, we may watch these stalwarts " flipping their alleys " with all the spirit and urgency of their ancestors of three hundred or more years ago. From all corners of both Surrey and Sussex will they come to do battle for tankard and trophy in their four-foot rink. Busmen, farm labourers, and apprentices, they will all be there, a staunch and steadfast crowd. And when the battle is won and the beer has flown fast and free, the results will be sent out to the far ends of the Empire for the benefit of those men who once took part in this time-honoured game in this one small corner of England.

The traditional countryman, as I said, is fast vanishing from the fields and woods of Surrey. But he has not yet entirely disappeared. At such ceremonies as these we shall meet with characters as good as any. A leading light at Tinsley, when last I was there, was a bearded octogenarian who, it appears, divided his life between working in the fields, gulping down ale in the "local", and sleeping the sleep of the just in a flour bin in a wayside barn.

Though, doubtless, he was exceptional in his choice —and it was his choice—of a "bedroom", we shall still find men who are ready to declare that, wherever the wind is on the first day of spring, there will it remain for the next three months; or that the length of the beam cast by the sun into the room of any house on Candlemas Day foretells the worst that may be expected in the way of snow during the coming winter.

Yes, the natives of Surrey may watch their lovely countryside being rent and torn asunder; but, like their counterparts of the West Country, they are not all willing to surrender their old beliefs without a struggle. Only the other day I got chatting with a man who, in all seriousness, bemoaned the fact that had he not been so foolish as to forget to tell his bees of all that was going on in his family circle a certain tragedy would have been averted.

" It was all me own fault, sir," and he shook his head : " I should have told them my son was going overseas. He'd never have been killed then, sir. Not then, he wouldn't ; the bees would have seen to that."

" Do you tell them *everything* ? " I asked.

" Yes, sir, *everything*."

Each morning, and again last thing at night, he confided, he walks solemnly down to his orchard, taps on each of his straw skeps, and proceeds to enumerate all the things that have happened throughout the day and all the plans that he has made for the morrow. Particularly careful is he never to forget to advise them of any death or illness, and at such times as these he will see that they are among the first to be informed, adding pathos to the performance by walking three times round the skeps before imparting the doleful news.

This belief in the power of the bees, like the belief that certain trees—such as the " shrew-ash " trees in Richmond Park—could cure childish ailments if the mother walked around them whispering charms to the rising sun, was once common in country districts, and it is pleasing to find it still persisting here and there in a county so close to the capital.

But then the desecration has *not* yet proved entirely fatal, and, just as we shall, now and again, bump up against some brawny veteran of the fields to remind us of Surrey's departing glory, so too shall we find men still plying some trade that has long brought fame to their district.

No longer can the mill at Mitcham grind down enormous quantities of tobacco leaf to make snuff for the Georgian dandies, but at Compton we may visit the unique picture gallery, to remind us of the time when G. F. Watts ran his famous potters' art guild there.

At Godalming we shall find men still quarrying ston

" A remarkably interesting place "—Tarring.

" *Sussex by the Sea* "—Beachy Head lighthouse.

"Some of the finest Regency architecture in England"—a corner of Hove.

and raising it by an unusual system of planks, while even Croydon—once a centre for private race-meetings and a haunt of Queen Elizabeth—is by no means without her interest. Here have been made some of the finest and noblest bells and clocks in the world. Here were cast the bells for the Rockefeller memorials of Chicago and New York, for the Houses of Parliament in Ottawa, the Wellington war memorial in New Zealand, the Royal Exchange in London, and the cathedrals of Manchester, Rochester, Derry, and elsewhere. To Croydon belongs the honour of casting the largest bell in the British Empire (that of Ottawa), while the two carillons—each containing seventy-two bells, of which one, I am told, weighs more than eighteen tons—for the Rockefeller memorials are the biggest in the world.

It was the monks who first made bells in England, and they were followed by itinerant craftsmen who travelled from place to place, setting up temporary furnaces, and casting the bells in the graveyards of the actual churches for which they were required. No longer are they beaten out from sheets of metal, yet at Croydon we shall watch men working upon almost exactly the same principle, and sometimes by much the same methods, as did those monks of ancient times.

A long and complicated business: not only must elaborate drawings, "strickle boards", and moulds be made before ever work can begin, but, when the bell is eventually cast, the harmonics must all be tuned so that each of the five notes—the "strike", "nominal", "hum", "tierce", and "quint"—is in harmony with the others. An important band, these bell-founders—it would be a sorry day for England if the little parish churches and the noble cathedrals could no longer ring out their peals to summon the people to Christian worship upon the Sabbath. Indeed, in some of the Surrey villages to-day, as in other parts, the very ringing of the bells has been reduced to so fine an art as to merit the continuance of the time-honoured contests between the local teams of ringers. Essentially English in character, the science of "change ringing", with its numerous methods—known variously as "Grandsire Triples", "Stedman Caters", "Bob Royal", "London Surprise", and so on—is one in which these village teams take special pride. The scope is as unending as is the music beautiful. With but thirteen bells, I am told, it is possible to ring no less than 6,227,020,800 changes, though that would take the best of teams as much as four hundred and eighty-one years of continuous ringing to accomplish!

No less important in their way are the walking-stick makers around Witley and Chiddingfold. Nowhere else in the world, they say, is such a colony as this to be found, for nowhere else are sticks deliberately cultivated for the purpose. It is in these Surrey woodlands that the familiar white sticks that guide the blind are grown. But here, too, are made the Service canes, the umbrella handles, the Scotsman's crook, and the shepherd's lambing stick. Hundreds of thousands of all shapes and sizes are sent all over the world from this quiet corner every year.

Ask one of these woodmen about his work, and you will soon see that, what with his manuring and trenching, his smudge fires and his hot sand and steamers, the making of a walking-stick is as full and detailed an industry as any. Ask him about the way he makes his handle, and he will show you how, on the strongest sticks, he grows this at right angles to the stem by uprooting his sapling after two years, and then laying it flat in a trench to allow one of the buds to shoot up and so form a new stem. Once he liked to keep this a closely-guarded secret, but, alas, secrets will out!

Strange how this area has sprung into prominence again in these last hundred years or so. For Chiddingfold was once the focal point of another industry, the birthplace of the English glass-making tradition. It all began when, in 1226, Laurence Vitrearius bought some twenty acres of land close by, set up his furnaces, and, with the aid of a number of Frenchmen and a few local charcoal-burners, proceeded to supply our entire glass needs. So important did little Chiddingfold become, that Edward I later granted the village a special charter and the right to hold Thursday markets and an annual fair in recognition of the part she was playing.

But a word of caution when talking of glass in these parts ; the men of Surrey speak with pride of Chiddingfold, but those of Sussex, on the other hand, contend that it was *their* woods that provided most of the fuel, and *their* charcoal burners who did all the work ! It is the Devon and Somerset cider rivalry all over again. And who shall deny that there is much to be said for the Sussex view ? After all, Chiddingfold is immediately on the border, and for several miles on either side the two counties are as one.

Nine — *Downland Glory*

IN the days of Elizabeth, and long before that, the Weald of Sussex, Surrey, and Kent—that still lovely stretch of woodland that separates the North Downs from the South, and takes in the forests of Ashdown, St. Leonards, Tilgate, Balcombe, and Worth—was once the principal iron-smelting district of England, before ever the North and Midlands rose to their industrial prosperity.

This whole long stretch of something like a hundred and twenty miles, extending in parts to a depth of about thirty miles, was once among the busiest and most important corners of England. Here would men fell the massive oaks—finer than any in the country, it was said, and known as " Sussex Weed "—for the shipbuilders ; here would they work the ironstone from the Wealden clay and smelt it in their furnaces. Here, too, more numerous than elsewhere, would be the " gangs " of charcoal-burners whose fuel fed those furnaces.

In some respects the Weald was once the mainstay of our island security ; so much so that when, in the reign of Elizabeth, a curb was imposed upon the wholesale felling of trees—at the expense of the charcoal-burners, and to the benefit of the shipwrights—Sussex, Surrey, and Kent were exempt from any such restrictions. Indeed, how could it ever have been otherwise, seeing that iron had been worked here at least since the time of the Romans? It was with ships built of Wealden oak and manned with guns of Wealden iron that Drake fought against the Armada, and at Buxted the talk is even yet of how the first cannon was cast there in 1543. Besides, where would the chivalrous knights of the Middle Ages have been but for the Sussex and Kentish armourers?

All over the Weald, then, but especially in Sussex, the iron-masters would be busy. Where there was a suitable stream within sufficiently close proximity of a good deposit, the lord of the manor would have it dammed to provide his hammer pond, until, long before the end of Elizabeth's time, there were close on a hundred and fifty such ponds in Sussex alone. It was the power from these streams that turned the water-wheels and operated the mighty hammers.

The discovery of coal has long robbed the Weald of her past importance; the industrial North and Midlands have taken on where these southern counties left off, the last furnace having put out its fires at Ashburnham in 1825. Still, the iron-masters of old have left their mark upon Sussex in no small way. As with the woolstaplers of Wiltshire, so here shall we come upon many a stately home and church that owes its splendour to the profits accrued by these old-time landlords. Along the highways and byways, too, shall we stop from time to time to ponder the name of some cottage or farmstead, or perhaps of some trackway or hill, whose very name provides a lasting link with this ancient industry. The Hammers, The Stokers, Smokey

Hole, Foundry House, Iron Hill ; these and many others equally fascinating we shall happen upon from time to time.

Many of the quaint tombstones in some of the churchyards are of iron smelted in the Sussex forests, as also are the fire-backs, spits, baskets and " dogs " that still grace many a cottage and manor house. Indeed, as far afield as Spain are to be found splendid examples of ironwork wrought in this once-busy corner of England.

Then again, here and there, we may even yet gaze upon the quiet waters of those ancient hammer ponds. The fumes of the forges have long since given place to the fragrant perfume of the water lilies, and the forests have shrunk to a fraction of their former size, and yet, in essence, these Sussex woodlands remain much the same. To this day—as in Charlton Forest, just north of Goodwood—you will yet occasionally meet with men of the old stock who will delight to talk of phantom riders spurring on their steeds through the sylvan glades as the night grows ever darker, or who will try to convince you that a pin pushed into an ash tree will cure warts. Admire the lilies-of-the-valley with which St. Leonards Forest is carpeted in springtime, and you may well be told that they first took root upon the spots where the noble St. Leonard spilt his blood during a long and gallant tussle with a dragon. The nightingale, it seems, is silent here. Once it sang in these woodlands as merrily as anywhere, until one day a neurotic hermit laid a curse upon the bird, since when it has sung no more. Or so the native of these parts will tell you. But then, Goodwood too has a " Birdless Grove ", I am told. The forests are not yet entirely devoid of their old characters !

As I say, the iron-masters have left their mark in no small way. For it is not only in the *material* relics that we are reminded of the past ; the very mood and temper of her natives have been framed and fashioned around the charcoal-burners' fires and the hammer ponds, and the influence has spread throughout the county.

If to the stranger these quiet Sussex folk often appear unfriendly, it is only long centuries of isolation that have made them so. In reality they are as kind and friendly as any, and their somewhat aloof manner is but a cloak with which to hide their inward shyness. For when the Wealden forest was in its heyday, Sussex, like Cornwall, was virtually a land apart. Once almost entirely covered by forest, her only roads were but little better than quagmires of sticky clay, along which only the foolish would wish to travel. A busy county within, it was, nevertheless, given a wide berth from without. But even within all was by no means plain sailing : Defoe tells of seeing a team of six oxen being called in to draw " a lady of very good quality " to church when the horses were unable to shift her coach. The oxen were certainly a god-send in this county, used alike for ploughing and moving windmills bodily, as at Brighton.

Then, too, the position has only been aggravated by the frequent invasions, and threats of invasion, that have kept the natives on their guard for something like two thousand years. The Romans, the Normans, and the French, all have landed upon the coast of Sussex in their time. Chichester, with her magnificent Gothic market cross set at the junction of four main roads, and the stately cathedral close by, was, under her older name of Regnum, a Roman port of entry, standing upon the famous Stane Street, which to-day stretches from Portsmouth, through Chichester and Halnaker, and so to a downland track to Bignor. And at Bignor is a Roman villa, with its fine pavements still in a splendid state of preservation, laid bare for all to see.

Remember, too, it was on Sussex soil that the Battle of Hastings was fought, on the spot where now stands Battle Abbey ; at Bosham that King Harold embarked for Normandy before all the troubles began.

Yet even after the Conquest, these stalwarts of Sussex could not relax their vigil. Philip of Spain, Napoleon, the Kaiser, and Hitler—to say nothing of the many French raiding-parties—have each, in their time, given them, like their neighbours of Kent, much food for thought. " Look ye well to the defence of Sussex," rang out Drake's Armada warning, and in many parts of the county—especially around Rye and Winchelsea—the cottagers will point to the gnarled and twisted beams upon the walls and ceilings of their homes, and tell you that they were salvaged from the ships of that once proud Spanish Armada ; ships that were battered to pieces along the coasts of Sussex and Kent. And on the beaches themselves are the remains of the Martello Towers that were set up for purposes of defence when, in later years, Napoleon was running riot.

In Sussex to-day we may talk with men whose ancestors stood guardian over the little towns and villages in those far-off days, just as they themselves have stood at arms in the very same fields and lanes twice in the present century. In one or two instances they remain the proud possessors of ancient privileges that were granted to their forebears by grateful kings and queens of long ago.

The people of Tarring, for instance—a village now absorbed into the Borough of Worthing—are even yet exempt from serving on juries by lawful rights granted to their ancestors by Queen Elizabeth. Nor is this their only charter. In the Middle Ages, when markets were of the first importance, and when the fair was a function not to be missed, the flower of Tarring's manhood used to set out for the markets of Steyning and Chichester, many miles away. At such times, French pirates would elect to raid the coast and plunder the village. As a result, Henry VI saw fit to grant them the right to hold their own market, on condition that it was not allowed to interfere with the regular fairs already long-established in other parts. Nor is that all. During the time of the Armada, the local church was used as a look-out tower for signalling messages concerning the movements of the Spanish fleet ; a fact which, to this day, is commemorated by flying the White Ensign from its flagstaff on state occasions. I believe that it is the only parish church in England to fly a naval flag. Whether, in fact, it is really privileged to do so seems extremely doubtful. But, no matter, it has fluttered at the mast-head during the lifetime of many generations, and doubtless it will continue to do so until it is worn out, which, however, may not be long hence.

A remarkably interesting place, Tarring, it was from here that the Henty family set off after the Battle of Waterloo to help found the Australian and New Zealand sheep industry ; here that the first plough ever to break the soil of Victoria was forged ; here that, centuries before Thomas à Becket, whose old palace still stands in part, planted the first fig tree which he brought with him from Italy in 1162. Though only the withered stump of that original tree remains, all around are flourishing fig gardens that have sprung from it.

As I say, the people of Sussex are *not* unfriendly ; they are merely shy and reserved. And who will deny that they have had good reason ? Get to know them, and you will find them as staunch and true as any. You will find, moreover, that, like the very downs, they differ both in speech and outlook, from east to west. If in the more populated eastern half of the county they sometimes appear rather " commercial ", in the west the pleasing influence of the large estates is still, happily, greatly in evidence.

They have certainly had much with which to contend, these Sussex folk. Quite apart from the question of invasion, the coast has been a perpetual source of worry since earliest times. Vast areas of land that once was Sussex now lie submerged and forgotten beneath the sea. Thousands of years ago, it is said, the coastline between Selsey Bill and Beachy Head was all but straight where now it forms an immense bay. Year by year the waves carve their way farther and farther inland until, in course of time, whole villages have gradually disappeared ; whole forests too. Around Selsey way, fishermen still talk of going to fish in the " park ", and beneath the waters over which their sailing boats—smart little craft, known locally as " Selsey crabbers "—will travel lie the remains of the old Selsey Cathedral, which served the Sussex diocese before ever the See moved to Chichester. A fisherman once told me that, on a still day, he could quite distinctly hear the muffled sound of the bells from the cathedral below the water. Maybe !

But the havoc goes on from year to year. It is only about a century since the little village of Middleton-on-Sea surrendered her original church to the waves. Indeed, an elderly native of these parts was able to tell me vivid stories of fragments of the church washed ashore by the high tides. Great times, he said, they were, the skulls from the submerged graveyard coming in particularly handy for football matches on the beach as soon as the waters receded again.

" We do say round here that the old village was destroyed as a punishment for the amount of smuggling that used to go on along this stretch of coast," he told me. "*Everyone* had a hand in it in some way or other. My old dad, why, he used to earn fourpence a time for carrying kegs of rum across several miles of fields to the various hide-outs. Now and again he'd be given a drop for himself too."

Middleton was not exceptional. Birling Gap, Rye, Pevensey, and many others, were once haunts that would have made even the Cornishmen stare in amazement, while along the courses of the rivers Arun, Adur, and Rother are small cottages and inns where the casks would be hidden in secret cellars. In a few of these cottages the special windows, through which the smugglers could look out without being seen themselves, still remain. Stern days those were; woe betide the "informers". Indeed, the harsh treatment meted out to any who "spilt the beans" must undoubtedly have contributed to the reticence of the Sussex folk. One such offender against the "smugglers' code", for instance, was whipped to death at Slindon. Such brutality was deliberately practised to ensure freedom from molestation and prosecution. Since smuggling was rife amongst all sections of the community, the wise were discreet in their words and action, and were careful to keep out of the way when a "run" was on, for fear of being called as witnesses. To most, the duties appeared as a deliberate infringement of their rights, and smuggling was practised accordingly.

"Has any of the coast disappeared in *your* lifetime?" I asked my friend.

"Lor' bless me soul, yes! Why, almost up to the outbreak of the 1914 war, I was ploughing the land under what is now Pagham Harbour."

Still, if the sea has eaten into the western end of the county, in the extreme east it is the other way about. Winchelsea, once a Cinque Port, now stands—like

Romney over the Kentish border—dignified and stately a mile or two inland, while the lonely Romney Marshes, of which part are in Sussex and part in Kent, were once completely under water. Here, perhaps three miles or more from the nearest hard road, men and women now drive the plough, harrow, and drill for the first time since its reclamation many centuries back. Where fish once swam, sheep now graze, and corn ripens into gold. So that what Sussex has lost at one end she has made up at the other.

Alas, it is not only the sea that has proved a source of trouble. Ever since the Georgians found that to brave the waves at that quaint little fishing village of Brighthelmstone—since shortened to Brighton—was as health-giving and enjoyable as to take the waters at Bath, Cheltenham, or Tunbridge Wells, the builder has run amok upon the coast. Once-lovely villages have gradually risen into the great seaside resorts we know to-day. So that now there is hardly an unspoilt stretch along the whole coastline from Hampshire to Kent, while such places as Portslade, Peacehaven, and Lancing stand out as hideous examples of development run riot ; as proofs of the menace before us.

Not that the resorts themselves are without their interest. Far from it. In Brighton and Hove we may still wander through whole streets and squares of some of the finest Regency architecture in England, as also may we yet visit the house in the Old Steine where Mrs. Fitzherbert once lived, and the curious Royal Pavilion the Prince Regent loved so well. How Cobbett hated it ; so do I ; but then that is purely a question of taste.

As we stroll through those lovely squares and in and out of the " lanes and twittens ", the ghost of the " First Gentleman " is ever beside us. And to many these old associations mean more than the piers, the sea front, or the Aquarium. For the people of Brighton

—the admirers of Brighton, that is—do not quickly forget the man who brought her fame, and, in the Regency Society, they have a body bent on the permanent preservation of the town's noblest architecture. Would that they would extend their activities into a nation-wide organization ! Such buildings must *never* be ruthlessly pulled down to make room for enormous blocks of flats, as some of the " planners " would wish. They are a precious and all too rare heritage that can never be replaced, and there is no conceivable reason why they should not continue to serve present-day needs.

Strange to think that Brighton was once a tiny fishing village ! Times have changed since Charles II arrived here one night to sup at a local inn, while arrangements were made with a man named Tettersall —who was afterwards made a captain, and who lies buried in St. Nicholas Churchyard—to carry him in his boat to France ; times have changed since the Regent himself employed his own " dipper ", who would accompany him into the sea, and make certain that the royal body kept always within safe distance of the shore. Times have changed . . . and yet, the " fisherman's quarter " has not quite shaken off the dust of the past.

Here it is still customary for certain of the fisherfolk to get out their skipping-ropes every Good Friday, as they have done since the Middle Ages, when skipping, for some reason or other, was regarded as a religious ceremony. It is still customary for them to take to sea buns baked on that day as a safeguard against disaster.

At Hastings, too—where the commoners were once empowered by law to break down the principal tenement of a bailiff who absented himself from duty—the fishermen, whose nets and boats are regularly blessed as of old, delight to run their strange Winkle Club.

It all began, I gather, just before the Boer War, when some fifteen fishermen, feeling a little bored with life, got together and decided to form a society. Subscription was to be a penny a week, and the idea was that every member should produce a fresh winkle when challenged by a fellow member to " winkle up ". Failure to do so meant a fine of twopence. As might be expected, quite a sum was raised from these and other fines ; sufficient, in fact, to provide for an annual dinner of bread-and-cheese with a pint of beer per head. As time went on, so the fame of the club and their dinners spread, until now many famous people all over the world, including at least one member of the Royal Family, are numbered among its patrons.

Indeed, one of the fishermen, who played no small part in forming this unique club in the first place, told me proudly that the funds have long since reached such proportions that every Christmas they are able to provide a dinner for something like two thousand children as well. The members' wives do most of the catering, and the children march through the streets of Hastings to the accompaniment of the Winkle Club Band. After dinner they are entertained and given presents.

The members' dinner, however, is still what really matters, and for this there is no limit to the spread. Twelve legs of pork, 140 lbs. of beef, vegetables of every class and description, and an almost unending flow of beer would not have been considered untoward in the pre-war days of plenty.

Hardly less interesting is Worthing, where John Selden was born at Salvington, now in the borough, and where Richard Jefferies lies buried. Here it was that the great glasshouse industry—not only of England but also of Belgium, Holland, and the Channel Islands—took seed in the middle years of last century. And West Sussex, along a belt stretching from Lancing to Chichester, is still the finest centre of the kind in the country, where tomatoes, grapes, beans, peaches, cucumbers, mushrooms, and many other such crops are cultivated by artificial means upon a prodigious scale. Moreover, Worthing is still the growers' " capital ".

It was the Great Exhibition of 1851 that gave birth to the idea, it appears. When the Prince Consort arranged to have his " beautiful glasshouses " dismantled and carted from Hyde Park to Sydenham, for re-erection as the Crystal Palace, a local doctor, whose name has been lost, bought some of the glass and built a special greenhouse in which to grow grapes for his patients. A revolutionary suggestion, it worked well, and the doctor seems to have done as well for himself as for his patients. His vines flourished as no outdoor crops had ever done before. Needless to say, he found a ready market for his produce ; so much so that a wily schoolmaster, one George Beer, who had been secretly watching the experiment with the keenest interest, soon set to work designing bigger and better houses—enormous affairs that became the laughing stock of the district.

Encouraged by his instant success, it was not long before the schoolmaster turned his attention to the indoor cultivation of " love apples ", or, as they have since become known, tomatoes. Despite his efforts at secrecy, news of Beer's venture soon leaked out, with the result that France, Holland, and Belgium were soon sending apprentices to Worthing to learn the tricks of the trade.

An elderly grower, whose grandfather was in the industry almost from the start, once told me that he could well remember his father proudly donning his frock coat and top hat to drive his horse and cart to the station to catch the special fruit train with his tomatoes.

Manures in those days, although as important as now, were regarded in rather a different light.

"Judged them by the smell, they did—the more potent the better," my friend assured me. "Offals and blood would be collected from the slaughter-house, and live sprats gathered from the beaches. Some of these sprats we would eat for our breakfast, but the rest would be mixed with the blood and offals and left to rot."

And there they would remain until no one could stand the smell any longer, when the whole concoction would be turned into the ground.

Times have changed since then, and perhaps it is as well. To-day the industry is a highly scientific one, giving employment to many thousands of men and women of all ages. Growers now spend as much as £200 an acre on having their land sterilized, while some go so far as to "inject" every square yard of soil with a special chemical designed to rid it of "undesirables".

The growing of food under glass is a complicated business in that the grower has always to keep pace with the weather and with the season of the year. His houses are fitted with hot water pipes controlled by a furnace, and with windows that can be opened to varying degrees; and I have seen men go round their houses no less than three times within as many hours to make some adjustment that will ensure the maintenance of an even temperature.

Yes, there is plenty of interest in these seaside towns. Shoreham furnished twenty-six ships and three hundred and thirty-nine seamen for the Royal Fleet in the time

" From then until picking-time, all will be at work "—in the Kentish hopfields.

" The ancient Admiralty Court still holds session in a barge every July "—at Rochester.

of Edward III, and Littlehampton was a cross-Channel port before ever Newhaven rose to prominence.

Even so, I sometimes feel that it is a pity that *Sussex by the Sea* should have become the county's favourite song. For to me her beauty lies not upon the coast but inland—upon the Weald, and upon those lovely South Downs (wooded to the west of the River Adur, more barren to the east, yet kindly everywhere) that roll on and on in gentle folds for something like eighty miles from beyond the Hampshire borders to Eastbourne ; those downs where the lights of beacons once gave warning of approaching foes, and the bonfires acclaimed the coronation of kings, and where, by Cissbury Ring, men made tools of flint before ever the iron deposits were dreamed of ; those downs with their two famous landmarks, Chanctonbury Ring and the " Long Man of Wilmington ", and their ancient windmills dotted about each on some vantage point as motionless relics of an age that is past.

If Cobbett disliked the Royal Pavilion he certainly found plenty to please him here :

> I have seen no wretchedness in Sussex and as to the villages in the South Downs, they are beautiful to behold. . . . I saw with great delight a pig in almost every labourer's home. The houses are good and warm ; and the gardens some of the very best that I have seen in England.

Another thing that Cobbett noted with pleasure was the friendly relationship that invariably existed between landowners and cottagers. And time has not caused that spirit to wear thin. Cobbett's description is as apt as ever : those downland villages are still beautiful to behold.

How picturesque and snug they nestle in or around those downs to-day : South Harting ; Didling, with its " phantom choir boy ", whose treble voice, a former vicar told me, has more than once been heard accompanying an all-male congregation ; Steyning, now just a fascinating little market town, but once among the most important places in England ; Heyshott, where Richard Cobden was born ; Fittleworth, where the smiths still ignite gunpowder in their anvil, as they have done since the Armada, to announce the end of hostilities to the more distant downland hamlets ; and Ditchling, long noted for its gooseberries, with the heavily-beamed house where Anne of Cleves whiled away her time after Henry VIII had finished with her, and where a colony of craftsmen are endeavouring to revive an interest in the arts and crafts.

The list seems unending. For we must not miss Cuckfield, on the edge of the Weald, with its hammer ponds and memories of Harrison Ainsworth and Shelley ; Groombridge ; Slindon, where Stephen Langton died, proud in the thought that he had been largely responsible for causing King John to sign Magna Carta ; Bury ; Amberley, beloved of artists ; Washington ; Alfriston, as famous for its apples as its age-old pilgrims' inn, *The Star*, where, incidentally, the natives still like to think that King Alfred burnt his cakes in this corner of Sussex rather than in Somerset ; East Dean (the one near Eastbourne), Ebernoe, Goodwood, or a whole host of others equally enchanting.

Gone are the days when Goodwood races meant a feast of entertainment in all the great houses for a week or more, and when the shops of Chichester would overflow with succulent dripping, the residue from these stately homes. Great times they were ! For whole weeks beforehand the district for miles around would be all agog. A furnished house within easy approach of the course might well fetch a hundred guineas or more in race week. Special police were drafted to Goodwood at such times, and on race-day water carts would be called in from near and far to lay the dust of the flint roads in the path of the carriages of the gentry. Indeed, for that week, the way to Goodwood was only a little less busy than the way to Brighton, with the innkeepers of Chichester working as fast and furiously as those of Crawley, the great stopping-place on the Brighton road.

Gone are those days. Yet Goodwood, with its famous Trundle Hill, where tradition has it that the golden calf lies buried, is, in parts, as beautiful as ever.

Fast disappearing, too, are the labourers' pigs that Cobbett was so overjoyed to see. Only at Ebernoe, a little to the north of Petworth, are they still in evidence to a really marked degree. But then Ebernoe is nearly unique.

Here men still work and live in much the same way as did their mediæval ancestors, clinging to ancient lore and shunning modern progress. They live in the past; they think in the past; and they are content to put up with some of the inconveniences of the past. In fact, they constitute the next thing to the self-supporting village community such as once existed all over England from the Middle Ages down to the advent of machinery at the turn of the eighteenth century. For Ebernoe folk live by the land, and, in Lord Leconfield, still have their lord of the manor. They retain their common rights as of old, and each man has his measure of land, comprising anything up to twenty acres, no matter what his job. Together they keep their cattle, grow their crops, and harvest their hay. The swineherd may no longer drive the pigs into the woods to feed upon the fallen acorns, but most villagers still like to salt, cure, and smoke the animals in their cottage homes. Some keep a cow or a goat in their back garden, too, and all have their poultry. They make their own cider and wines, brew their own beer, and have their mill for grinding the corn. Just as every mediæval village had its own " headman " to organize social life, so Ebernoe has her " king " to-day.

At Ebernoe the radio is looked upon askance ; the telephone is regarded as a quite unnecessary evil ; well-water, oil-lamps, and candles yet prevail ; the nearest bus passes twice a day along a road three miles away ; and, of course, there is no such thing as a shop or inn. The inhabitants are cut off from the rest of England both geographically and spiritually, but they would not have it otherwise.

It is on the village green, then, that social life really gets into its stride. Here the villagers celebrate a centuries-old custom—the Horn Fair—every summer, when a sheep is killed and roasted on a spit in one corner while eleven of their stalwarts engage some neighbouring team at cricket. The sheep is put to roast at eight in the morning, and the older folk take it in turns to baste the animal. At one-thirty all settle down to feast upon it, and, at the end of the match, the horns are awarded to the batsman who has made the highest score for the winning side.

In the evening there will be fun and merriment, too, as the old folk mingle with the young men and maidens and dance upon the green until midnight. No one seems to know the origin of this ancient fair ; no one greatly cares. Possibly it is a survival of the ancient " boon day " feasts of the Middle Ages, when, at the end of the work on the demesne, a sheep would be brought on to the field in full view of the commoners. If it stopped to graze it could be claimed by the peasants ; if it escaped, it was lost to them.

Incidentally, if ever you should have occasion to ask the time in Ebernoe, beware ! They carry their independence to their clocks and watches, refusing to alter them for summer time. Surely enough, before ever he gives you an answer, the native will first look you up and down, and remark :

" Now let me see, you don't come from these parts, so your time won't be quite the same as mine."

Whereupon he will start his calculations.

I once chaffed an elderly inhabitant about this reticence to recognize summer time.

" There baint no such thing," he scoffed. " The old sun be the only thing what gives us the time, so we goes by him here. If the rest of England likes their clocks and watches wrong, then, dammit, there be only their selves to thank ! "

But if the cottagers' pigs are dwindling in numbers, so, alas, are the downland sheep—horned in the west, but " polled " in the east—whose wool and mutton have long brought fame to the downs. The friendly bobtail sheep dog—ever a pet in the home, but as reliable as you make them in the fields—and the old-time shepherd, with his special smock and crook, are characters of the past, just as the soft tinkle of the sheep-bells is sweet music we shall hear no more. Flocks that once numbered perhaps a thousand can now be counted in hundreds : foreign imports have spelt their doom. The life of a shepherd is too hard and lonely for the modern generation ; the smock has become but a museum piece.

So with the cattle, whose bulls have done so much to improve the herds of the Argentine and of South Africa.

And yet, for all that, the downland scene never alters greatly ; at least, not materially. The people of Sussex are too proud of their heritage for that, and are ever at pains to preserve it. Not only have the county councils of both East and West Sussex formulated protective planning schemes, restricting the amount of building according to the various heights, but more than a thousand downland dwellers, including many influential landowners, keep constant watch over their destiny in the form of the Society of Sussex Downsmen.

Many a battle have these men and women fought and won against the would-be despoilers of our fair countryside ; against jerry-builders, whose first thought has been for money rather than for beauty.

A noble body, their aims and duties are manifold. As an instance, they have divided the entire stretch of the downs into eleven zones, with a district officer in charge of each. In these zones regular patrols are organized on horseback, cycle, and foot, to ensure that no damage is done either to the wild flowers or saplings, and that motorists respect the byelaw that makes it an offence to drive their cars more than fifteen yards on to the turf.

But perhaps their greatest achievements lie in the work of the special " trust ". For not only have they prevented much building from taking place by buying up threatened land, but, in cases where houses have been recognized to be necessary, they have often been instrumental in persuading architects to design ones that are at least in tone with their setting. Even the colour of a telephone box on a village green has been altered at their request ; electricity cables have been taken underground instead of overhead ; designs of shops have been modified ; a road scheme has been diverted to avoid shaking the foundations of an ancient church ; unsightly notice boards have been removed.

Moreover, the work of these Sussex Downsmen is stirring the imagination of others, so that many villages, too, now boast their own preservation societies.

Yes, the men and women of Sussex are proud of their downs and are ready to work for them. If only other counties would look to their future in like manner !

Essentially a farming county, in many of the village schools the children are now being encouraged to run their own small-holdings, which, in turn, also form the backbone of their classroom education. Thus, from earliest childhood the boys and girls of Sussex are given a rural bias. Not only are they taught the practical side of life in the fields, but indoors, too, they are given the opportunity to study the " whys and wherefores " of the many things they have seen for themselves in hedgerow, garden, and farm alike.

As an instance, a typical arithmetic problem now set in one school that I visited recently reads : " If lime is used at the rate of six ounces per square yard, how much would be needed for an allotment ninety feet long by thirty feet wide ? " Similarly, other questions dealt with the feeding of rabbits, and with the bacon value of pigs.

Classroom English is taught in much the same way, oral lessons taking the form of talks on certain aspects of farming or craftsmanship. In some cases a carefully planned three-year syllabus, designed to teach them about the soil, plants, and œcology, and about the life of animals, birds, and insects, has been adopted.

Weaving and spinning, basketry, smithing, carpentry and turnery, the curing and making-up of skins, leatherwork, pottery, and so on, all take their place in the school calendar, while rural rallies, too, are staged from time to time to enable the children to see the village craftsmen and farmers at work.

Nor is it only in the schools that these old traditions are being fostered. In company with the West Sussex Church and Countryside Association—an undenominational body, sponsored to a great extent by the Bishop of Chichester, I believe—the local Young Farmers' Clubs are fostering a renewed interest in the church festivals of Plough Monday, Rogation-tide, Lammas-tide, and Harvest-tide. At these festivals the young farmers themselves take all the speaking parts, while on Plough Monday a plough is drawn by them before the entrance to Chichester Cathedral, there to be blessed, together with their county banner, by the Bishop himself, after the manner of the beloved St. Richard of Chichester.

More than any other county, perhaps—with the possible exception of Devon—is Sussex mindful of the fact that, if England is to retain the fertility of her soil and maintain a balanced agriculture, her sons must continue to follow in their fathers' footsteps with that same traditional regularity : a position that can be achieved only by moulding them in the spirit and atmosphere of the fields from earliest childhood.

And in Sussex, happily, tradition dies hard. In the fields and woodlands, upon the smooth turfed down-land slopes, and in the little village workshops, we shall find men following the same calling that their fore-fathers pursued in the very same spots centuries back. Their link with the past is as unbroken as their love of the soil and all that it stands for.

Old industries fade and die as their need grows less and less. No longer is marble excavated at Petworth, Plaistow, Kirdford, Streat, Ditchling, and Plumpton, to provide materials for the little parish churches and for Canterbury Cathedral ; no longer do they flake stones at Horsham to the same extent to provide those lovely roofing slabs that are such a feature of some of the old Sussex manors, or knap flints with which to build the cottages. A common sight was the roadside flint-cracker once. In summer time the hedges would be all white with their dust, and it is said that the reason why so many of the cottagers of to-day are still averse to opening their windows even on the hottest day is simply that they have not yet forgotten those times of everlasting dusting and sweeping up.

The truffle-hunters have left the woods of Patching and of Goodwood, as also have the glass-blowers deserted Kirdford, the needle-makers Chichester, and the salt-workers Appledram.

Old industries fade and die . . . and yet in Sussex, more than anywhere, shall we find men still plying the trades their ancestors knew and loved so well. In the woods and copses men still make hurdles and sheep-feeding-cages as of yore. Blacksmiths, potters, and charcoal-burners, wheelwrights, saddlers, tanners and lime-burners, ladder and rake-makers—we shall meet them all, though their number dwindles decade by decade. So, too, at Robertsbridge shall we find the cricket-bat makers, and at East Hoathly and Hurstmonceux, the " truggers ". For in private garden and on farm alike, the all-wood trug basket, made of strips of ash and chestnut—all carefully split, seasoned and steamed to shape—is held in high esteem.

It is from such countrymen as these that we shall learn the real spirit of Sussex to-day ; from their speech —as from that of the few remaining old-time downland shepherds—that we may yet glean some odd word or phrase that was once common in these parts but which, for the most part, has long since been forgotten.

The motto of the Sussex countryman is still " we wunt be druv ", just as " sure*lie* " is yet his favourite way of expressing either agreement or surprise. " 'Ackle ", too, is a word of which he is particularly fond ; one that he will employ as much to describe a piece of farm machinery that fails to work harmoniously with his tractor as to tell of a man who fails to live harmoniously with his wife.

" There 'tis, they don't 'ackle," he will say, shaking his head resignedly. " Still, best let bide."

Incidentally, if you want to avoid being dubbed a " furriner ", be chary how you pronounce the Sussex place names. To talk of *Sea*ford, *Kird*ford or *Ard*ingly —as do most people—is entirely wrong ; always must the emphasis be placed upon the *last* syllable.

As you wander over the downs and lanes of Sussex, you will meet with all sorts and conditions of men and women. Most unusual, perhaps, is the little religious sect around Loxwood, Northchapel, Warnham, Kirdford, and Chichester, who hustle and bustle about their work in Victorian dress, adopting the old-world courtesy that went with crinolines and bone collars.

Founded by a London shoemaker named John Sirgood, they glory in the name of the " Cokelers ", by dint of the fact, some say, that large quantities of cocoa used to be brought from London to provide drink for their meetings at a time when such a beverage was unobtainable in Sussex. Their aim, it seems, is to help their neighbours according to the teachings of the Bible, and to run communal produce stores. A delightful band, these Cokelers, they have certainly brought much happiness to their district, and they are a joy to meet. Quite possibly they constituted the first co-operative movement in the country.

Never so superstitious as those of the West Country, the people of Sussex nevertheless still cling to certain of their legends and customs. Ask a native of Midhurst why his town has fallen from grace to such an extent that it is now controlled by a parish council, when once it was a borough boasting two Members of Parliament ; ask him this and, most likely, he will shrug his shoulders and, pointing in the direction of the beautiful Cowdray Park nearby, will say :

" There 'tis. 'Tis the curse of Cowdray."

And thereon, around the ruined remains of Cowdray House, hangs a story. Built in 1530 by the Earl of

Southampton, and considered to be one of the finest houses of the period, it became at once a popular haunt of the highest in the land, from kings and princes downwards. Among its most frequent visitors was a particular court favourite of Henry VIII—one Sir Anthony Browne—who immediately held high revel there, and turned away the monks from the door with insults.

As might be expected, the monks resented all this ostentation and ridicule, and so their words, " the house of the despoiler shall perish by fire and water ", proclaimed the lasting curse. And so it came to pass. Sir Anthony eventually became the rightful owner, and, though the mansion was never to be destroyed in his lifetime, it was ravaged by fire at the end of the eighteenth century at a moment when the eighth Viscount Montague, who had inherited the property, was abroad. The Viscount was on the point of returning home to be married, when one of the workmen, preparing the mansion for the wedding, left some rubbish burning in the north gallery. Nor did the curse end with the fire. A week later the Viscount was drowned while trying—against orders—to shoot the Laufenburg rapids in a frail boat. One tragedy followed another. Five months after that, a cousin, who succeeded him, died. Whereupon a woman inherited the family fortunes, only to learn that her two sons had been drowned off Bognor.

A pleasing place, Midhurst, with its fine main street, its grammar school, its stocks, and the funny little chemist shop where H. G. Wells once rolled pills, broke a dozen soda-water siphons during a friendly brawl with an errand-boy, dusted coloured water-bottles, and learnt to serve patent medicines. They still sell " Mr. Wells's cough mixture " here. But then they still do lots of things in Midhurst—they still toll the bell at midday on Shrove Tuesday, for instance, to remind the housewives to put on the pancakes, just as they still ring the curfew in memory of a man who lost his way in these parts far back in the Middle Ages. At Chichester, too, the Curfew is rung daily, the number of tolls varying according to the day of the month.

But to return to the legends. At Bosham, that fascinating little yachting centre ("Happy Bosham", the villagers call it) where King Canute's daughter was drowned in the moat, and where her ashes lie buried inside the church—at Bosham they will tell you a legend of bells that will outshine anything that Kintbury may have to offer.

One morning, the tale runs, there sailed up Bosham Channel a fleet of Norsemen bent on attacking and plundering the village. They landed, sacked the place, and made off with the tenor bell. After appealing in vain to the pirates to return it, the monks proceeded to ring a peal from those that were left as a sign of their gratitude that at least their lives had been spared. But, strange to tell, the stolen bell at once moved in sympathy. Then, lo and behold, it fell through the bottom of the ship. Eventually a team of pure white heifers, together with a brand new bell-rope, were brought into action in one great salvage operation. But it was all in vain; the rope rent in two at the crucial moment, due, it is said, to the fact that one of the wretched animals was found to harbour a single black hair in its tail.

Not even the vicar would care to decry such a story: "The bell," he writes, "remains to this day where it sank, but it cannot be silenced. Beneath the tidal waters its lament is heard to harmonize with its sister bells."

At Lyminster, too—where no one seems quite sure

how to spell the name of the village—they will tell you a story of a knight and a dragon and a bottomless pit, or " Knuckler Hole ", as they will call it.

Then, of course, there is the legend of the *Labour in Vain* inn at Westergate, and its queer sign depicting a white woman vainly endeavouring to scrub a black baby white. A previous owner, it seems, went with his wife to the tropics. The wife was unexpectedly called home, but no sooner had she returned than she gave birth to a black son. Fearing her husband's wrath, she at once set to work with her scrubbing brush. But it was all in vain. When at last the house became an inn, the landlord, a man with a sense of humour, named the pub after this strange story.

As I say, some of the time-honoured customs still survive here and there. Every February, on the evening of the Monday nearest to the full moon, a group of farmers and others around Arundel way will meet at an inn within the shadows of the castle to hold their annual dinner, whereat, as the drink flows free, they will talk about things they have never done and arrange plans that they will never pursue. They are members of the local Society for Prosecuting Felons, Thieves, and Other Miscreants ; the last survivors of the parish police forces such as once operated in most country districts before the time of Sir Robert Peel. In the days of the cattle-rustlers they were all-important, all-powerful too. Not for thirty years or more have they brought anyone to justice, yet they still display their handbills around the town, offering tempting rewards of anything from ten pounds for a murderer to two pounds for a petty thief.

More serious, perhaps, is the office of Tenant of the Tolls at Petworth, where, in Leconfield House—famous for its magnificent art collection—lives the county's lord-lieutenant. Every time a hawker sells fish in the streets of this ancient town, it means, by centuries-old rights, an extra penny in the pocket of the " Tenant " ; and when vegetables are sold from a barrow of a Saturday morning, the toll is worth double. Petworth's unofficial " mayor ", his name is " law " both in the square and on the common. Many a tale will he tell you of fights with gypsies on the common. But that was in the old days—he has long since proved his might. Even the police, I gather, hesitate to act in square or on common without first having " a word with the Tenant ".

But then, that may well be because it is he who is largely responsible for organizing the seven-hundred-year-old fair ; and no one would wish to see anything go wrong in that direction. For Fair Day is the day of days at Petworth, just as Whit-Monday is the great occasion at South Harting, and November 5 at Lewes and Rye, both long famous for their bonfire nights, with the burning of effigies of Guy Fawkes and the Pope, firework-displays, and religious services. How deep the bitterness of religious persecution bites !—in this ceremony, the people of Lewes still remember those harmless country folk who were burnt at the stake in Tudor times for following their Protestant faith.

Strange, how quickly the scene becomes transformed at South Harting every Whit-Monday ! Where all had been serene and quiet the night before, the little village is all agog on this one day of the year, as one of England's last-surviving friendly societies proceeds to prove that " club day " is by no means a thing of the past in these parts.

Scarcely have the last hours of darkness passed, than a little group of men will be busily decorating the old *White Hart* with beech boughs. On to the square they will then pass, there to set up the largest bough of all, which they will lovingly adorn with streamers of red, white and blue. By the time that all is set and ready, and the members have paid their subscriptions, it will be time for lunch. After which will come the procession. From the steps of the old inn some doughty veteran will call the roll. At once the standard-bearers take their place at the head ; next comes the band and, behind them, the " rank and file ", each proudly wearing a club rosette and carrying a peeled hazel-stick as a symbol, some say, of the days when the Canterbury pilgrims carried staves.

Slowly—though somewhat noisily—the procession will pass through the village, down to the square and back again, and so up to the church to listen to a sermon from the rector. And woe betide the man who shirks the procession, and, instead, stays gulping beer at the bar ; surely enough the stewards will be hounding him down, ready to collect a shilling for his negligence !

Not all, of course, can attend. Down in the baker's oven in the square, one man will be " basting the roast " while in the *White Hart* itself another will be equally busy attending to the silverside and vegetables. Then, too, there will be the seventy-two gallons of beer to look after. For club day without its feast would be unthinkable. They do things in a big way in this little Sussex village. Here is a menu that may well make the " Winklers " of Hastings sit up : six yards of suet pudding, three gammons, 40 lbs. of veal, with a like quantity of salt beef, 14 lbs. of top side, a couple of legs of pork, and an unending supply of home-grown vegetables—good stuff, all of it !

As the procession returns, men will emerge from all quarters, wheeling their hand-trucks or carrying bowls, each proudly bringing forth the dishes for which they personally have been responsible.

A happy day is club day ; the day on which all will

like to test their voices in song and merriment to the full. And these Sussex folk are by no means lacking in traditional songs and dances. " Over the Sticks " and " Bonny Breast Knot " ; " The Old Sow ", " The Triumph ", and the " Shepherd Boy " ; " The Sussex Sheep-Shearing Song " and the " Littlehampton Collier Lads "—are all still in evidence, though, alas, fast fading out. Nor are they lacking in their plays : at Boxgrove and in one or two other villages, we may yet watch the Christmas performances of the " Tipteers ". Like the Mummers of other parts, these players once wandered from hamlet to hamlet of a winter's night, brightening the long evenings of the rustics with their unwritten plays. Strangely confused in parts, and sometimes wellnigh unintelligible, these plays are far older than Christianity, dating their origin to the pagan festivals of winter, when the country folk all over the world would pray to their deity to revitalize the fertility of their soil and ensure a harvest in the coming season. Once pagan but later turned Christian, the performances are a kind of cross between the two, with such characters as Saint George, the Turkish Knight, and Beelzebub or the Devil, taking the principal rôles.

It is, perhaps, surprising that a custom whose main object has so long passed away, and one that is now, to outward appearances, so meaningless, should still survive with such tenacity. The reason is simply that such plays as these were once performed by the farm labourers, who, long after their old beliefs had begun to fade, continued to find in them a convenient means of adding to their meagre earnings between harvest and sowing when all was comparatively quiet on the land and overtime-pay out of the question. Also, before the days of cinemas and wireless sets, the lonely villagers welcomed their shows.

But if the Tipteers and the " bonfire boys ", Petworth Fair, and South Harting club day, are but isolated survivals, I do not believe that there is a village in Sussex —and certainly not a town—that does not merit exploration for some reason or other.

While at Houghton we may sip ale in the little beer house where Charles II, in more of a hurry than ourselves, stopped on his way to Brighton before taking ship at Shoreham ; at Newhaven we shall enter the inn where another fugitive, Louis Philippe, started his exile. At Findon, famous for its sheep fair, we shall dally a while in conversation with the village blacksmith in the forge where Derby and Grand National winners have been shod, just as at Burwash and Rottingdean we shall think of Kipling, at Rye of the dramatist Fletcher, whose home still stands, at Felpham of Blake, and at Horsham of Shelley, who was born at Warnham nearby.

Bramber will show us the strangest museum in England, with such scenes as *The Death of Cock Robin* portrayed in minute detail by stuffed animals, while at Sompting, not too far distant, we may worship in the only Saxon church of the kind in the country. Built on three levels, with a strange helmet-shaped tower, and once used by the Knights Templars and the Knights Hospitallers, there are, in fact, only two others like it in the world, and, since both are on the Rhine, these may well have been bombed.

Indeed, the churches of Sussex alone provide an endless source of interest. While that of Hardham can boast some of the oldest wall paintings in England, at Berwick, by contrast, we shall see a splendid example of what modern artists can do to brighten walls. Then, again, at Lurgashall we shall marvel at the unusual wooden cloister that was built and roofed with Horsham stone in Stuart times. Less noble, perhaps, but no less interesting is the " watch house " in the churchyard at Warblington—a relic of the days when armed guards would stand watch over the graves in readiness for the coming of the body snatchers.

If Glyndebourne is world famous as the place where, in 1934, John Christie started his festivals of Mozart operas, Cade Street is hardly less notable as the place where Jack Cade met his death after the failure of his rebellion. If Rottingdean was the first village to have electricity, it was between John Butt's timber yards at Littlehampton and Trafalgar Street, Brighton, that the first experimental telephone line was installed in Great Britain.

From north to south, from east to west, Sussex is steeped in history ; only Kent can vie with her in this respect, and even Kent cannot boast of the prehistoric Piltdown Man, as can Uckfield. Perhaps it is on account of this very closeness of purpose and interest that a certain friendly rivalry exists between the natives on the borderland of these two counties.

It often happens that along this border—on the Romney Marshes, for instance—the men of Sussex and those of Kent will find themselves working side by side upon the same job. It is then that the fat is in the fire ! When things go wrong, as, for example, when the village painter mistakenly wrote " Sir John Flagstaff " instead of " Sir John Falstaff " upon the signboard of a local inn, the old gibe outs :

" Silly Sussex ! Silly Sussex ! "

Once there was real feeling in these words. In recent times, however, certain learned men have come to the rescue of the Sussex country folk by pointing out that " silly " is derived from an Anglo-Saxon word, and can as well mean blessed, happy, fortunate, prosperous, innocent, or harmless, as the less complimentary things their neighbours have in mind. Also, these Sussex folk have gained confidence in the thought that an old carol refers to Christ as " the silly child ".

Still, silly or no, the people of Sussex and Kent are, in the main, good neighbours. They remember the storms and vicissitudes they have weathered together for more than a thousand years. Besides, in the Cinque Ports they have a lasting link that no gibes could hope to sever.

Ten *The Garden of England*

As far back as the time of the Romans, such Kentish ports as Dover, Richborough, Lympne, and Reculver, together with Pevensey in Sussex, took their place among a chain of fortified stations that stretched along parts of the South and East coasts as bulwarks against the northern pirates. When the Saxons came, these stations were reduced in number, but not in importance, and it has often been said that it is from these ancient shore forts that the Cinque Ports (known in Kent and Sussex alike as the " Sink Ports ") have sprung.

Be that as it may, it was in the reign of William the Conqueror that they were incorporated as a definite fortified defence group, bearing grave responsibilities but enjoying numerous unusual privileges in return. Dover, Sandwich, Romney, Hythe, and Hastings constituted the original five, and to these were added Rye and Winchelsea, both of which, however, were later to be merged with Hastings for administrative purposes. After a while, eight corporate members, including Deal, Folkestone, Tenterden, Faversham, Fordwich—the mediæval port of Canterbury—Lydd, Pevensey, and Seaford, together with twenty-four " limbs ", or non-corporate members, were brought into the scheme.

Upon these Cinque Ports, as upon no other named towns, rested the defence of this realm during centuries of war and rumours of war. Together they were obliged by charter to provide a fleet of their own—each ship to be manned by a " rector ", " constable ", twenty-one men, and a boy—and to maintain it at their own expense during the first fourteen days of any national emergency. In a way they formed the nucleus of our naval strength.

How bitterly must the French and Spaniards have resented this fleet ! The Cinque Ports kept the French at bay in the thirteenth century, and sent a hundred and five ships and more than two thousand men to the Siege of Calais ; and, in later years, rallied by the side of Lord Howard of Effingham when Hastings alone sent twenty ships to fight the Spanish Armada.

By no means easy was it to maintain such a fleet ; great were the financial burdens imposed upon those Kentish and Sussex ports. Even so, such hardships, although to prove their downfall in the end, were, for a time, more than offset by the enormous benefits meted out to their citizens ; benefits that made them, on occasion, just a little swollen-headed.

Under the terms of their charters, for instance, each port could send two barons to Parliament, while collectively they could also claim the right to appoint representatives to hold the canopy over the King's head at a coronation, and to sit upon his right hand at all royal entertainments and at certain State functions. All-powerful, they were, in many respects, also untouchable by common law. Not only were they exempt from many taxes, tolls, and other dues, but they could also impose certain local levies and collect flotsam and ietsam upon their seas and beaches. And if any offended against the law of the land, they were entitled to demand to be tried by their own courts at Shepway, Brodhull, or Guestling, no matter what the nature of their crime.

Alas, how are the mighty fallen! Towns that once boasted flourishing harbours now stand a mile or two inland, their ancient ports long silted up and entirely useless. Like Winchelsea, Rye, Hastings, and Pevensey in Sussex, such Kentish towns as Sandwich, Faversham, Fordwich, Deal, Folkestone, and Romney remain but interesting hunting grounds for relics of a bygone era in our island history. Dover alone of the Cinque Ports Confederation maintains any semblance of her old importance; Dover, with her castle high above the famous White Cliffs—the "lock and key of the Kingdom", the Conqueror called it, when he appointed his half-brother, the Bishop of Bayeux, her governor and proclaimed him Earl of Kent—her Maison Dieu, and her badly war-scarred Round House. But even Dover is more important (except in times of war) as the leading cross-Channel base than as a naval centre now, for the Cinque Ports have long been ousted by Portsmouth, Plymouth, and Chatham.

Even so, these ancient harbours can never quite surrender their glorious past. With Walmer Castle as his official residence, the Cinque Ports still have their Lord Warden, a post once held by the Duke of Wellington and now entrusted to the great Winston Churchill, the 158th holder of the office.

It was in this castle that Wellington died in 1852, after living here for something like a quarter of a century, and we may still visit his bedroom and see some of his personal belongings, such as the chair in which he breathed his last breath, the camp bed he brought from Waterloo, and the silken-covered mattress upon which he slept each night, covered by a velvet blanket that had once belonged to Blücher. It was in this castle that William Pitt talked with Villeneuve after Trafalgar ; here that he and Nelson first met, and so sowed the seeds of France's fate and of England's glory.

How proud must Kent be of such close affinity with these three !—Pitt, Wellington, and Churchill ; each in their time the saviours of mankind ; each as staunch and steadfast as the White Cliffs themselves. But for them Kent—and England too—might well have been a sorrier land to-day.

It was at Hayes that Pitt was born ; at Westerham that Churchill chose, some twenty-five years ago, to make his country seat. And if the great house where Pitt first saw the light of day, and where his no less famous father, the Earl of Chatham, died, is, alas, no more, Chartwell is to be saved for the nation, bought by a group of Mr. Churchill's friends to be handed over to the National Trust upon his death as a lasting memorial to the man who inspired the world to fight the cause of freedom in the dark days of 1940 ; Chartwell, where "Winnie" once laid the bricks of a cottage at the rate of one a minute, and gained a trade union ticket for which, however, he was later deemed to be ineligible.

Over this old manor house to-day proudly flutters the flag of the Lord Warden. And this post is by no means merely a titular one. Like many of the ancient boroughs and "limbs" themselves, it still enjoys certain of the age-old rights and privileges that once meant so much to those who went down to the sea in ships.

Vanguard of England since before the Coming of Christ, there is hardly a corner of Kent that has not, at some time or another, played her part in shaping her destiny.

Was it at Deal, Dover, or Walmer, or was it, after all, perhaps, at Lympne, that Julius Caesar landed, those two thousand years ago, after being well and truly baffled by the tides of the Straits of Dover that proved so very different from those he had known in the Mediterranean? Was it the tales of the rich booty in our midst—tales told by the itinerant merchants—that prompted the great emperor to venture upon his two hazardous raids on the shores of Kent? We cannot tell. All we know is that it was here, here in this south-eastern-most tip of our island that the great era of Roman domination—extending over some four centuries, and gradually spreading throughout the South and Midlands—was eventually to begin. From Dover to Chester, passing through Canterbury, Rochester, and London, stretches their famous Watling Street; at Canterbury, Bobbing, Brengett, Rochester, Cuxton, and Folkestone, are relics of their occupation. But, then, all Kent was Roman once, and in towns and villages far and wide we shall be shown souvenirs of this bygone, but enterprising, age, or be told tales—as at Chilham and Barham, for instance—of bloody encounters between the invaders and the Ancient Britons before, at last, the latter were finally subdued and the two began to live together in peace and harmony.

What a fund of history lies buried beneath the soil of Kent! Whether upon the coast or the banks of the Medway, upon the wooded North Downs, the Weald, or the low-lying Romney Marshes, there is hardly a town or village that cannot recall its days of trial and stress. From end to end Kent is the very foundation-stone of English history as we know it to-day; the county that has more than once lain at the proud feet of a conqueror, but which, as a kingdom unto herself, has risen again to stand as a sure bastion against further would-be conquerors for close on a thousand years.

It was at Ebbsfleet, tradition has it, that Hengist and Horsa landed in 449 ; at Aylesford—where, many centuries later, the Carmelites established their first religious house—that they eventually mustered their forces and set up their standard of victory by those strange prehistoric stones that have long been world-famous as " Kit's Coty House ".

Gravesend—for long the Thames Pilot Station, and once the assembly point of the sailing vessels of Martin Frobisher and Sebastian Cabot—was an important Saxon shipping centre when the shore forts were in their heyday, while Bapchild, Faversham, Canterbury, and Bearsted have all been the scene of those Saxon parliaments that gloried in the name of " witenagemot ". Indeed, at Bearsted—famous alike as the camping ground of Wat Tyler's followers, and as the scene of a fierce battle between the Royalists and Roundheads, and of less bloodthirsty tussles between cricketers great and small, from the days of Alfred Mynn to those of our own time—at Bearsted, in a hollow a little to the south of the church, can still be seen the amphitheatre where those rulers of old were prone to meet of a fine summer's day.

Sandwich, too—thrice burnt by the French in the time of Henry VI—can tell of the landing of King Canute in 851 ; Sandwich, that pleasing little town with her Fishergate and her Barbican, where the children still race for buns and biscuits on St. Bartholomew's Day, in memory, it is said, of the time when the pilgrims to Canterbury were given free food.

Yes, Kent has seen momentous times ; momentous people, too.

To Sandwich came Richard Cœur de Lion after his imprisonment in Austria ; to Dover, Charles II upon his Restoration, and then what a scene to behold as the exiled king, greeted upon his landing by General Monk, arrived in triumph at Rochester, to bide a while before continuing his journey to London. How different to the scene at Shoreham, that now distant eve, was the one witnessed by John Evelyn as he journeyed into London on that far-off day in May 1660 :

> With a triumph of above 3,000 horse and foot, brandishing their swords and shouting with joy, the way strewed with flowers, the bells ringing, the streets hung with tapestry, fountains running with wine, the Mayor, Aldermen and all the Companies in their liveries, chains of gold and banners, lords and nobles clad in cloth of silver, gold and velvet, the windows and balconies all set with ladies : trumpets, music, myriads of people flocking even so far as from Rochester, so as they were seven hours in passing the City. . . .

How different, too, to the scene at Faversham that greeted his less noble brother, James II, when, in later years, he tried to beat a hasty retreat to the Continent as soon as it became obvious that William of Orange was more palatable to the people than he. There are men and women alive to-day who will tell you how their ancestors were among that band of argumentative fishermen and others to whom the miserable monarch, in desperation, distributed three hundred guineas (taken from the Mint in London before he left) in five-shilling silver pieces as payment for his safety.

Momentous people, indeed. At Faversham, too, lies King Stephen, and here, it is said, came William Shakespeare as a strolling player.

Farningham may boast the manor house where lived Captain Bligh of the *Bounty*, and Westerham can tell not only of Pitt and Churchill but of General James Wolfe, the founder of Quebec, who was born in the old vicarage here, a strange house, seemingly built of white bricks that are, in fact, " mathematical tiles ", brought from Ashford. An embarrassing moment for the incumbent, the Rev. George Lewis, must that January evening of 1727 have been. Little did he expect, when he issued his invitation to his neighbour of the stately red house close by, that a tremendous thunderstorm would break, and that, before the rains ceased, his guest would give birth in his house to a boy who, thirty-two years later, was to scale the cliffs on to the Plains of Abraham and bring all Canada under the Union Jack.

Westerham may talk of Wolfe, Pitt, and Churchill, but at Penshurst the hero is ever Sir Philip Sidney, around whose stately birthplace, with its magnificent baronial hall, the entire village appears to cluster. For ever will this quiet corner of Kent be linked with this "brightest gem of Elizabeth's court"; this poet, statesman, and soldier, who fell into disfavour for opposing the Queen's French marriage, who was betrayed by Drake, but who died a hero's death in battle; this man whose words Charles I saw fit to repeat shortly before his execution:

> Let calamities be the exercise but not the overthrow of my virtue. Let the power of my enemies prevail, but prevail not to my destruction. Let my greatness be their pretext, my pain be the sweetness of their revenge. Let them, if so it seems good unto thee, vex me with more and more punishment; but, O Lord, let never their wickedness have such a head but that I may carry a pure mind in a pure body.

As dignified and stately as the family who brought her fame stands Penshurst Place to-day. Once the property of the Crown, but later presented by Edward VI to Sir William Sidney, hero of Flodden, it was here that Henry VIII, who was largely responsible for extending the parks, courted Anne Boleyn, having first met her when he lost his way on a hawking expedition. It was a convenient meeting, for it so happened that at that very moment Henry was engaged in correspondence with the Pope concerning an idea he had in mind for ridding himself of Katherine of Aragon, whose presence he was now finding increasingly tedious. If all went well—and there was surely no doubt of that—he would soon be in need of a second wife.

Thus, when Anne, who lived at Hever Castle, conveniently close at hand, appeared on the scene, the plan seemed complete. And so it proved. The once joyful Anne, who had played as a child so happily upon the spacious lawns of Hever ; who had skipped merrily down the lanes of Kent, stopping now and again, no doubt, to pick wild flowers from the hedgerow, was soon to become the Queen Consort ; the mother of the future Queen Elizabeth. Yet how bitterly must the proud Boleyns have rued that chance meeting with the King of England ! Not only were they to see their daughter beheaded, but their son too, and soon Hever Castle itself was to be seized by the Crown.

Particularly fond of Kent was Henry. Allington and Charing, on the Pilgrim's Way—where he dined in Cranmer's palace on his journey to the Field of the Cloth of Gold, and expressed such a liking for the place that the wily archbishop took the hint—were especially high in his affections. But, then, Henry would also have liked to have lived at Otford, had not the local climatic conditions proved so cruel to his already crippling " rheumatics ".

As I say, momentous people have trodden the soil of Kent. While at Chislehurst they will still describe the burial of the third Napoleon in 1873, at Acrise they will tell you that it was here that King John laid the crown of England at the feet of the Pope's Legate, and so lifted the Interdict. How joyfully must the bells of the little parish church have rung out the glad news that the five years' curse upon our land had been raised, and that village priests everywhere could now christen the young and bury the dead once more !

While at that quaint little village of Brenchley, with her furnace pond and wealth of timbered cottages, they will point the way to Wat Tyler's home. Barham folk will talk with greater pride of Simon de Montfort, the founder of our parliamentary system. Lydd will recall the days when Cardinal Wolsey was her vicar, or Downe of when Charles Darwin was a noted citizen. Tonbridge, with her mass of interesting old buildings and her famous public school, will tell of links with Jane Austen, some of whose early ancestors were Kentish cloth-makers ; Margate of Turner and Gray ; Boxley of Tennyson and George Sandys ; Maidstone of Hazlitt ; Canterbury of Christopher Marlowe.

But it is of Charles Dickens and of the Rev. Richard Barham, author of the *Ingoldsby Legends*, that we shall think first if we would make a literary pilgrimage of Kent. If the area around Rochester will ever be known as the " Dickens country ", Canterbury, where he was born in 1788, Denton, where he succeeded to the manor of Tappington, Upper Hardres, where his father, the " fat alderman ", lies buried, Ashford, where he obtained his first curacy, much of the Medway and the Romney Marshes, and the whole north coast, including the Swale and the Isle of Sheppey, must always belong to Barham. To the people of Kent these two names—Dickens and Ingoldsby—are ever immortal ; as much the epitome of their countryside as Thomas Hardy is of Dorset, or Jane Austen of Hampshire.

Before he was ten, young Dickens came to Rochester. His father was a dockyard worker, and Charles was sent to a school in Rome Lane. After a while the family removed to London, yet never could the author forget this ancient and historical cathedral city, and for close on a quarter of a century, until his death in

1870, chose to live at Gad's Hill, three miles out on the old Rochester to Gravesend coach road; that hill, once wooded, where Shakespeare is said to have laid the scene of the exploits of Sir John Falstaff, and which gained its unusual name from the remarkable number of vagabonds who at one time were wont to frequent it.

"Mudfog", "Our Town", "Dullborough", and "Cloisterham", all are Rochester; Rochester whose streets, though "lively and animated", Mr. Pickwick saw as "dirty", and whose principal productions were but "soldiers, sailors, Jews, chalk, shrimps, officers and dockyard men". Here it was, at the Bull Hotel, that Mr. Pickwick and his companions alighted from the Commodore Coach at the end of their journey from the Golden Cross; here that they set off for Dingley Dell; here that Jingle insulted Dr. Slammer at the charity ball, an unhappy incident that resulted in arrangements being made for the staging of a duel in Fort Pitt Fields. . . .

But it is not only in Rochester and Gad's Hill that we shall think of Dickens: at Chalk, we shall picture him on his honeymoon in Nash's Cottage, and visit the forge that figures in *Great Expectations;* at Broadstairs, we shall pity him living in the *Bleak House* near the harbour; at Cobham—perhaps the most fascinating of all Kentish villages—envy him as he makes his way into that "clean and commodious alehouse", the *Leather Bottle*, for so long the haunt of his admirers.

In any of these places we may expect to bump into Mr. Pickwick, Mr. Snodgrass, Mr. Winkle, or Sam Weller as we round the corner, for in Kent these delightful characters become at once as real as the man who created them. But then, of course, they are not all creations. In many a Kentish town and village to-day are men and women whose parents and grandparents as much provided the spiritual inspiration of his books as did the houses in which they lived, and the lanes along which they trod, supply the material background. Only recently I got chatting to a nonagenarian who figures in *The Uncommercial Traveller.* Bearing a distinct resemblance to the author himself, with his great beard and pleasantly wrinkled face, he told me that once, as a small boy, he had been dashing enough to climb on to a fruiterer's cart at Gad's Hill when the owner's back was turned. The consequences were disastrous, for the horse at once took fright and elected to bolt, upsetting the fruit and vegetables to the ground in the general pandemonium. Dickens, it seems, was coming up the hill at the time, and went to the youngster's aid, and so tickled was he over the whole affair that he could not refrain from making use of the incident in years to come.

But if Dickens, by birth, should really belong to Hampshire, Barham claimed a Kentish ancestry of at least six centuries. It was his proud boast that he was descended from that notoriously ignoble knight, FitzUrse, who, in the darkness of that December day of 1170, drew his sword with three others and lashed at the skull of St. Thomas à Becket within the Cathedral of Canterbury. So revolting did the name of FitzUrse become that his brother changed it to De Bearham. Later, it was shortened to its present form, and it is said that it is from this family that the quaint little village of Barham—where Caesar, King John, and Simon de Montfort, each in his turn, camped on the bleak downs nearby—takes its name.

Alas, once wealthy and all-powerful, the sins of their father were visited unto many generations of the Barhams. Little by little did their estates fall asunder, their fortunes to be redeemed only in the eighteenth century when one John Barham had the good sense to take unto himself for a wife the daughter of a certain Thomas Harris, whose fortunes, gained from the hop-fields, were truly astonishing.

It was through this marriage that Richard eventually inherited Tappington Manor, that most interesting house where the stain of blood upon the stairs still bears testimony to a tragedy enacted some three hundred years ago. Two brothers, it seems, occupied the house at the time. One was for Charles ; the other for Cromwell. To say the least of it, the atmosphere was tense ; so much so that the two were forced to agree to have their separate quarters in the house, and never to address a single word to one another again. All went well for a time until, by unlucky chance, they met one night upon the stairs. That was the end : next morning the Royalist was found sprawling on the ground, a dagger through his back.

Surprising is it that this man who, with his keen sense of wit and his love of delving into the past, this man who kneaded together fact and fiction to such an extent as to make Kent appear the most legendary land in England, should have completely ignored this tragedy on his very doorstep. But no matter : as " Mr. Thomas Ingoldsby ", he built for himself a niche in the history of Kent that is as undying as the many superstitions of the Romney Marshes that he unravelled and twisted and made for ever famous.

Rich in variety of scenery, this land of Kent has provided inspiration for artists through countless ages. Did Shakespeare really find his soul in this " garden of England ", as did Bunyan his in Surrey or Bedfordshire ? Were the rough seas and the cliffs, the forests and the weavers' homes, really the inspiration of his plays, as has so often been said ? Can Kent claim affinity with Shakespeare, too, or shall that proud privilege belong only to Warwickshire ? It is a mystery whose answer we shall probably never know.

Times have changed since the great Elizabethan came this way. The Cinque Ports have dwindled to obscurity ; trees have given place to houses in many parts ; the majority of the weavers' looms are active no more ; the ancient windmills that once made flour for the village bakers now grind only cattle-feed or else are still and derelict ; fast cars now hurry along the roads from London to the coast where once the pack-horse ambled, slow but sure, over the unmade tracks. The old order changes . . . and yet, somehow, Kent is still the " garden of England " just as she will continue to be the " lock and key of the kingdom " for as long as there are yet ships to pass through the Straits of Dover.

What scene more entrancing than those richly wooded North Downs—with their clumps of beeches to add to the belief that this may well be the only tree indigenous to our island ; the Medway, with its sailing barges of perhaps a hundred and fifty tons, so constructed that they can be manned by but one man and a boy, passing on to Rochester with their cargoes of wheat, oats, linseed, cement, and sundry other forms of merchandise ; or the Weald, with its most fascinating assortment of villages ? Even the Romney Marshes, with the three-miles-long Dymchurch Wall still keeping the sea at bay, as when the Romans first built it, have a lure of their own.

Indeed, to the native of these parts the Romney Marshes, with their age-old sheep runs and dykes and their banks of primroses, are the finest of all, just as to others the more open eastern end of the county will appear every bit as entrancing as the winding wooded lanes and hills of the western section. For in the eyes of those who live in it, each district is a jewel beyond compare. Proud of their county, they are prouder still of that part of it that gave them their birthright. So much so, in fact, that to confuse a " Man of Kent " with a " Kentish Man ", or vice versa, is just insulting. While to talk of the former is to refer to one born to the west of the Medway, the latter term applies only to those hailing from the eastern side. It is a fine point of etiquette with which it is as well to be acquainted; the aftermath of an old feud, they will tell you, that dates back to the time of the Conqueror, when one side supported him and the other opposed him tooth-and-nail.

Incidentally, talking of the Conqueror, until quite recent years the people of Kent enjoyed a system of land inheritance that for centuries was almost unique, one known as " gavelkind ". Under this system a man who died intestate had his land divided equally between his sons—or, failing sons, daughters—instead of its passing to his heir. A tenant could dispose of his estate by will, or alienate his holdings by feoffment on attaining the age of fifteen, while a wife received a half share in any property. Similarly, a widower became a " tenant by courtesy " of a like share until such time as he re-married. It was a full and well-laid scheme which, among other things, provided a safeguard against escheating for felony, and which, if for no other reason, was popular as ensuring that " every son is as great a gentleman as the eldest son is ".

A solicitor, with whom I discussed this matter, explained that gavelkind formed an important feature of Saxon law, and that the Conqueror, finding it an uphill task to subdue these Kentish folk, deemed it wise policy to allow them to maintain this section of the old laws of the land in the hope of keeping them quiet, whereas the rest of the country was to bow to Norman legislation.

As varied as the landscape scenery is the village architecture. Here we shall come upon a cottage of weather-boarding; there a Tudor manor house of black and white. Around the corner we may stumble upon as neat an example of tile-hanging as we shall find anywhere, and, next to it, maybe, a mellow brick house with a tiled roof as wavy and uneven as they made them. All kinds and descriptions of homes, built of divers materials by men of succeeding ages, each portraying the changing modes of the times, may go to make up a single village. And yet all will be in perfect harmony.

In many respects I do believe that these Kentish towns and villages are the prettiest of all. What more captivating than Smarden or Chilham—where, under the terms of a bequest of 1638, the local lasses about to be married held annual races on the "Old Wives Lees" for a prize of ten pounds, designed to help the winner set up her first home. What better than Bishopsbourne, Aylesford, or Fordwich, Benenden, Cobham or, Appledore, Ightham, Eynsford, or Tenterden?

Remarkably interesting too, some of them: Biddenden, the most easterly site of the iron-manufacture from the Hastings beds, where the poor still receive an annual dole of bread and cheese in memory of those famous twins, Eliza and Mary Chulkhurst, who, joined together at the hips and shoulders, lived here some eight hundred years ago; Lamberhurst, where much of the wrought-iron work for St. Paul's Cathedral was forged in Bedgebury Woods; Saltwood, plotting-ground for the murder of St. Thomas à Becket; Offham, with its quintain to remind us of the chivalrous knights of long ago; New Romney, where the crowning of the Boy Bishop is still celebrated, I believe, and where, as Duke of York, the King started his famous schoolboy camps ; or Sissinghurst, where prisoners were quartered during the Seven Years War, with freedom to walk out on parole as far as the *Three Chimneys*, a few miles out on the road to Biddenden. And Sissinghurst once housed lunatics too : I am told that there are people there still who can remember seeing them chained up outside the castle. Great times has this little village seen ; leading through the woods right down to Rye is a track once trodden by smugglers. . . .

Then, too, there is Gun Green, where the cannons were proved. No longer is there a green, but, no matter, it is yet pretty. Surprising how many Kentish villages and hamlets still bear the name of " green " when all trace of common land has long since disappeared. This, I am told, is due to the remarkable number of squatters who, in days gone by, found Kent a happy hunting ground wherein to spend their years of peaceful and unchallenged possession before staking their claim to rightful ownership.

Equally surprising is the number of places that bear the name of " forstal " or " fostal ", as, for instance, in the case of St. Lawrence Forstal or Hunter's Forstal. Some say that the name owes its origin to the mediæval system of assarting, and that a forstal comprised a triangular-shaped clearing in a wood where a few odd cottages were built, without, however, the sites ever being developed to the proportions of either a village or hamlet, as had originally been intended. There are many theories, but this, to me, appears the most convincing.

Perhaps the most interesting of these places, though, is the little group around Cranbrook, with its picturesque mill towering above the roof-tops—Goudhurst, Tenterden, Hawkhurst, Lamberhurst, and Headcorn, for example—where the Flemish refugees set up their looms and brought fame to Kent in that now distant past. The looms have long since disappeared, but the families of Oyler, Rumens, and Unicume, who are the descendants of those refugees, yet remain.

How busy were those districts once !—as busy as the clothiers' towns of Wiltshire. How prosperous too did the owners of those looms become, when once they were shifted from the cottage homes to the factories up the street ! At Cranbrook the talk is still of the day when Queen Elizabeth spent the night at the *George*, and craftsmen and women wove a carpet of grey broad-cloth to lay in the road before her all the way from their workshops to Coursehorne Manor, perhaps a mile distant. A proud day that was !

Still, it was not only here that the weavers were active. Around Sevenoaks—with its famous cricket ground and its stately mansion, Knole, where a former Lord Sackville played cricket in a team captained by his head gardener before ever Hambledon rose to fame —around Sevenoaks and Canterbury (still an important centre for the repair of church organs), they were no less busy making brocaded silk, stockings, and muslin.

Among the refugees to come to Canterbury was a band of Spanish Protestants, who gloried in the name of the " Walloons ". Arriving at Winchelsea in 1561, they made their way to the city on mules and horses, there to be dubbed " the Strangers " by the natives, by dint of the fact that their dress and ways of life were as strange as their language. Yet so beautifully did they weave their bayes and sayes, their taffetas, bonbazines and serges, their ribbons and their laces, that Queen Elizabeth not only granted them a licence to ply their craft within the walls of the city, but, moreover, permitted them to use the cathedral undercroft as their place of worship—a privilege which their descendants enjoy to this day.

Year by year, as their fame spread, so their numbers

multiplied. By 1574 they had gained full rights as citizens, with authority to appoint their own sub-magistrates. In course of time they were to become a flourishing community, working upon a thousand looms and giving employment to close on three thousand men and women, before, at last, foreign competition spelt their doom and caused them to scatter to Spitalfields and other industrial centres.

Though we shall no longer see the red-sailed barges, piled high with silks and wools, passing along the river, or hear the voice of some master craftsman as he shouts his unloading orders, we may even now visit the house in King's Bridge where they worked, and watch a group of modern weavers employing the self-same methods upon those self-same looms.

Strangely varied were the activities that once took place in Canterbury. For here, too, were burnt the heretics at two shillings and eightpence a time—two shillings for the load of wood, and eightpence for the stake and staple. Quite an art it was, this burning business : sometimes a small bag of gunpowder might be placed behind the head of the culprit—when the flames reached the bag it went off bang, and that was that ! A penny extra the gunpowder cost, but doubtless, it was well worth while. . . .

But who shall say which corner of Kent is really the most interesting ? Every town and village, almost, draws us like a magnet, beckoning us to explore her streets and buildings for evidence of the part she, too, has played. Though there is little—apart from the Pantiles—to show for it now, we must not forget the splendour that once belonged to Tunbridge Wells. We must not forget that Margate was an important Tudor and Georgian port for the Low Countries, or that it was at Folkestone that the mysteries of the circulation of the blood were first unravelled.

Nor shall we overlook the Dartford and Crayford Ship Canal, or the Royal Military Canal, built at the time of the Napoleonic troubles, or the little islands off her coast—from lonely Elmley Isle, with a population of little more than twenty, to Sheppey, with her many legends, or Thanet, where, somewhere about a hundred years ago, a poor boy named John Swinford amassed a fortune of three hundred thousand pounds, largely, it seems, from the gathering of seaweed for use on his farms.

As I say, all Kent is steeped in history : a veritable gold mine of information for the inquiring traveller.

It is in springtime that we shall see Kent at her most beautiful ; in springtime when all to the west of the county is pink and white with blossom, with the swinging cowls and the tiled roof-tops of the oast houses peeping through, here and there, to remind us that hops, too, will be coming along before summer is out. Not even the orchards of Devon or Somerset can, I believe, quite equal the glory that is Kent's at this one time of year. Hardly a cottage home is there that does not boast its share of trees to add to the sea of blossom on the fruit farms. And even where there is neither cottage nor farm, we shall often come upon an odd wild cherry or apple that has seeded itself within a copse or hedgerow. Amidst such a blaze of colour, the humming of the bees as they journey between hive and blossom appears to hold an added significance, while even the song of the birds sounds more joyous than ever as they twitter their farewell to winter and greet the dawn of a longer and brighter day.

It is, indeed, a joyous and important time for all ; the time when the riches of the year depend to a large extent upon whether there be sun or wind before the buds have set. For the growing of fruit has long been a thriving Kentish industry, and all through the summer, apples, pears, plums, cherries, soft fruits, strawberries, and raspberries will, each in their turn, be leaving the orchards and gardens for the markets and the roadside fruit stalls.

It was Henry VIII—or so they will tell you—who first brought the cherry to Kent, and it is around that tree that the lore of the fruit farms has long been centred. Every Easter, in days gone by, the young people would go " a pudding-pieing ", visiting the village pubs for miles around to eat flat pies—the size of saucers—with raised crusts filled with custard and sprinkled with currants, and drink " cherry beer " made from the juice and pulp of the previous season's fruit. All along the route from Canterbury to London the innkeepers would be busy serving these tempting drinks and pies to the sore and weary travellers.

And when the year's harvest had been safely picked, then would come the cherry fairs, when villages far and wide would turn out to make merry, and eat and drink the precious fruit in every conceivable form and in truly astonishing quantities.

Ask a Man of Kent to-day to name his favourite fruit, and the old adage will out :

A cherry year, a merry year ;
A plum year, a dumb year.

And should that same countryman invite you to step into the snugness of his cottage home, he may well turn and ask :

" Be you a dry, met ? "

Whereupon, if you answer " I be ", he may take from his cupboard a bottle of that delicious wine which he still delights to make from his cherries whenever the harvest is good. For to him, as to his ancestors, the cherry is still the symbol of all that is best in the English countryside.

Still, it is for the growing of hops that Kent is perhaps

most famous. Ever since the crop was introduced from the Low Countries in the late fifteenth or early sixteenth century, and the first Kentish hop field was planted out at Little Chart, the industry has steadily spread throughout the western end of the county.

Before ever the blossom bursts upon the fruit trees, the hoppers will be busy skinning and pickling their poles in hot tar, and long before winter is out those poles will be ready in the plantations. By March the stilt-walkers will be passing down the rows, engaged upon their intricate system of stringing, and from then until picking time all will be at work with their special ploughs, " kufs ", " spanes ", " becks ", and so on, harrowing, hoeing, and preparing the soil, spraying against " red spider ", and, maybe, protecting the crops against dust and smoke by means of hessian.

So that, as spring gives place to summer, it is upon the hop fields, with the quaint little oast houses standing proudly by, rather than upon the orchards, that we now gaze. And soon those fields, where all seems still and peaceful now, save only for the movements of the natives who go so quietly about their work, will be a hive of activity ; of laughter, merriment, and excited chatter. For when September comes and picking time is here, what joyful scenes there will be. All Cockney London, it seems, will be there, perhaps twenty thousand strong ; all ready to enjoy that holiday which, to them, is the crowning glory of the year. Here will be an old woman of eighty odd—not above three years in sixty has she missed—and with her will be her daughter, grand-daughter, and even, perhaps, her great-grand-daughter. And there trundles an elderly man with three nippers in a pram, each with a remarkably dirty face, but no matter. In one corner are the huts in which the pickers will sleep, and not far off the first-aid centres, fully equipped with dispensaries and ready for any contingency. Here comes a fish cart, and there a baker's van, for these Cockneys will be hungry before the day is out.

What a scene indeed, what laughter and merriment will echo through those now silent fields ! And when the picking is done, and the hops are drying in the oast houses, then will come the crowning of the Queen of the Hops, for which honour each farm will surely enter three of its fairest damsels.

To-day the hops are picked into canvas-covered wooden frames, known as " bins ", and carried to the oast houses in " pokes ", where they are spread out on a platform of battens that has previously been covered with horse-hair mats. And there, above a charcoal and anthracite furnace, they will be left to dry under the care of two men who, for twelve hours or more, will take it in turns to move them about with their enormous wooden shovels to see that that they are evenly baked throughout.

An elderly hopper told me that he could remember the days when each load picked was recorded by the cutting of notches on to tally sticks, for the benefit of those who could neither read nor write, and when the drying process was in the charge of but one man. Strenuous days those were. Not once in a month would a drier take off his clothes for a good night's sleep ; instead he contented himself with dozing upon a straw bed beside the furnace in any odd moments he could spare. And, since the hops were turned every hour then, those moments were, naturally, few and far between. Nor did they get much time for meals.

" Roasted their onions and potatoes in the ashes, they did, and cooked their rashers of bacon over the flames. Tasty meals they were, though, mind you," my friend assured me, as he smacked his lips in envious meditation.

And well he might, for Kent has long been renowned for her foodstuffs. The flesh of her deer and her pheasants were once considered the most succulent in the land, while the oyster fisheries of Whitstable, Milton, the Medway, and elsewhere, have been famous for perhaps two thousand years. With what pride and satisfaction did the ancient companies and guilds of fishermen collect them in the past! Indeed, at Rochester, the ancient "Admiralty Court" still holds session in a barge every July, when a jury of fishermen sits to discuss the control of the Medway fisheries, and to see that all who have served their seven years' apprenticeship to any fisherman or dredger enjoy their time-honoured rights.

A great centre for fishing is Kent. While Deal has long served as the headquarters of the British Sea Anglers Association, at Folkestone, where they still prefer the hook and line to the best of nets, it is customary for the fishermen to set aside the eight best whiting out of every boat, and to pool the profits from these sales for their Christmas-time "Rumbald Feast".

But the people of Kent by no means rely only on food-production for their livelihood; their industries are as many and varied as their village architecture. Around the coast and along the inland waterways shipwrights and boat-builders may still be found plying their trades with that same devotion as when the Cinque Ports were in their prime. By the inland waters, too, around Eynsford, Ashford, and Maidstone in particular, they still make paper, as at Wookey Hole in Somerset, while at various points are to be found far larger mills, run on modern mass-production lines. Ever since the last year of the seventeenth century have the paper-makers of Eynsford been busy, and at Dartford, close by, lies the oldest craftsman of all, Sir John Spielmen, upon whose paper, it is believed,

Shakespeare's first plays may have been printed. No longer is salt recovered from the Isle of Thanet, or gunpowder prepared in almost every other sizeable village ; the iron-foundries are as dead as those of Sussex, and the copperers and calico bleachers have long since departed. Not for a hundred years or more has that lovely Bethersden marble, of which so many Kentish fireplaces are made, been excavated. But chalk is still cut in many parts, as since the days before Caesar came this way ; Kentish flints are yet sent to the potteries of Staffordshire ; " ragstone " is still cut along the Medway for road-making, as is marl dug for the making of cricket-pitches and the manuring of the fields. Up and down the country the quarries and brickfields are active yet, with the " yellow " brick for building, and the remarkably hard and durable " blue " for the flooring of stables, held in special esteem.

Then there are the coal-fields too, whose first workings were made from the disused borings of the Channel tunnel ; but, then, Kent does not wish to become another " Black Country ". . . .

Despite her nearness to London, the old-time countryman has by no means yet entirely deserted the fields and lanes of Kent. Here and there at harvest time we may still find a sheaf of corn tied to a farm-gate to denote that all is safely gathered in and that the gleaners may now enter. And there are plenty still who will declare as emphatically as ever that, when the cowls on the hop-kilns turn in different directions, a storm is brewing, or that, when the frogs brighten to yellow, a change of weather may be expected.

Whether to " Man of Kent " or " Kentish Man " a horse is still a " hoss ", the stem of a leaf a " strig ", a reap-hook a " begging hook ", a fire a " blake ", a woodlouse a " monkey pea ", and a shallow pond a

" sole ". So, too, does " cater " yet remain his favourite word for describing anything angular.

As we wander from place to place throughout the length and breadth of this delightful county, there is one name that is for ever cropping up in our chats with these natives ; everywhere the finger-posts beckon us to her midst. That name is Canterbury.

Nearly a hundred and fifty years after the arrival of Hengist and Horsa—in the spring of 597, it was—King Ethelbert and his good Queen Bertha sat peacefully talking within the shade of an aged oak tree in this self-same spot, when there sailed up the Channel St. Augustine and forty black-robed monks, come from Rome at the bidding of Pope Gregory to convert the people to Christianity.

As their ship neared the coast it was an anxious moment for all. Only with misgivings had these missionaries agreed to make the journey, for the reports they had received of the barbarity of the people had been cruel indeed—so cruel that they had once turned back to plead with Gregory to excuse them their hazardous adventure. But it was an anxious moment for Ethelbert too, who was somewhat in awe of these " mystery men ", fearing that if he did but invoke their wrath there would be no limits to the miracles they might perform.

Doubtless it was the very tenseness of the moment—coupled with the fact that Bertha was already a Christian—that saved the situation.

Soon Augustine and his band of followers were treading their way to Canterbury, " bearing a silver cross for a banner, and the image of Our Lord and Saviour painted on a board ". As they neared the city, they began their weird Latin chants. People darted madly here and there to catch a glimpse of this strange band ; excited chatter filled the streets, where all had been comparatively quiet before ; all were agog. The story of Canterbury had begun.

That Whitsun, Ethelbert himself would be baptised a Christian in the river, and, after him, on Christmas Day, some ten thousand of his subjects. Soon the little church that the Romans had built during their occupation would rise as Canterbury's first cathedral, with Augustine, safely ensconced in the King's own palace, her first archbishop.

How sacred the wide world over has the name of Canterbury become since then. Gone is St. Augustine's church ; gone too the one built about a hundred and fifty years later by Archbishop Cuthbert. Yet Augustine and Ethelbert, are both with us still, buried in the ruined abbey just outside the city walls.

It was in 1070, when Lanfranc, Abbot of Caen, became archbishop, that work on the present cathedral was begun, the original church having by then been "reduced almost to nothing by fire and rain ". But much has happened since the completion, within the space of but seven years, of this new building. Time has not stood still at Canterbury. Archbishops have come and gone, century has followed century, and all the while the once little cathedral has steadily risen to greater magnitude. William of Sens, William the Englishman, and Henry Yevele, master-mason to Edward III, these and many after them have left their mark upon this noble place, until to-day it stands as dignified and beautiful as any in the land ; a great and stately edifice, whose fine proportions and magnificent interior no other, surely, can ever quite surpass.

Fire and brimstone, murder and destruction, bombs —all have cast their gloom upon Canterbury ; but the great cathedral still stands.

Let those of us who come as pilgrims to Canterbury to-day think back on St. Augustine and the martyred

St. Thomas, and on those famous archbishops who have followed them down the centuries and whose tombs are all around us. Let us think back on the countless thousands of footsore travellers who have trodden the way before us to worship at the famous shrine, and of the little parish churches and cathedrals we ourselves have visited in reaching here—Truro, Exeter, Bath, and Wells, Salisbury, Wimborne Minster, Winchester, and Chichester. . . . Then, before leaving, let us spare a silent moment in thankfulness that this great cathedral has survived all ravages, to remain one of the jewels of this, our England.

Bibliography

British Calendar Customs.

Hone's Year Book.

Chambers's Book of Days.

Moonrakings (Edith Olivier).

English Custom and Usage (Christina Hole).

The Berkshire Book (Women's Institute).

Dorset Up Along and Down Along (Women's Institute).

The English Woodland (John Rodgers).

The Romance of Canterbury Cathedral (Margaret A. Babbington).

A History of Rochester (F. F. Smith).

The Hambledon Cricket Chronicle (F. S. Ashley-Copper).

The Story of Hungerford (W. H. Summers).

Cornwall and Its People (A. K. Hamilton Jenkin).

Index

Index

Index

Index

Index

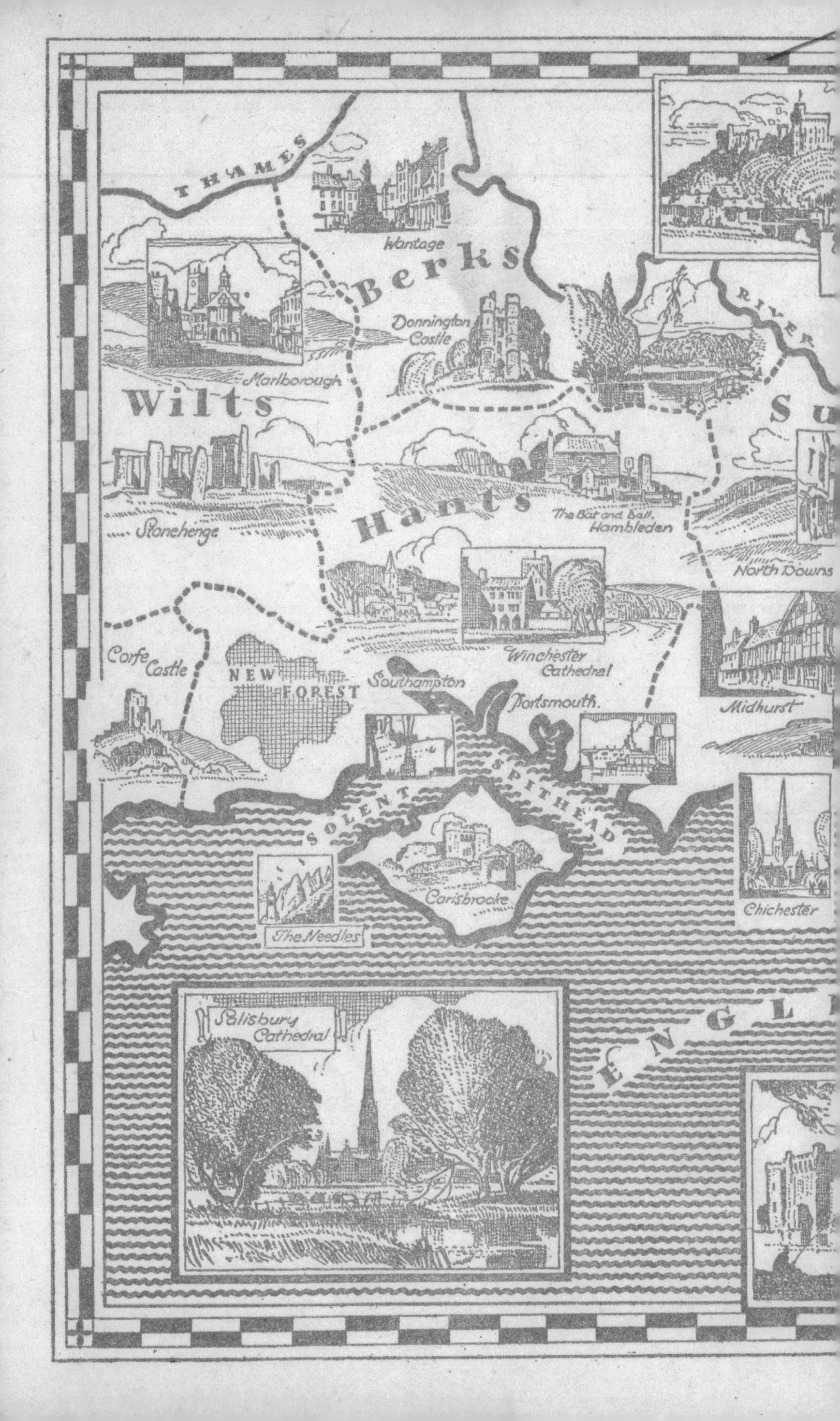
THAMES
Wantage
Berks
Donnington Castle
Marlborough
Wilts
RIVER
Su
Stonehenge
Hants
The Bat and Ball, Hambleden
North Downs
Corfe Castle
NEW FOREST
Southampton
Winchester Cathedral
Portsmouth.
Midhurst
SOLENT
SPITHEAD
Carisbrooke
The Needles
Chichester
Salisbury Cathedral
ENGL